SHROUDED IN LIGHT

NATURALISTIC PLANTING INSPIRED BY WILD SHRUBLANDS

SHROUDED IN LIGHT

NATURALISTIC PLANTING INSPIRED BY WILD SHRUBLANDS

**KEVIN PHILIP WILLIAMS
& MICHAEL GUIDI**

filbert press

FOR JESSICA HANNAH JONES,
You are the wild west.
I love you.
Kevin

FOR JOSH,
Forever Ago.
Michael

First published in 2024 by Filbert Press
filbertpress.com

Published in collaboration with Denver Botanic Gardens
botanicgardens.org

DENVER BOTANIC GARDENS

Text © 2024 Kevin Philip Williams and Michael Guidi

PHOTOGRAPHS by Kevin Philip Williams and Michael Guidi unless otherwise noted on page 240
DESIGN Michael Whitehead

All rights reserved. No part of this book may be reproduced or utilized in any form or by any means, electronic or mechanical, including photocopying, recording or by any information storage and retrieval system, without permission in writing from Filbert Press.

A catalogue record for this book is available from the British Library

ISBN: 978-1-7399039-5-4

Printed in China

MIX
Paper | Supporting responsible forestry
FSC® C014688

FRONT COVER **Desiccated flowers of chamise (*Adenostoma fasciculatum*) develop a burnt red glow that contrasts with silver bursts of *Ceanothus crassifolius* (hoaryleaf ceanothus) foliage. Seasonal changes provide visual relief and reveal the diversity of species in the dense chaparral vegetation.**

PAGE 2 **Environmentally dwarfed *Caragana jubata* (shag-spine peashrub) blending with mountain grasses and glacial choss in the subalpine shrublands near Barskoon, Kyrgyzstan**

CONTENTS

Foreword *by Nigel Dunnett*	6
PREFACE	14
American Hardcore *by Kevin Philip Williams*	16
Collaborative Creatures *by Michael Guidi*	18
Welcome to the Thicket	20
PART ONE / UNDERSTANDING SHRUBS	24
Why So Shrubby?	26
STEMS	28
Shrubs as Caretakers	30
FRUITS	34
Global Weirdness	37
How Shrubs Exist	39
LEAVES	44
Gimme Danger, Little Stranger	47
FLOWERS	52
Walk Among Us	56
BRUSH BEASTS	60
The Divine Language of The Soundless	63
PART TWO / SEEING SHRUBLANDS	68
Model Shrublands	70
The Grand Repeater	74
Neo-Expressionist Remixes	77
HEATH	78
INLAND BARRENS	84
BALDS	90
SHRUB-STEPPE	96
DRY MONTANE SHRUBLANDS	104
WET MONTANE SHRUBLAND	110
DESERT SCRUB	116
CHAPARRAL	122
COASTAL SCRUB	128
Alternative Shrublands	134
Shrub Love Coast to Coast	138
THE DISTURBED	144
THIS AIN'T NO MEADOW	148
CHILDREN OF DUNES	150
SHRUBS OF DARKNESS	154
SWAMP THINGS	157
PRICKS AND PINHEADS	160
NANOSCRUB	164
BIODOMES	168
WHAT DO YOU CONSIDER A TREE?	172

PART THREE / MAKING SHRUBSCAPES	176
Model Shrubscapes	178
The LA WAVE (Est 2017)	180
SummerHome Garden (Est 2020)	182
Fear of a Shrub Planet: Beyond the Bushes	184
Landscapes of Cohabitation (Est 2000)	186
Sky Scrub	188
Moda Building (2007)	189
One South Van Ness Avenue (2010)	190
Gardens of the Post-Anthropocene	192
Lands End Lookout (Est 2012)	194
The High Line (Est 2009)	196
Tuning In	200
Cyberpunk Shrubscapes (Est 2022)	202
Further Strategies for Naturalistic Design	204
Wildness and the Post-Humanities	204
Anthropogenic Wild Systems	205
Non-Anthropogenic Wild Systems	210
Sympoietic Systems	212
Embracing Wilderness	213
Wild Systems Emulation	214
SummerHome Garden (Est 2020)	218
Alien Dream Worlds Meow Wolf Denver: Convergence Station (Est 2022)	219
Denver Art Museum Sensory Garden (Est 2020)	221
Mesh Not Matrix	222
Do What You Want	224
Endnotes	
Kevin Philip Williams	226
Michael Guidi	227
RESOURCES	
Glossary	228
Bibliographic references	231
About the Authors	233
Index	234
Acknowledgments	240

FOREWORD
Nigel Dunnett

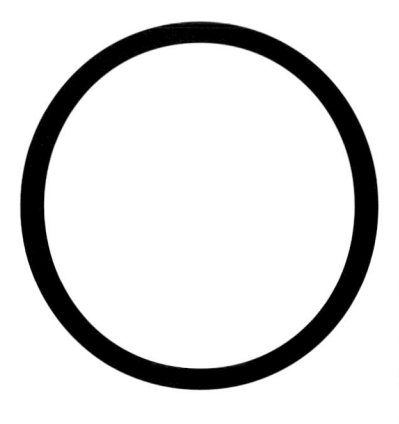

OVER RECENT DECADES, PERENNIALS AND GRASSES have dominated the move towards a more naturalistic approach to planting design: the so-called "new naturalism" has focused almost exclusively on herbaceous plants to create beautiful evocations of nature. Given the wealth of spectacular flowering landscapes and plant communities around the world, it is hardly surprising that designers and gardeners have chosen diverse grassland types such as prairies, meadows, and steppe as their starting point. And because their attention has been on flowers and abundant growth, they have taken inspiration almost exclusively from sunny and open habitats. Until now, shrubs and other woody plants have been largely left out of the equation.

The disappearance of shrubs from contemporary discussions of naturalistic planting design is incredibly ironic because overall shrubs remain the most ubiquitous and widely used type of landscape and garden plant, dominating the displays and offerings from garden centres and retail outlets. But this ubiquity has proved to be their downfall. The New Perennial movement started in Europe in the second half of the 20th Century as a direct counter-reaction to the previous shrub-based regime that held sway. The stodgy shrubbery, a feature of British gardens during the 1950s, 60s and 70s and usually a jumbled-up mix of a diverse range of shrubs (one of each) that fused together into a chaotic mess, was very dispiriting and uninspiring. During the same period in the public landscape, endless hectares of shrub mass plantings – monocultural blocks of a very limited range of low-maintenance shrubs, often trimmed into unnatural shapes, and sitting in sterile bark mulch – was equally, or even more, dispiriting (it is hugely depressing that we still find so much of this around today).

It is no wonder then that in the 1980s perennials and grasses offered such a refreshing sense of dynamism, colour, movement and change, compared to the rigidness of these tired shrub plantings. They also seemed to present a much more direct connection to the natural world and chimed with a growing sense of ecological awareness. At the same time, in the United States, a movement against the importation of European garden styles and the dominance of the (irrigated) lawn led to a renewal of interest in the indigenous landscape, most notably the prairie ecosystem, as a basis for garden and planting design. The prairie aesthetic is now dominant in contemporary planting design, but one if its characteristics is that it's mostly a no-go area for shrubs.

And the name doesn't help either: "shrub" lacks a certain sexiness, and the American equivalent "bush" isn't much better. Shrub-dominated landscapes also often have negative connotations recalling scrub, for example, a term used to describe poor agricultural land that has been overgrazed or dominated by impenetrable thorny vegetation. So, for many reasons, the shrub has become an under-rated element in refined gardening circles. However, that also means that the time is ripe for a complete reconsideration of their place within a more ecologically-informed, naturalistic and sustainable approach to the way we plant our gardens and designed landscapes. That's why this book is so important and timely. Let's hear it for shrubs!

BELOW **The Beech Gardens at the Barbican in London demonstrate how well woody plants fit into naturalistic planting design. They also bring the huge benefit of a permanent three-dimensional structure with additional biodiversity benefits and habitat opportunities.**

The good news is that, as this book shows so well, shrub-based planting can fit so easily within the orbit of contemporary naturalistic planting design – there is absolutely no reason why all its principles should not be applied to woody plants. In essence, naturalistic planting design takes "natural" plant communities and vegetation types and uses them as the base and inspiration for creating enhanced, amplified versions for gardens and designed landscapes. This inspiration can be applied by using the actual plant species and combinations that occur in the wild, but equally it can come from studying the visual essence of that vegetation, noticing the plant patterns and distributions, and using these as a design starting point. This book is full of such inspiration and reference points. The examples draw upon the experience of the authors and are predominantly North American in their geographical locations, but the same principles apply wherever shrubs are the main component of the vegetation anywhere in the world. Different words or terms are used to describe shrublands depending on their geographical location. The Californian chaparral features in this book, but we also have the maquis of France and the Mediterranean, the Italian macchia, the mattoral in Spain, Chile and Mexico, the fynbos in South Africa and kwongan in south-west Australia, to name but a few. Within this global distribution there is such huge variation in character from dense thickets of closed scrub to more sparse open scrub and from tall shrublands and savanna through to low heathlands.

Scrub may be an unflattering name, but some of the most valuable and attractive starting points for shrub-based planting design are the more open types of scrub, where shrubs are mixed with other plant types. Scrub can be a magical mix of shrubs and small trees scattered among meadow or grassland, so typical of chalk or limestone areas; these are often also a veritable biodiversity hotspot for birds and insects as well as plant life. Equally, the roadsides, prairie edges and woodland edges of the eastern United States and the Midwest often contain intimate mixtures of herbaceous perennials and suckering clonal shrubs that produce visually spectacular displays in autumn. Like British chalk downlands and limestone dales, central European steppe combines a wide diversity of shrubs and small trees (primarily from the Rosaceae) in a mosaic comprising sun-loving herbaceous perennials and grasses. So instead of scrub, how about using a different, more evocative name for these wonderful vegetation types, perhaps shrub mosaics?

Although most of the examples given above are from sunny places, shrubs are found in shade as well, for example as vital components of woodland- or forest-edge habitats and providing the understory layer in forest vegetations. It is important to remember that in most temperate parts of the world, the natural vegetation state is woody. By focusing on naturalistic herbaceous plantings, almost by definition, means that increased energy and resources are needed in the management of grassland-based plantings to keep them as grasslands year after year. Conversely, shrub-based plantings will require much less input because they are closer to the natural state of things. Adding shrubs into the mix also brings with it the huge benefit of permanent three-dimensional structure – meadowy plantings tend to appear rather two dimensional and flat. Furthermore, having a permanent presence of woody plants brings with it additional biodiversity benefits and habitat opportunities.

BELOW A scattering of trees and shrubs with other plant types is often seen in wild shrub landscapes and makes a magical mix here at the Beech Gardens in London.

ABOVE **Shrubs planted in patterns that evoke the natural coastal landscape at Juan Grimm's Bahía Azul garden in Chile.**

This book includes some fantastic examples of naturalistic design with shrubs, using reference wild landscapes as a starting point. While the focus here is on North America, exactly the same principles of working in tune with the local and regional vegetation types or biotopes apply across the world. Some examples of naturalistic planting design with shrubs include the incredible gardens and designed landscapes of Olivier Filippi in France, who works in highly stressed Mediterranean environments. He draws upon the wide range of native shrubs and sub-shrubs to create shrubscapes that are highly textural, due to contrasts in plant shape and form, and so successful that it is often difficult to tell where the garden ends and the surrounding wild landscape begins.

Similarly, the Chilean landscape architect, Juan Grimm, creates spectacular gardens dominated by shrubs in patterns that emulate the natural landscape. While many of the plants used are native plants, not all are indigenous to the locality. The crucial point is that they all share a visual ecology in that they fit with the character of the surroundings. Grimm is an unashamed modernist who doesn't go in for rustic charm and his planting is often juxtaposed with modern and contemporary architecture and industrial materials – the rounded and natural forms of the woody plants making a great contrast with the rigid lines of the built elements.

In my own work I have deliberately included the shrub form to give a solid framework among or above loose and wild perennial plantings. For example, the shrub-steppe plantings at the Beech Gardens at the Barbican in London integrate low-density shrubs within naturalistic dry meadow and steppe plantings in this public roof garden. Shrubs used include *Amelanchier lamarckii* (for spring flower and autumn foliage), *Philadelphus* 'Belle Étoile' (for summer scent and flower), *Euonymus europaeus* 'Red Cascade' (for autumn fruit and foliage), *Viburnum* × *bodnantense* 'Dawn' (for winter flower and scent), *Hypericum* × *hidcoteense* 'Hidcote' (for summer flower and evergreen leaves), and *Sambucus nigra* f. *porphyrophylla* 'Gerda' PBR (for foliage, flower and fruit), and multi-stemmed *Cornus kousa* var. *chinensis* (for flower, fruit and autumn colour). These are all used to create an open woodland-edge framework for the perennial plantings and have been essential to the success of the scheme, in particular for creating a three-dimensional quality and structure to the plantings for much of the year when the perennials are not at their peak. The seasonal dimension of autumn leaf colour and fruit has also been important.

The hazel coppice at Trentham Gardens, Staffordshire, UK is another example of shrubs providing a solid framework for underplanting. A grid of native hazel (*Corylus avellana*) was planted at 3-5-metre (10-15-ft) centres, beneath which is a ground layer planting of native ferns and perennials with year-round interest, including the evergreen hart's tongue fern, (*Asplenium scolopendrium*), oxlip (*Primula elatior*), sweet violet (*Viola odorata*) and lungwort (*Pulmonaria* 'Blue Ensign'). Periodic coppicing of the hazels (every five years) retains their shrub form in addition to which they contribute early spring flowers, fruit, autumn colour, and textural winter bark. The complete planting almost makes a whole ecosystem and without the three-dimensional woody plant component, it would be a simple and much less interesting green carpet at ground level.

These few examples, along with the others in the book, are only scratching the surface of what's possible. There is so much natural inspiration to be discovered, studied, and learnt from. This book is the first to totally devote itself to opening our eyes to that inspiration, and I hope that it will be an important and much-needed starting point to bring shrubs back in from the cold, so that they can take their rightful place as essential components within naturalistic planting of gardens and public spaces.

FOLLOWING SPREAD *Coleogyne ramosissima* (blackbrush) scrubland in the Needles District of Canyonlands National Park, Utah. Blackbrush is drought-deciduous, losing its leaves during periods of intense heat or drought, giving these shrubs a charred, skeletal appearance.

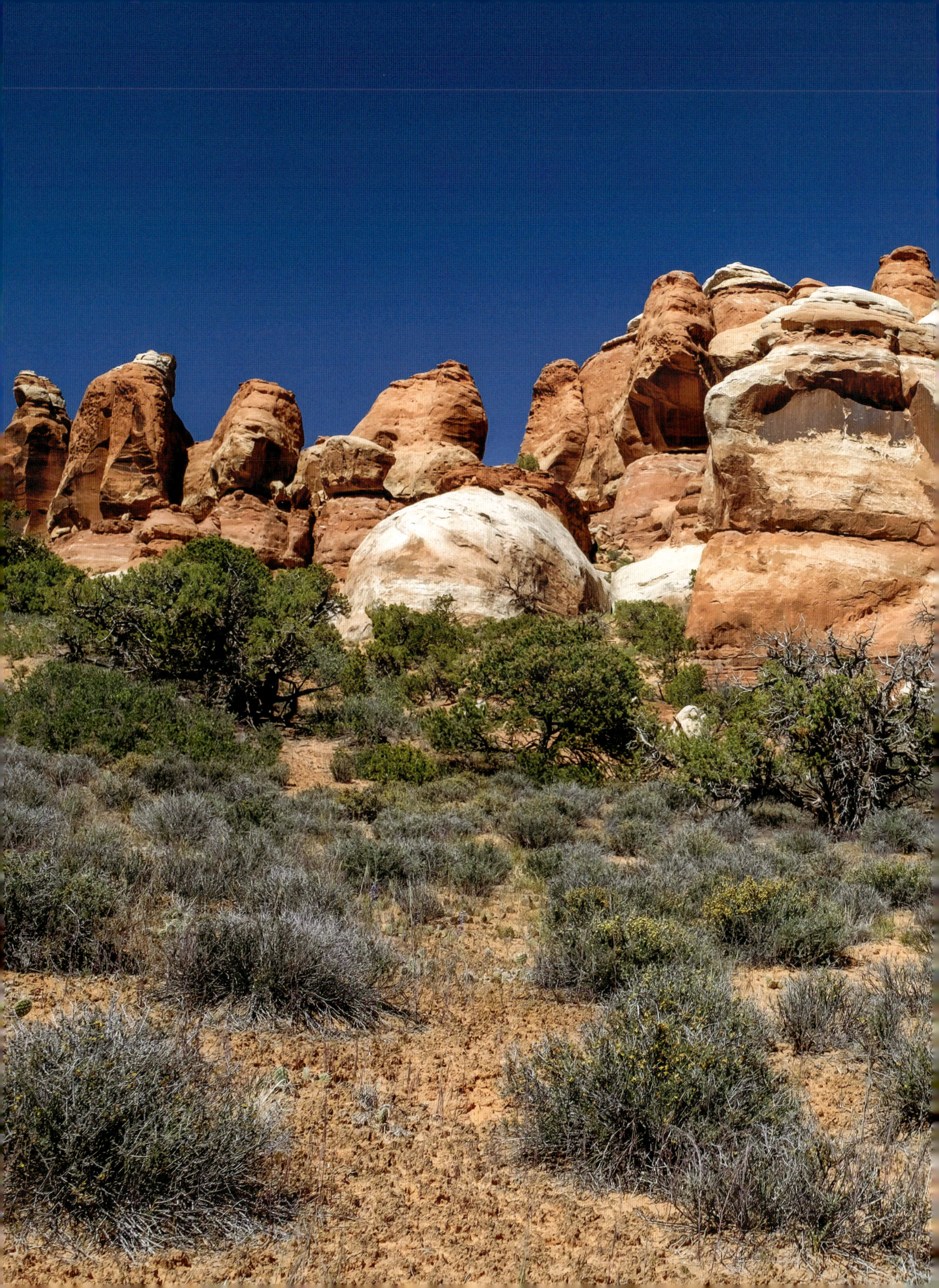

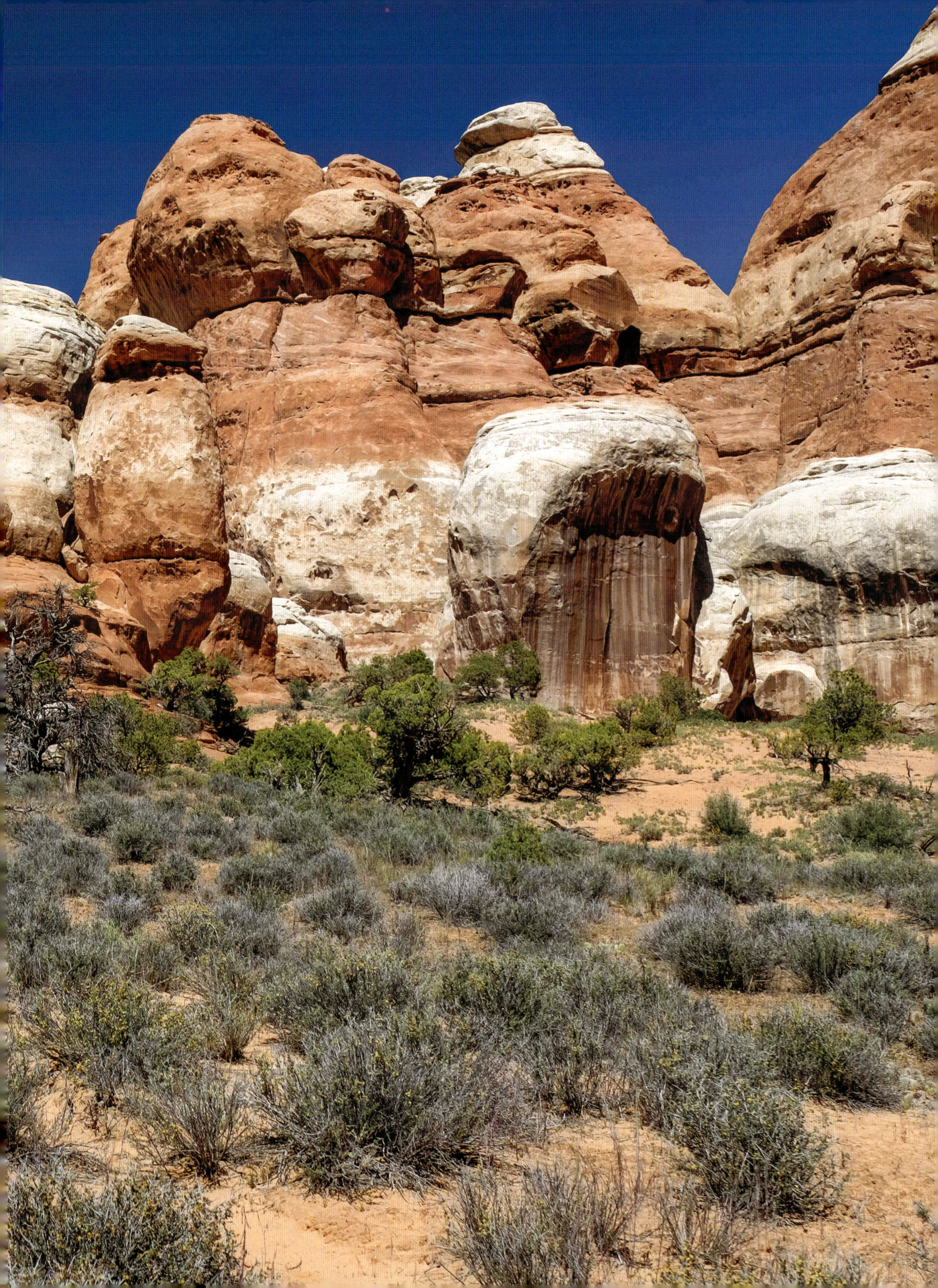

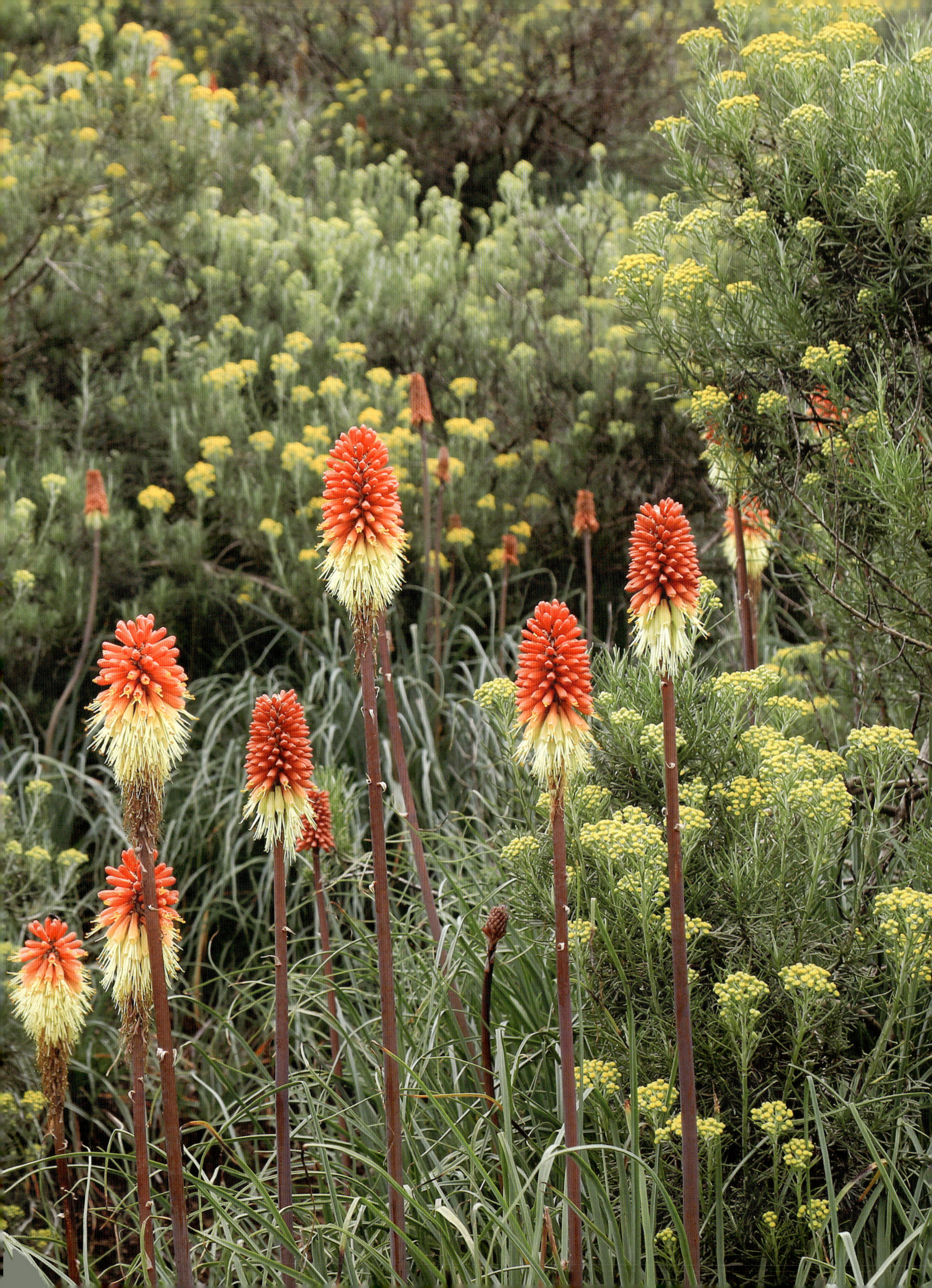

PREFACE

Parallels between floristic and morphological expression in plant communities can be seen throughout the world. In this case, the pairing of *Kniphofia caulescens* (red-hot poker) and *Inulanthera thodei* (lelingoana) is reminiscent of the Central Asian combinations of *Eremurus* (foxtail lily) and *Helichrysum* (everlasting) or the North American *Liatris* (blazing star) and *Ericameria* (rabbitbrush).

AMERICAN HARDCORE
Kevin Philip Williams

"We are creatures shaped by our experiences; we like what we know, more often than we know what we like."

Wallace Stegner | *Thoughts in a Dry Land* [1]

MY MIND MELTED THE FIRST TIME I saw a thicket of rabbitbrush and sagebrush shrouded in harsh western American light. I understood that these were Other things in a place very different from anything I had yet experienced. The bluffs and washes frothed with silver and teal, breaking against cinnamon earth and cresting in charcoal and gold. Wading into the tumult and walking among the glowing shrubs was intoxicating. This was a cartoon world; a type of magic; a wish. These colors, forms, and geologies seemed alien and improbable, albeit common and primally terrestrial. My eyes had been opened to a different beauty. My veil was being shredded, my grasslands plowed under, my forests of perception burned to the ground. I was standing at the edge of the vast shrubland known as The Great Sagebrush Sea, and it was raging. This was my gateway to shrublands. I started to notice them everywhere that I traveled. They fill deserts, surround forests, permeate grasslands and hold back the oceans. They are expansive and liminal, permanent and temporary. I felt energized by the intensity of these places and their inspired compositions.

These ecosystems are our future gardens, and partnering with shrubs to create new worlds out of our fragmented, highly altered, mutating planet is imperative for the survival of all things. Shrublands are simultaneously vibrant, complex ecosystems and hard places, refuges built on environmental economies of extremes. Shrubs are exceptional creatures, providing for their communities and connecting all threads with their endurance.

Shrouded in Light is a celebration and exploration of shrublands and the shrubs that make them. It is an invitation for you to design, work, live, and play with shrubs. Internalizing the mantras of shrublands will allow you to see the world differently, more complexly, and hopefully, more holistically. Do you have the courage to enter the thicket? To explore hard places? To stare into the void and listen to the dissonance?

Fluid Creatures Shrouded in Light (2019)
HOUSE PAINT ON CANVAS
Sean McNamara
This painting is an exploration of the treatment and arrangement of objects and Others at the intersection of scrublands and abandoned spaces. It plays with the interchangeability of the forms and utility of organic and inorganic things in the landscape while highlighting the details (flowers versus mortar) that undeniably separate them. The cartoonish glare of the main subject blows the entire scene apart — a reminder that the observed has intentions of its own.

COLLABORATIVE CREATURES
Michael Guidi

"To use the world well, to be able to stop wasting it and our time in it, we need to relearn our being in it."

Ursula K. Le Guin | *Forward, Deep in Admiration* [2]

Shrubs are the growth form of the Anthropocene. Their familiar shadows follow us across the landscape where humans harrow, graze, and develop in economic pursuit. Shrubs thrive in the hottest of desert regions, roadcuts, and abandoned pastures, and they march reliably northward into the Arctic tundra as we warm the earth. They are collaborators in our earth stewardship, boldly occupying space in the rapid, inevitable disturbance of human enterprise. Their intermediate and in-between nature, like our own, prepares them to inherit changing planetary conditions and thrive in the new wilds of the world.

Shrubs exist like all organisms, by transforming energy into the sinuous threads of life, but their efforts are only possible because of their extensive partnerships with other creatures. It is now believed that the success of all living things is best understood through the lens of collaboration. "We are all lichens:"[3] an amalgamation of different organisms that exist in symbiosis to sustain life. This biological revelation has muddied the waters of classical biotic interaction and evolutionary theory and ultimately leads to the conclusion that a biological individual as commonly understood does not exist. Rather, life is assembled from symbiotic interactions that are so thoroughly embedded within biota they disrupt all of the traditional boundaries that have historically defined an individual organism. Just like lichens, we all require the ever-present effort of our symbionts. The individual, then, is an emergent property of a complex biological system, and shrubs with their enmeshed limbs and dense thickets embody this notion of convoluted interaction. Shrublands are the living embodiment of Darwin's entangled bank and Alexander von Humboldt's nonlinear knotted fabric – places that converge and bind life. They aggregate, divide, and pulse across every major biome, acting as conduits of biodiversity and eco-evolutionary change in real time.

This book is a call to incorporate the aesthetic lessons from shrub-dominated landscapes into our planted spaces but also poses a deeper challenge to bring their collaborative way of being into practice. From the open sagebrush steppe to the chaos of mixed shrub ecotone, shrublands inspire and evoke human reaction; let us take this as an invitation for partnership. Let's bring shrubby chaos into the garden and be shrouded in its light.

Ferricrete Fynbos (2022)
WOOL ON LINEN REGISTER,
40.6 x 35.6cm, approximately 37,856 stitches
John Feek

A cascading shrubland on the shoulder of the Beartooth Plateau, Wyoming. Ribbons of silver *Artemisia tridentata* (big sagebrush) and red *Ribes aureum* (golden currant) integrate a spectrum of senescing textures in this mixed-structure landscape.

Welcome to the Thicket

Shrubs are their own creatures. They are Others – individuals with their own intentions and agency worthy of our attention and respect. In order to fully appreciate and accept them, we have to think beyond ourselves.

Throughout this book we offer artistic inspirations, philosophical ideas, cultural touchpoints and atmospheric tones that are necessary to understand the variety of moods, thoughts, emotions and aesthetics that are inherent to, and evoked by, shrublands. These are varied, marvelous, extraordinary, challenging, mysterious places and their potential is best experienced if we meet them with equal depth.

Gardens can be more profound places than many people let them be. They do not have to be one-dimensional, built solely for human enjoyment. They need not be spaces that reinforce notions of contemporary beauty or be justified by a measurable function that they perform. Gardens do not have to exist at all, but since they do, we should make them as complex and interesting as the world needs them to be.

This book is broken into three sections: *Understanding Shrubs*, *Seeing Shrublands*, and *Making Shrubscapes*. In *Understanding Shrubs*, we discuss the nature of shrubs and the ecology of shrublands, and explore how we think about and respond emotionally to these plants and their communities. *Seeing Shrublands* investigates the cultural conditions and visual appeal of the major and minor shrublands of the world, while *Making Shrubscapes* offers techniques, ideas and examples for working with shrubs to create dynamic, resilient landscapes.

View of Bordighera (1884)
Claude Monet
Of the Mediterranean maquis of Bordighera, Italy, Monet said "It is too thick, and there are always parts with lots of details, a jumble terrible to render, and of course, I am the man of isolated trees and vast spaces."[4] But Monet did paint the jumble, and in the intricate, light-catching, sclerophyllous menage was pushed to create a thicker, wilder Impressionism. In *View of Bordighera* (1884), he depicts a city barely carved out of the land. Between a frame of sinewy pines and dense, upper elevation scrub he captured foliage hued between black and yellow, and a sea of cool-toned shrubs rushing to and through the city even more active than the sea beyond. In this scene, the only visible path back to humanity is seemingly impassable. Instead of a mass path, the traditional rural trail, shrublands create the negative, the path of mass.

There isn't a single right way to appreciate and interpret these landscapes, and we don't want you to see them only in the way that we do, but we're asking you to look, possibly with a wider lens than you have before. We want to show you possibilities, not certainties, and above all, inspiration, not instruction.

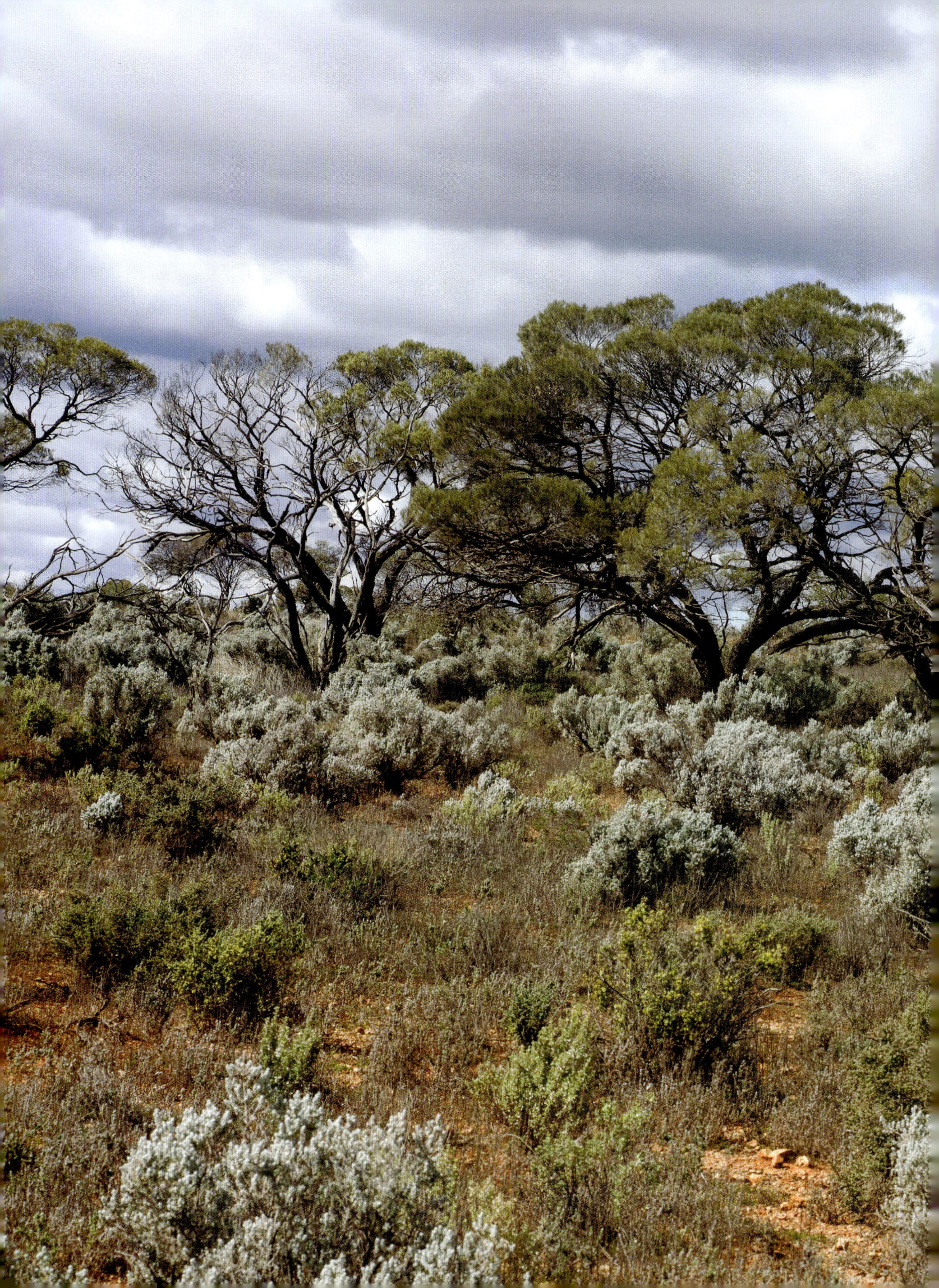

The remnants of an *Acacia* (wattle) woodland mixing with a chenopod shrubland in South Australia. This harsh, tortured landscape holds an intrinsic and extrinsic beauty that's compelling beyond conventional standards. The subtly shifting hues of faded green, the red earth, and the contrast of silver with the charcoal trunks provide a sophisticated earth-tone palette, while the twisting and self-contained forms communicate experience, reliance and self-assuredness. The limitations imposed on this environment have created a refined composition. Often the most interesting and important expressions occur in the face of oppression.

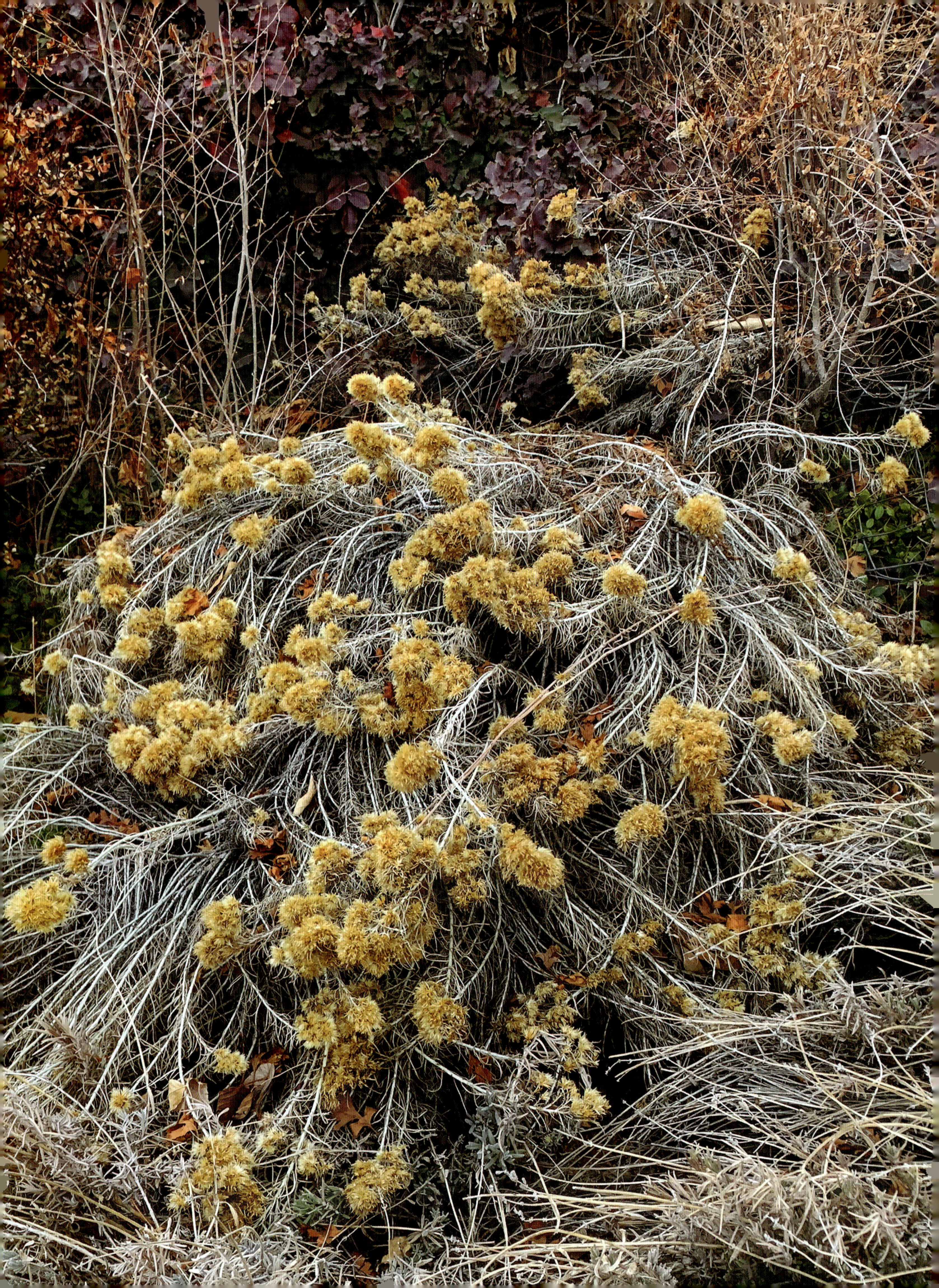

1

A mixed shrub garden of *Berberis aquifolium* (Oregon grape), *Berberis thunbergii* (Japanese barberry), and *Lavandula* sp. (lavender) featuring grotesquely attractive *Ericameria nauseosa* (rubber rabbitbrush) as its centerpiece. Denver, Colorado.

UNDERSTANDING SHRUBS

"So many ecological beings are 'Excluded Middles'
and so much ecological action is in the realm of 'not quite'
and 'slightly,' gradations of yes."

Timothy Morton | *Dark Ecology: For a Logic of Future Coexistence*, 2016[5]

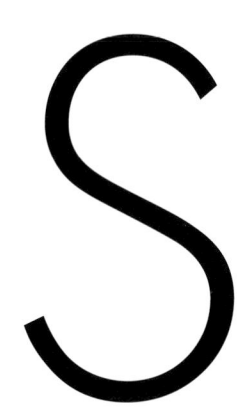

SHRUBS ARE UNDERSTUDIED CREATURES compared to their herbaceous and arboreal relatives. The categorization of plant growth forms into herbs, shrubs, and trees is an ancient distinction dating back to Greek philosophers and has remained largely intact since. Clearly, humans have long been in agreement that there is something distinct and intermediate about shrubs: we know them when we see them.

Why So Shrubby?

Though vague, the definition of a shrub usually contains some consistent elements: a multi-stemmed/trunked, wood-producing plant, usually smaller than a tree but larger than herbaceous vegetation (attempts to assign a height range are usually contradictory and futile). Of course, most plants are multi-stemmed, producing wood does not have to define a plant as a shrub, and trees can be almost any size. Still, there has been tireless dispute about the basic definition of a shrub.

Shrubs, as an intermediate growth form, are increasingly understood to have a number of advantages, especially under harsh environmental conditions. They are able to allocate biomass into a greater number of woody stems, each requiring less resource investment than the primary stems of a tree. This growth strategy allows shrubs to exist in unforgiving environments where loss of one or more stems will still allow for growth and reproduction. Frequent fire, hailstorms, or other environmental damage mean that shrubs must balance their energetic investment into persistent above-ground tissues. For similar reasons, trees are conspicuously absent in the steppe and desert regions of the world, including the North American prairie, where frequent disturbance and scarcity of resources do not incentivize the evolution of woody growth forms.

UNDERSTANDING SHRUBS 27

LEFT The succulent scrub and evergreen bushes of the Argentine steppe populate one of the driest regions in the country. Here *Pleurophora patagonica* (tomillo rosa) blooms profusely among dormant bunchgrasses near the town of Sarmiento.

BELOW The high contrast between the dark cinnabar of *Eriogonum fasciculatum* (California buckwheat) and the copper green *Ceanothus leucodermis* (chaparral whitethorn) defies the idea of a summer-dry, washed-out world. California.

Stems

We peered into each mass

Crouching Hunkering Crawling Wondering

When does soft tissue become rigid?

When does bark peel, fissure and blush?

When does wood crack open?

When does it dress itself in Others?

When does damage become decor?

When does disease become desirable?

UNDERSTANDING SHRUBS   29

Arctostaphylos glauca (bigberry manzanita)

Larrea tridentata (creosote bush)

Lichens on *Ceanothus* (California lilac)

Pieris floribunda (mountain andromeda)

Rhododendron catawbiense (mountain rosebay)

Prunus pensylvanica (fire cherry)

Aralia racemosa (American spikenard)

Shrubs as Caretakers

Shrublands have some of the highest animal biodiversity outside the tropics, partially owing to their complex vegetation structure that allows them to harbor high numbers of plants and animals.[6] In North America, arid and semi-arid shrublands are hotbeds of endemism, with a high degree of specialization to soil types and environmental conditions. Here, the very nature of environmental harshness provides a multitude of microclimates and ecological niches for plants and animals to inhabit. The harsh environmental conditions of many shrublands mean that ecological interactions among shrubs and their co-occurring species are critical for plant communities. Shrubs can facilitate the establishment, growth, and persistence of other plant species beneath their canopy, acting as nurse plants that help to temper harsh sunlight, lessen evaporation, and draw precious water to the surface with established root systems. In part, shrubs become caretakers for plants because they are first caretakers of other creatures; birds and mammals rest, nest, and feed in their branches and root systems, carrying and dropping seeds that find nooks in the organic duff beneath in which to germinate – a fitting synergy that has earned shrubs and shrublands the designation of fertility islands.

The saguaro cactus (*Carnegiea gigantea*) was one of the first species identified to be a beneficiary of nurse plants, shown to establish only under the canopy of Sonoran Desert shrubs, including creosote bush (*Larrea tridentata*) and mesquite (*Prosopis glandulosa*). Since then, ecologists have identified nurse plant effects from ecosystems as diverse as pinyon-juniper shrublands to high-elevation alpine cushion and shrub communities. The common feature among all systems with strong nurse plant effects are harsh environmental conditions; from blistering heat to pitifully short growing seasons, plants help other plants to prosper in these settings. It's increasingly clear that facilitative effects, like the nurse plant phenomena in shrublands, are critical for structuring and maintaining plant communities and far more widespread than initially recognized by plant ecologists.

In gardens, shrubs can also act as caretakers, not only for other plants, but for animal life as well. In planted environments, just as in natural ecosystems, vegetation structure is a primary driving factor in promoting biodiversity. Simple landscapes such as lawns lack species diversity, whereas landscapes with a mix of herbaceous and woody plant material of varying heights and emergence times will harbor many more species. Shrubland-inspired

UNDERSTANDING SHRUBS

LEFT The Embrace. Nursing and coddling shrubs in Saguaro National Park East, Arizona

BELOW Regionally, rhododendron thickets have been dubbed rhododendron hells because of the difficulty of passing through their dense and deeply tangled, scraping branches. Does the sentiment transfer when we work with these plant communities to create shrubscapes? Does hostile ecology create hostile horticulture? Do we create our own Hells? Dolly Sods Wilderness, Monongahela National Forest, West Virginia.

"Alone above a raging sea"[7]
Frangula californica (coffeeberry), *Ceanothus thyrsiflorus* (blueblossom), *Ericameria ericoides* (mock heather) and *Eriophyllum staechadifolium* (silver seaside wooly sunflower) raging in their own cove, full of the movement of the Pacific Ocean. Big Sur, California.

landscapes also have the advantage of year-round presence, remaining structurally intact during the winter months, providing a welcome refuge for birds, invertebrates, and other creatures. And just as in natural areas, shrubs influence their surrounding environment with regard to co-occurring plants. Shade from a nearby shrub may represent the required environmental alteration to support a rich primary layer of grasses and herbaceous perennials. As designed plant communities change over time, the high ecological heterogeneity of shrubby landscapes provides the necessary conditions for diverse plant communities to prosper. In ecological time, annual or biennial plants may persevere only under the shady protection of a nearby shrub in dry years, but spread back throughout the landscape in subsequent years with more precipitation. Persistent perennials that require less exposure may find the necessary respite within the environmental modification of shrubby growth that might not be available in the matrix of an herbaceous planting.

No plant community is static, whether natural or designed, and by harnessing the innate collaboration between different plant growth forms we can thoughtfully chaperone relationships – rather than dictate positions – between plants for a more resilient landscape.

Shrubs play a key facilitative role in desert environments, improving plant establishment and influencing community structure. Seemingly inert stems of *Fouquieria splendens* (ocotillo) splay outward in dormant intercession while *Agave deserti* (desert agave) patchily skirt around their bases in Mojave National Preserve, California.

Fruits

The ritual of *seeking out that which is offered* The entitlement of consumption The passion of consummation The gratitude of nourishment, satiation and relinquishment

UNDERSTANDING SHRUBS

Prunus americana (American plum)

Prunus maritima (beach plum)

Notholithocarpus densiflorus (tanbark oak)

Fuchsia paniculata ssp. *paniculata* (shrubby fuchsia)

Arbutus xalapensis (Texas madrone)

Berberis repens (creeping Oregon grape)

Cascabela thevetia (bushy dogbane)

Larrea nitida (jarilla)

Ephedra ochreata (caman)

Rhododendron canadense (rhodora)

Alnus alnobetula (green alder)

Ribes roezlii (Sierra gooseberry)

Global Weirdness

In an era of profound global change, shrublands are generally prospering. Global warming is thawing permafrost in the Arctic, allowing willow shrublands to advance across the tundra. Intensive grazing practices and suppressed fire regimes are causing graminoids of perennial grasslands to lose out to shrubs[8], which are better able to endure persistent grazing pressure. In areas of the American West which are experiencing more frequent, intense wildfires, shrublands are replacing previously forested landscapes. We should expect consistent changes like these as ecosystems react and adapt to shifting baseline conditions. It's clear, however, that shrubs are well-made for the ubiquitous ecological disturbance of the Anthropocene.

Eriogonum umbellatum (sulphurflower buckwheat), *Ericameria nauseosa* (rubber rabbitbrush), *Ribes cereum* (wax currant) and *Holodiscus dumosus* (mountain spray) carving out a new life on the cinder fields of Newberry National Volcanic Monument, Oregon.

Mixed chaparral regrowth, three years after the Whittier Fire. The blueprints of succession are still looming. It's important to remember that humans most often define what is disaster and what is recovery, but the shrublands set their own terms. California.

Shrubs may also provide practical solutions to our climate and biodiversity crises. Landscape design and vegetation management in our parks, nature preserves, and gardens offer an opportunity to mitigate atmospheric greenhouse gasses through carbon sequestration while simultaneously creating ecologically valuable space. Embracing shrubs as part of the greater, integrated landscape, and looking to shrublands for models on how to design dense, regenerative spaces will help to realize these codependent goals.

How Shrubs Exist

Shrubs are an idea, both real and imposed. That is to say, shrubs certainly exist, but they do so along a spectrum of thoughts about what a shrub is and is not (ultimate size, wood formation, architecture, lifespan). Clearly, the classification and blueprint for what a shrub is remains complex and unresolved. They are plants in a quantum state, and to define them is to misrepresent their true qualities. In this way, shrubs escape definition. And yet, it's mostly obvious what a shrub is when we are face-to-face with one.

Salicylic acid bath on the talus slopes of the Rocky Mountains.

Tamarix (salt cedar) and *Ericameria* (rabbitbrush) breaking around the tufa formations of Mono Lake, California.

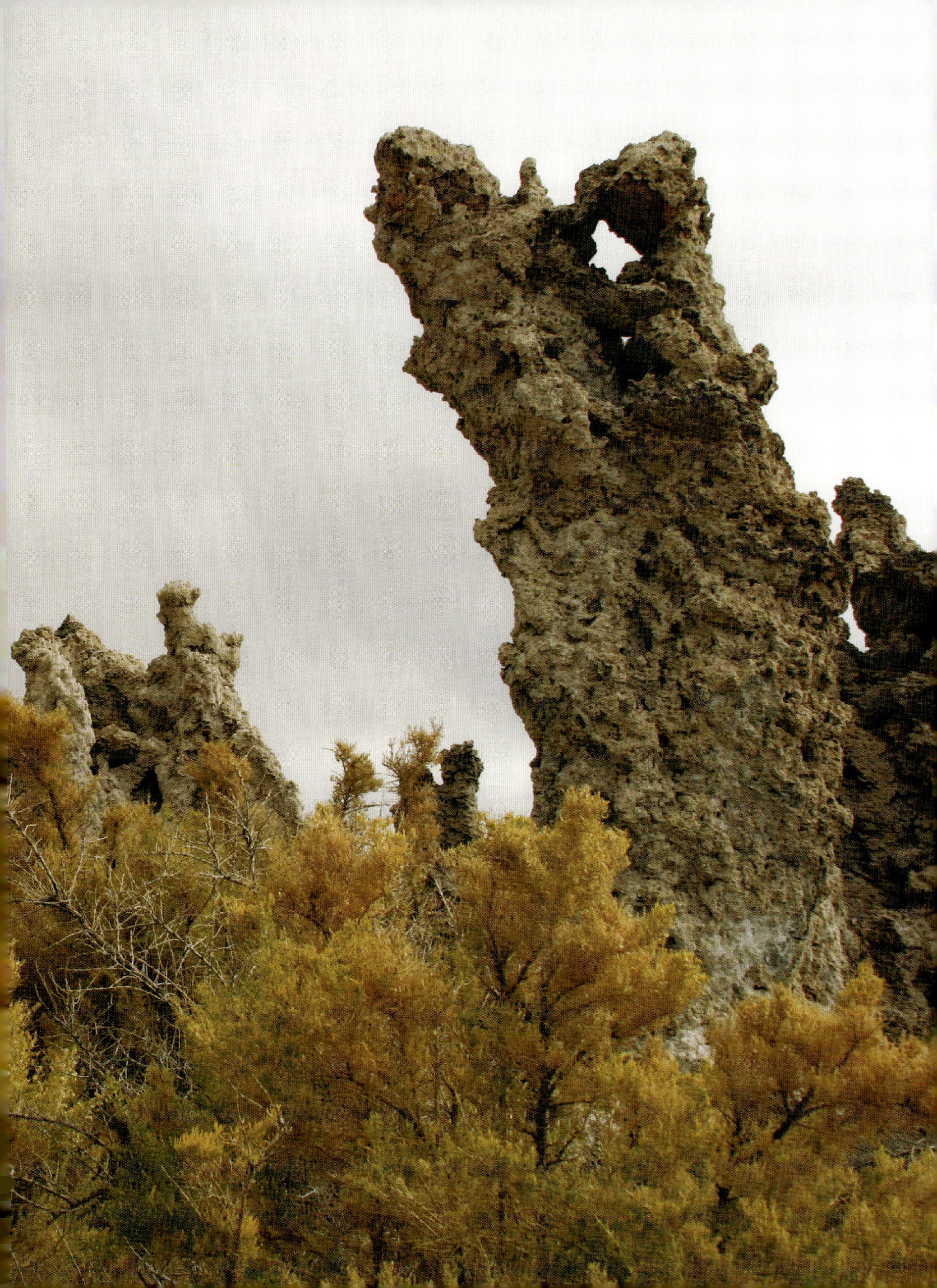

Shrubs (2022)
INK ON PAPER
21.6 x 27.9 cm
Kevin Hennessy
A flash plexus of transmogrifying parts; shrub to human and human to shrub.

Definitions, labels and classifications cannot illustrate the vibrancy of life contained within most creatures. Biological simplification and compartmentalization can no longer be relied upon in an age of DNA sequencing and post-humanist semiotics, and so, we shall not try to define what a shrub is, but rather how it is through the expanded lens of art, philosophy, culture and natureculture.

Shrubs live in the world of excluded middles, as floristic expressions that defy any attempt at definition by existing simultaneously as gradients of multiple things. They are slightly what they are not, and slightly not what they are. Shrubs are constantly in the process of becoming. They are nothing more or less than themselves. A shrub occupies a certain space in the world. It is not the space of flora that we walk over, nor the space of flora that we walk under. It is the space of the flora that we walk with. Shrubs are human-sized, humanoid vegetation[9]; anthropometric flora growing on a scale that we cannot easily dominate. If forbs are fodder and trees are gods, then shrubs are our equals.

The word "shrub" finds its origins in the Proto-Indo-European word sker or ker, meaning to cut. Sker was also used in the creation of the words scrap, shard, carnal, carnage and scrape. Could this mean that shrubs cut and scrape, do they separate or are they separate? Or do they protect? Shroud is of Old English origin, but also finds its origins in the base terms cut or shred. Is a shroud a shrub? Is a shrubland a shroudland? Do they cover, encase or envelope? Where is the carnage of a shrub directed? What does it shield?

Are shrublands cities populated with interfloric citizens? Are they analogous anthroflora (flora that is most related and relatable to the function of people) and if so, how do we relate to a flora that exists on our scale? The natureculture of shrubs and shrublands is as deeply embedded in our cultural practices, languages, and thoughts as any other landscape.

UNDERSTANDING SHRUBS 43

Leaves

We rub ourselves with anything aromatic *Tearing at leaves* Crushing them between our fingers *Breathing* Oblivious to irritation *Looking for abrasion* Begging for chemicals Energy inhaled, ingested, absorbed An elemental condition

UNDERSTANDING SHRUBS 45

Shepherdia rotundifolia (roundleaf buffaloberry)

Arctostaphylos columbiana (hairy manzanita)

Cercocarpus intricatus 'Green Cliff' (Green Cliff little leaf mountain mahogany)

Berberis fremontii (Fremont barberry)

Viburnum 'Pragense' (Prague viburnum)

Vauquelinia californica (Arizona rosewood)

Graptophyllum pictum (caricature plant)

Larrea nitida (jarilla)

Nassauvia glomerulosa (colapiche)

Euphorbia collina (Pichoga)

Quercus marilandica (blackjack oak)

A livestock paddock of Helichrysum trilineatum (hokubetsi) and Pentzia cooperi (lebaila) carved out of the shrublands of Lesotho.

Gimme Danger, Little Stranger[10]

Along with grasslands and forests, shrublands are part of our archetypal landscapes[11] and experiencing them triggers specific senses, thoughts, emotions, and memories. But what exactly is being triggered?

Grasslands and forests are reminders of abundance. They conjure images of fire-regimented hunting grounds and shaded grazing grounds – agricultural and pastoral scenes that promise harvest, security, and comfort. They are spaces that exalt human control; landscape intoxicants of ease and relaxation. Shrublands, by comparison, are perceived as challenging places; they are spaces of hidden rooms and impenetrable walls, concealers of predators and prey. They are also providers of forage and fuel; well-browsed shrubland may indicate a nearby ungulate. Any simplification of a deeply complex, constantly changing system is an injustice, so while shrublands are demanding, the road to partnering with them means understanding why.

Historically and contemporarily, shrublands have been met with destruction and disdain. They are burned, chained, plowed, chopped, shredded or completely disregarded; seen as useless, dangerous, unproductive, and uninhabitable. Our human ignorance and biases have, in small ways, benefitted these landscapes. Many shrublands remain lightly touched,

OPPOSITE, TOP Double Take. A trailside shrub witch echoes the adjacent shrubby forms in a birch-spruce forest understory outside Anchorage, Alaska.

OPPOSITE, BELOW LEFT A strange shrub-witch on the edge of a winter thicket in Great Sand Dunes National Park, Colorado

OPPOSITE, BELOW RIGHT *Agave lechuguilla* (lechuguilla) and gnarled *Juniperus deppeana* (alligator juniper) scaffold the night sky, framing Milky Way star clusters above Chihuahuan Desert scrub in Big Bend National Park, Texas.

under-subjugated, and wild, with the result that shrublands have now become viewed as intriguing, exotic, arousing, covetable, and dangerous. They command attention, interaction and respect. And shrubs are themselves physical and emotional microcosms of shrublands. Their masses and voids can be both attractive and sickening, offering teasing uncertainty and creepiness. The allure and danger of the familiar Other is the offer of something known, yet the menace of difference.[12]

This is an evocation of the uncanny valley, a perceptual phenomenon in which the closer something gets to looking or acting like a human (while not perfectly replicating a human) the more repulsed we are by it. A shrub pruned into cartoonish topiary, or a bush with googly eyes nested in its branches can feel endearing, but a gangly form full of twisted limbs and shadows, rustling from inner life, can feel repellent. In this way, shrubs have become something of a botanical monster[13]. They are a close likeness to ourselves, but they act just beyond the realm of our kingdom. They create thickets, occupying and obstructing our fantasy forests, and reclaim our perfect pastures, competing with our crops. The destined inhabitants of post-humanity, their species and adaptations outnumber ours by many magnitudes.

In response we have tamed them, mutilated them, and pushed them to the literal fringe of gardens. In the dreaded foundational planting, a design concept that has been rallied against almost since its inception[14], the shrub became relegated to the margin between lawn and home, and conceptually to the edge between grassland and forest, and the idea of the wild shrubland was destroyed. We threw out the baby with the bathwater, without realizing the value and potential of both.

Shrubscaping promises to be our first real prospect into dangerous gardening. Through shrubscaping, we create gardens and landscapes that emulate shrublands and celebrate their ability to surprise, allure, and exhilarate. Shrubscapes allow us to have deep and resonant conversations with places that we cannot control. They are reminders that the willful non-human Other exists.

UNDERSTANDING SHRUBS 49

ABOVE On the natural podium known as the Rostrum overlooking Yosemite Valley in California, *Arctostaphylos viscida* (whiteleaf manzanita) grinds on the edge of balds too extreme to support pine and hemlock. The skeletons of the manzanita occupy the same space they did when alive. Their wintergreen leaves and red trunks are an incredible pairing. The slime-green lichen and mosses and cool granite further set this world off. Geologic plants for a geologic world; creeping life;

RIGHT *Thicket #2* (2021)
OIL ON WOOD PANEL 20.3 × 15.2 cm
Mark Laver
Palpable textures unify the thick mesh of dark landscapes and beckon the viewer to enter — a sickening, exhilarating pleasure.

UNDERSTANDING SHRUBS 51

Flowers

It's not the reason, but another reason

It's not sexual It's not subsistence

It's jealousy, adoration, respect

Fashion and representation

Confidence and vulnerability

The ephemeral tradition

Fallugia paradoxa (póñil)

Chilopsis linearis 'Desert Willie' LIPWILLA™(Desert Willie desert willow)

Purshia stansburiana (Stansbury's cliffrose)

Rosa Northern Accents™ 'Sven' (Sven shrub rose)

Ericameria nauseosa (rubber rabbitbrush)

Kalmia latifolia (mountain laurel)

Mimosa borealis (pink mimosa)

Lupinus arboreus (coastal bush lupine)

Amorpha canescens (leadplant)

Sorbus scopulina (western mountain ash)

Rosa acicularis (prickly wild rose)

Salix arctica (Arctic willow)

UNDERSTANDING SHRUBS 55

Diplacus aurantiacus (sticky monkey-flower)

Rhododendron × (hybrid white spider azalea)

Vaccinium angustifolium (lowbush blueberry)

Quercus marilandica (blackjack oak)

Rhododendron prinophyllum (early azalea)

Justicia californica (beloperone)

Walk Among Us

Shrublands are mazes. Structurally, they are self-organized into complicated networks of passageways, rooms, and walls. Walking through a shrubland can be an exercise in confusion and disorientation. Navigating through a thicket takes time, patience, and tolerance, since seemingly clear paths lead to dead ends. The decision to squeeze through two bushes seems logical, until their tangled lower branches clutter your steps and pull at your legs, ultimately revealing no true break in the canopy. You spend more time moving laterally and chasing breaks than moving forward. Doubling back only reveals new confusing passages and patterns.

Shrubs themselves are fractal microcosms of their larger communities. Their labyrinthine structures are due in part to their distinction as organisms

Tumbled sandstone boulders perfectly in scale with the surrounding shrubs create raised pathways through the otherwise unnavigable chaparral. How often do garden paths deliver relief and refuge in addition to perspective?

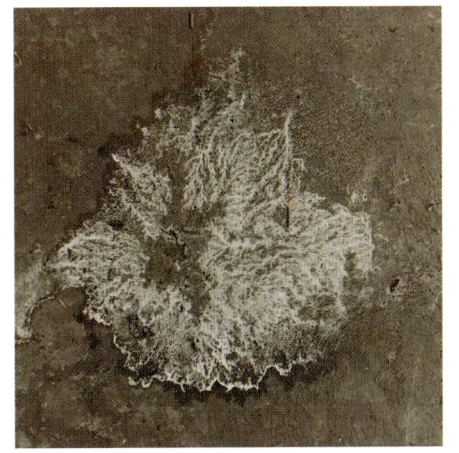

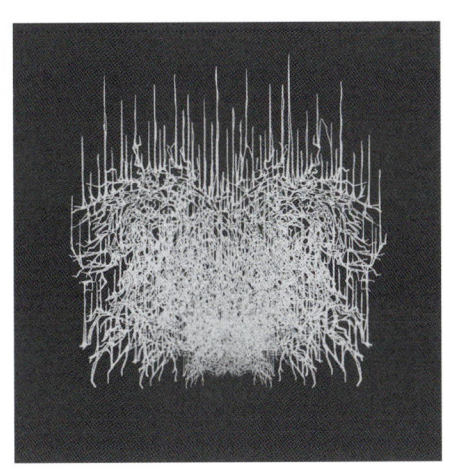

TOP LEFT Lichen, the quintessential partnering organism, negotiating a primal pattern on the forest floor

TOP RIGHT Evaporated salt crystal formations displaying intricate growth patterns; shadows of organic structures based in a chemical world

BOTTOM LEFT Dynamism in death: creeping, sinuous deadwood of *Arctostaphylos viscida* (whiteleaf manzanita) seemingly existing on the same timescale as the granitic substrate it overlays in Yosemite National Park, California. Low-disturbance regimes often build up an abundance of dead biomass which is seen as a sign of neglect or mismanagement in garden settings. Can we embrace these vibrant and persistent reminders of death in our gardens? Listen to the album *Seizures in Barren Praise*[15], stare into the necroarchitecture and embrace the bleak.

BOTTOM RIGHT *Shrub Emblem* (2022)
DIGITAL DRAWING
Alpen Grob
The high-contrast, extremely stark, and somewhat bleak violence of black metal band logos are inspired by natural forms and phenomena, connecting these emblems to the awe and reverence that we feel for ancient, complicated and autonomous organisms and processes.

that are assemblages of living and dead parts. Beneath their leaves, many shrubs have deeply layered and interior branching structures formed from a necroarchitecture of lignified, dead, and broken branches. This intricacy of design and significance is only approximated by black metal sigils, the stylized band names and logos composed of spiky, drippy, gooey, entangled systems. As a genre, black metal strives to create an expression of extreme music inspired by the surrounding environmental atmosphere, and much like the natural landscapes that inspire its musical textures and iconography, a whole new world is unlocked for those who can understand and appreciate them. The living and dead architecture of shrub branching also creates a type of sigil, representing the meaning, purpose, and power of the shrub. Contemplating these structures is a kind of meditation. If we could read them well enough, would they reveal the true name of the shrub?

What other kinds of stories does the tangle tell? These intricate spaces provide food, shelter, refuge and protection for innumerable other creatures. By accepting the deep, dizzying and disorienting aesthetics of shrublands we are accepting the aesthetics of life. We are accepting a deeper understanding of what beauty is, beyond what just makes us happy. To make something really beautiful and unique for this world we need to think about what other beings find beautiful. We need to allow and get lost in non-human messes.

FOLLOWING SPREAD Glacial moraines punch through the fairy-tale forests outside Gothenburg, Sweden. A true heathland, *Erica* dominates the thin rocky soils and a corrosive spectrum of *Vaccinium* color forms nestle into their preferred microclimates. Even after a severe summer drought which aborted flowers and defoliated the most exposed shrubs, the distinct and haunting beauty of the heath remains intact.

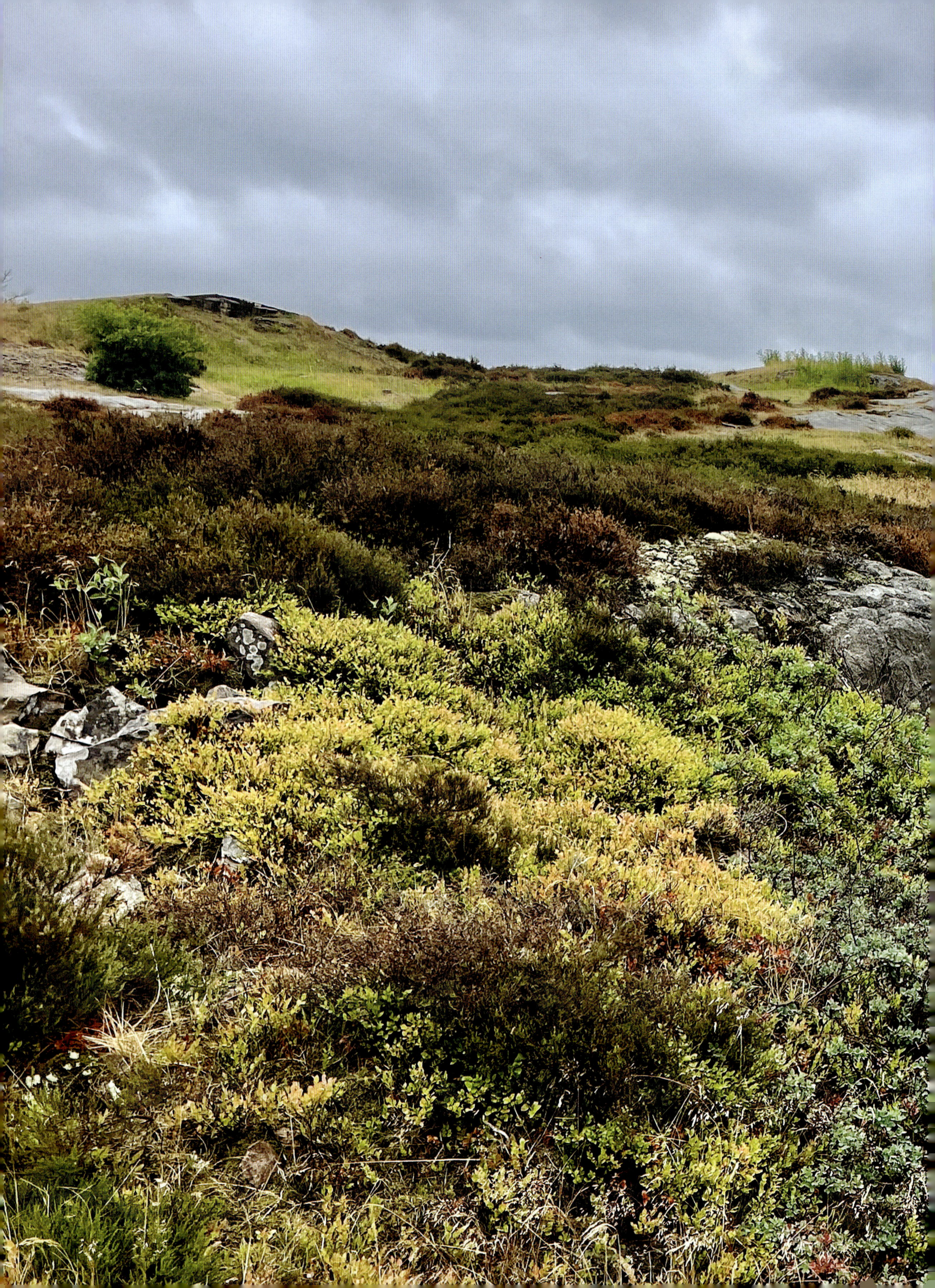

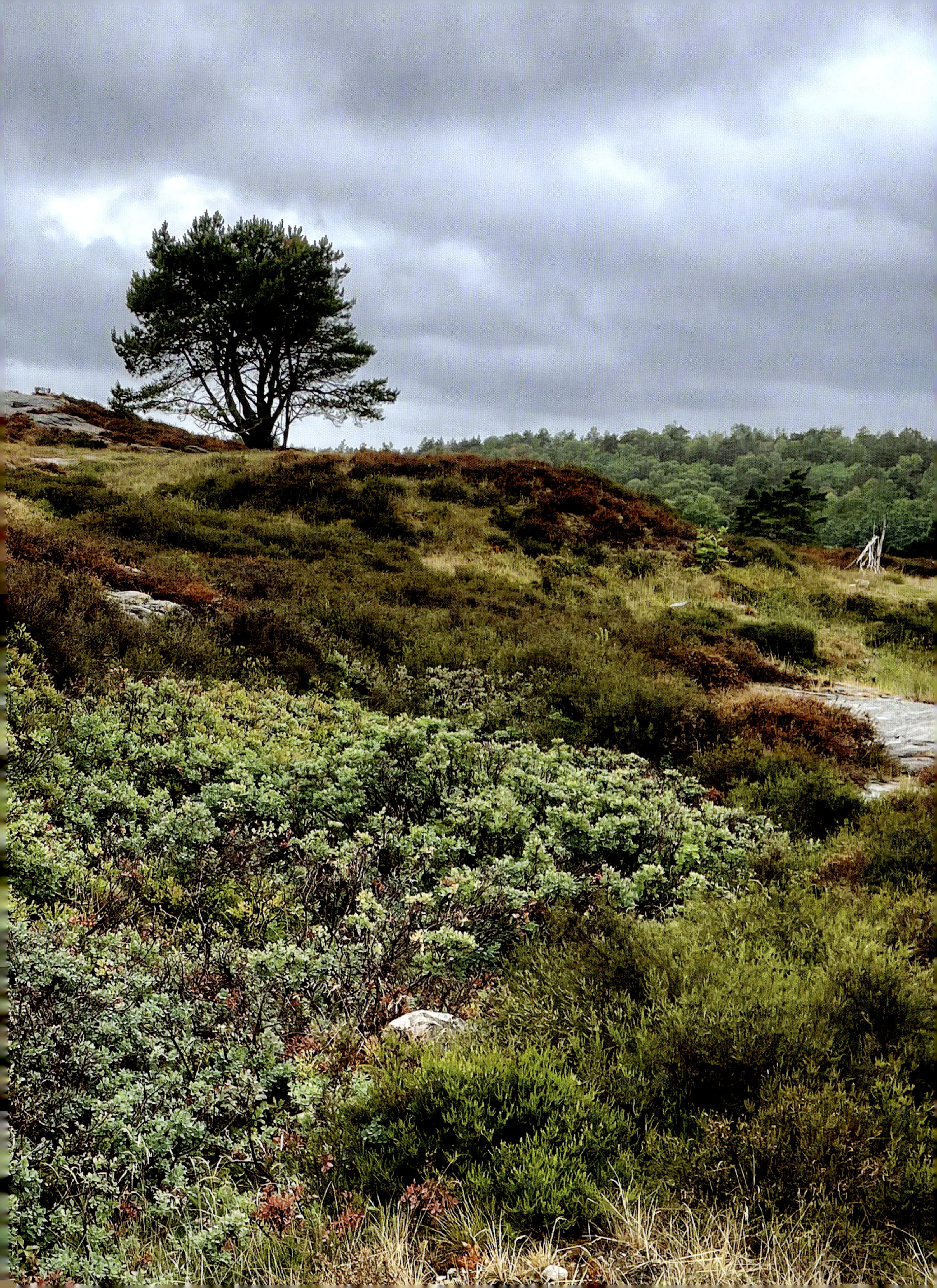

Brush beasts

What draws us here, to walk through
the shrubs together? The mass path
or the path of mass? To hide from
each other? *What do we leave behind?*
Blood, bones, fur, shit, Broken branches
and impressions in the duff
Why do we leave and why do we return?

UNDERSTANDING SHRUBS 61

Piggies in Patagonia, Argentina

Yak in Tibet, China

Uncharismatic megafaunal surrender in the shrublands. Chama, New Mexico

Sunbathing horse in Monument Valley Navajo Tribal Park, Utah

Mule deer in Big Sur, California

Elephant seals and the coastal scrub of San Simeon, California

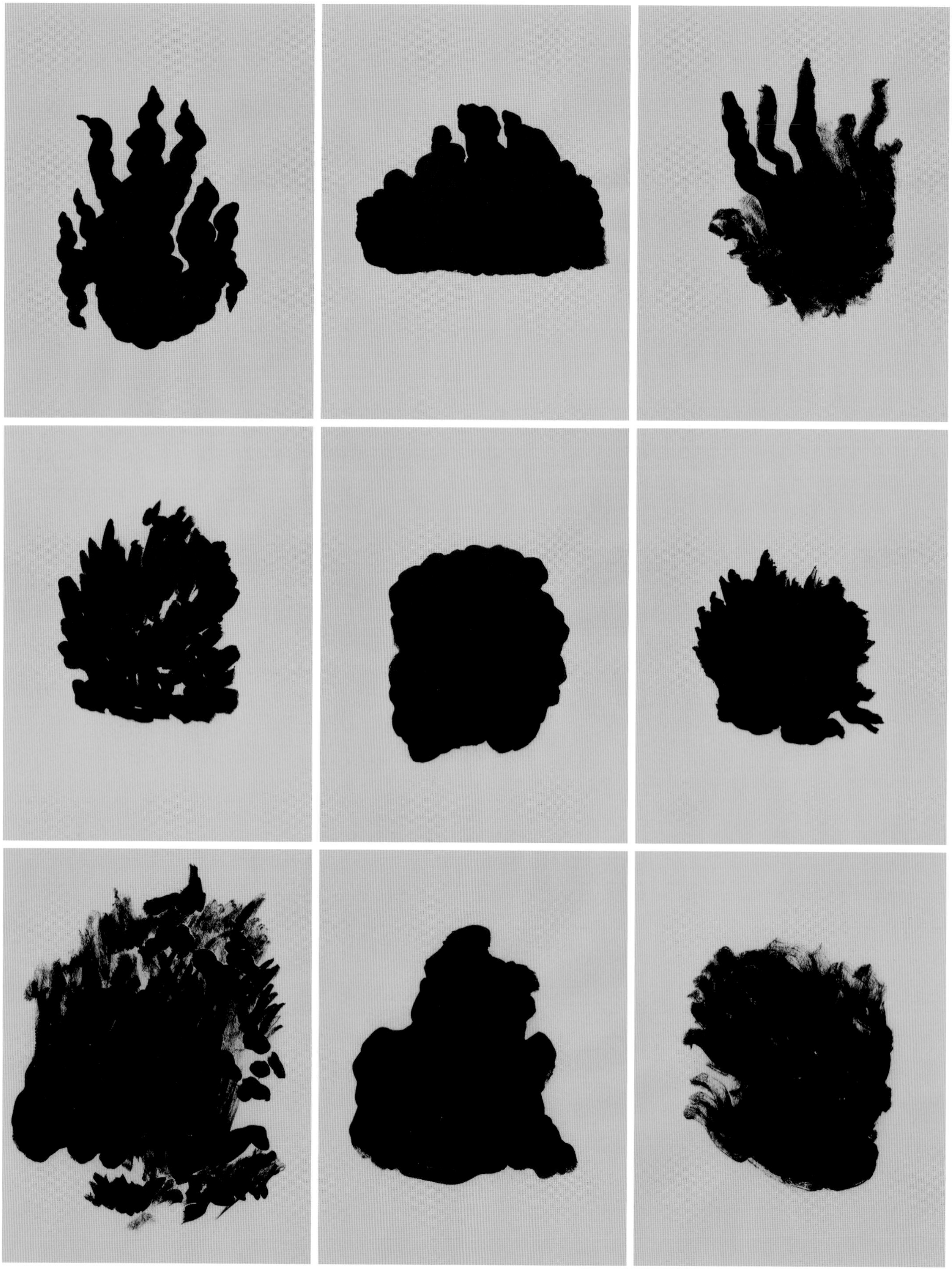

The Divine Language of the Soundless

Gardens are full of non-linguistic, representational communication[16] that we use to create a dialogue with the non-human world. Gardening itself is the act of expressing, reading and writing, hearing and saying, this information. Through these processes, in this headspace, we garden as we dream, which is to say we garden indexically. We use a thing itself to represent its meaning and potential[17]. When we create landscapes with shrubs, we use the shrub itself as an icon, an emoji worth a thousand words. The shrub speaks to us through its very presence. Holding the image of a shrub in our thoughts affects and infects our own language, thoughts and expectations.

OPPOSITE PAGE **Selections from** *The Yellow Paintings* **(2019)** ACRYLIC PAINT ON COLORED PAPER **Kevin Philip Williams**

BELOW **Selected images from Allison Cekala's American Pile (2017) about which she documents, "Mountainscapes sculpted by humans across the contiguous United States."[18] These, often human-scale, mounds reveal a universal impulse to build, organize, and contain, and possibly suggest aesthetic preferences. If arranged en masse, these piles would create moundscapes, not visually disparate from shrublands.**

Bald Head Island, North Carolina. 2018

Taos, New Mexico. 2018

Untitled, Hadley, Massachusetts. 2018

Untitled, Hadley, Massachusetts. 2018

Shrubs tell us that they exist, en masse, strongly and quietly, full of meaning and potential. They are visually arresting creatures. Their appearance reveals certain things, suggests others, but hides most. A bush standing solitarily in the middle of an open field is a focal point: a greeting, a threat, a loner, a vagrant, a pioneer, a remnant. It promises an encounter and harbors all tangible and intangible possibilities of that encounter. XOXO. All of this untapped potential exists for us to use in our gardens. To communicate with shrubs, and through shrubs, we have to make shrubscapes.

ABOVE A Gordian knot of neutral-toned, divaricate shrubs at Ōtari-Wilton's Bush, New Zealand illustrating the dynamic contrasts that come from subtle differences in form and color even when texture remains a constant.

OPPOSITE PAGE Shrub-steppe in the Little Missouri National Grassland, North Dakota, with *Rhus aromatica* (fragrant sumac), *Amelanchier alnifolia* (western serviceberry) and *Shepherdia argentea* (silver buffaloberry) forming dense shrub islands among grass rivers. These islands provide strategic refuge and gradients of habitat use by fauna.

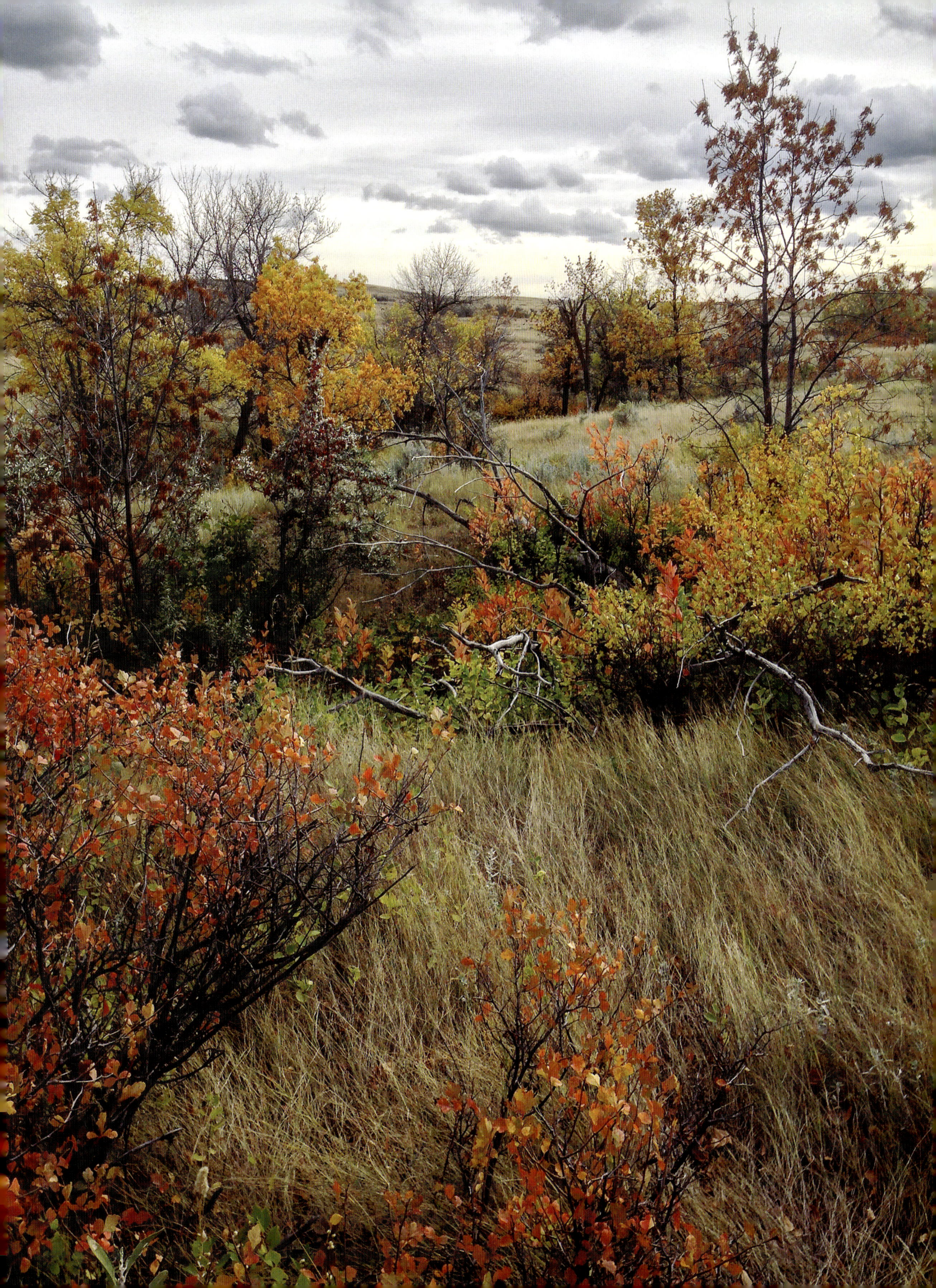

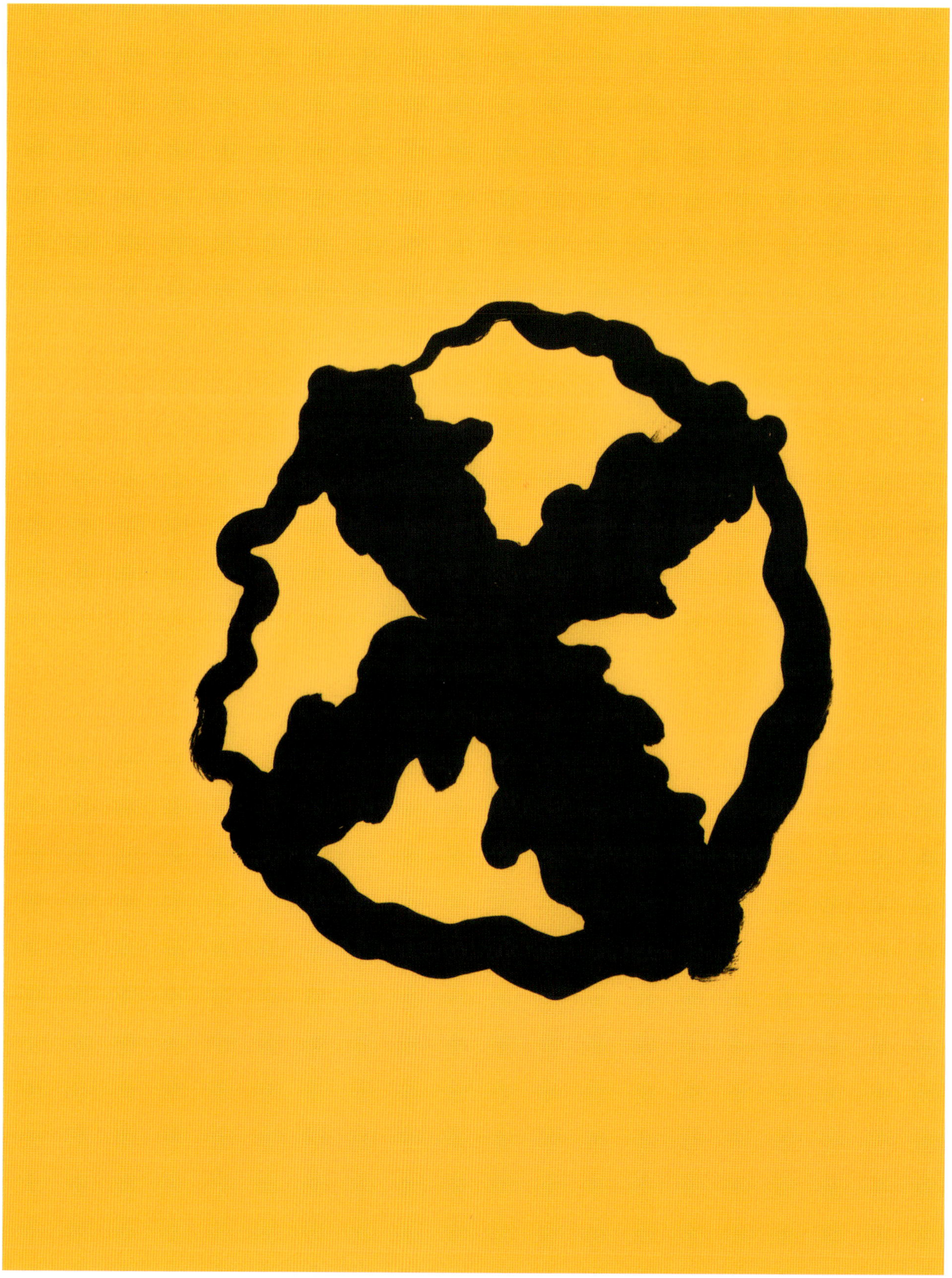

As icons, shrubs communicate information embodied by both the X and the O. X is a symbol of defiance. An obstructive mass. A hug. An embrace. A warning. Keep off. Be here. A wall. A focal point. O is an opening, a kiss, a portal, a circle, a path, an endless return, a cycle, a hole.

OPPOSITE, LEFT *X* (2019)
ACRYLIC PAINT ON PAPER
Kevin Philip Williams

BELOW *Shrub Juice Ensō* (2023)
BERBERIS REPENS (CREEPING OREGON GRAPE) INK MADE FROM WILD-COLLECTED DRUPES, BLENDED, STRAINED, AND APPLIED TO CALLIGRAPHY PAPER
TS Mushin Crisman

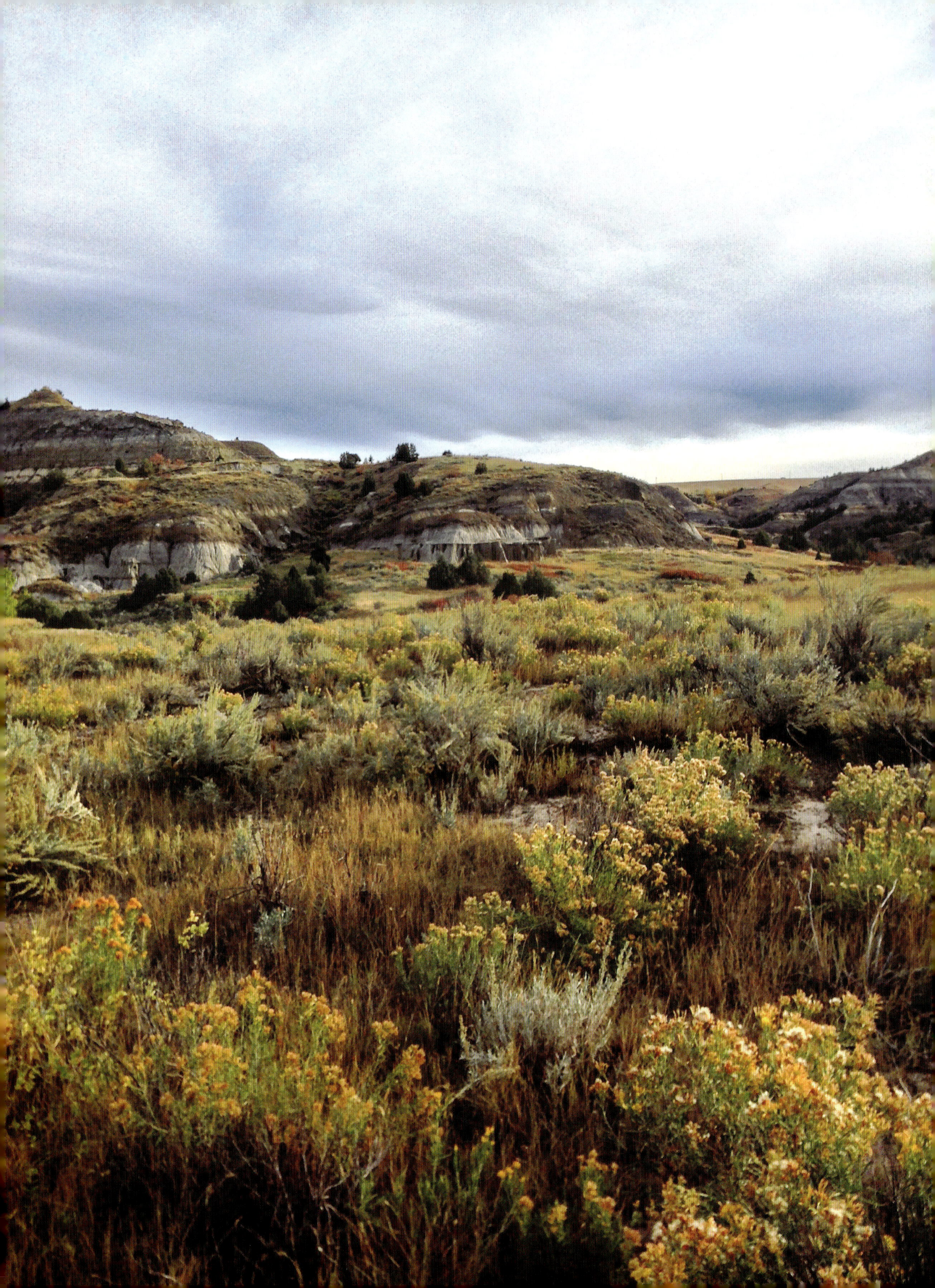

2

Autumn in the shale badlands of the Little Missouri National Grasslands in North Dakota. The mass of *Ericameria nauseosa* (rubber rabbitbrush) billows forward, punctuated by puffs of smoky *Artemisia cana* (silver sagebrush). These communities are enhanced visually by introduced range grasses, such as *Bromus inermis* (smooth brome), which fill areas that are otherwise too altered to support the pre-disturbance plant community. This creates codominant pathways, ribbons of life, often alternating between shrubs and grasses, creating visual and practical roadways, passages and browsing stands through the labyrinth of shrubs.

SEEING SHRUBLANDS

"Should I pursue a path so twisted?"

Patti Smith, *'Pissing in a River'*[19]

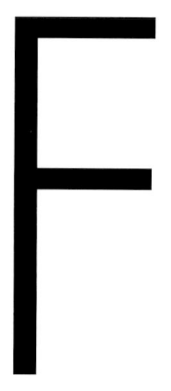

FROM A HUMAN PERSPECTIVE, shrublands are predominantly landscapes of scarcity, prevented from becoming something more desirable by environmental constraints. Yet our projections of ideal landscape conditions blind us to the deep and enduring productivity of shrubby landscapes.

Model Shrublands

Shrublands are everywhere, and depending on where you find yourself, you might call them any one of myriad names: boscage, bramble, briar, brush, bush, carr, cedar scrub, ceniza, cerrado, chaparral, copse, fynbos, garrigue, heath, karoo, kwongan, macchia, mallee, maquis, matorral, monte, moorland, petran, phrygana, pindan, pocosin, restinga, roee, sand sage prairie, scrub, scrubland, shinnery, shrub swamp, shrubland, shrubsteppe, strandveld, thicket and thorn are just some.

They appear where environmental conditions place plants under considerable stress. Aridity, nutrient-poor soils, disturbance, poor soil aeration, intense temperatures, short growing seasons, and windy environments can favor shrubby growth and contribute to the presence of shrub-dominated plant communities.[20] The classic models of stable shrubland biomes occur mostly in deserts, semi-arid continental interiors and the five Mediterranean climate regions of the world, covering more than ten percent of the Earth's terrestrial surface area.[21] However, the very conditions that promote shrub-dominated growth also present challenges to human settlement and development. It's no coincidence that the North American prairies – and not the shrublands – were plowed under for agricultural use. The very environments that hewed such resilient growth forms translate poorly to agriculture. Thus, the utility that we can extract from these landscapes is something more akin to respect and appreciation, rather than domination and coercion.

SEEING SHRUBLANDS 71

The copper-green flash and faded tones of exposure and oxidation. *Artemisia tridentata* (big sagebrush) and *Grayia spinosa* (spiny hopsage) are perfect in this ecstatic place. Anything vibrant would feel misplaced. Smith Rock State Park, Oregon.

Arctostaphylos pungens (pointleaf manzanita) and *Yucca baccata* (banana yucca) form an impressive thicket beneath the airy canopy and rainbow trunks of *Cupressus arizonica* (Arizona cypress) in Coconino National Forest, Arizona.

FOLLOWING SPREAD The washed-out colors of the Argentine Monte or Low Monte, a cold, arid steppe dominated by scrub. *Baccharis* (baccharises), *Azorella* (mulinum), and *Ephedra* (jointfir) are typical denizens of these ashy soils near Bariloche, Argentina.

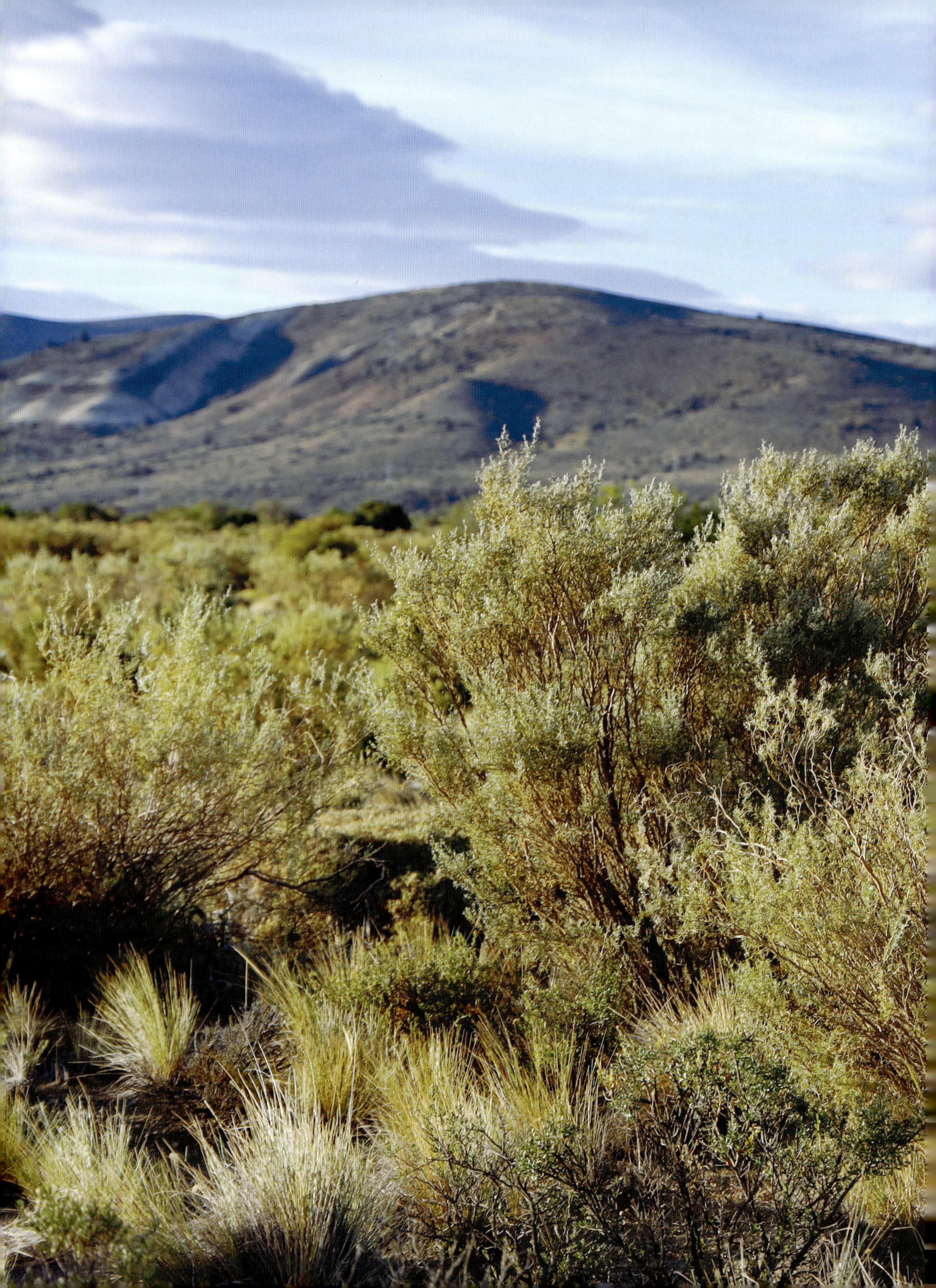

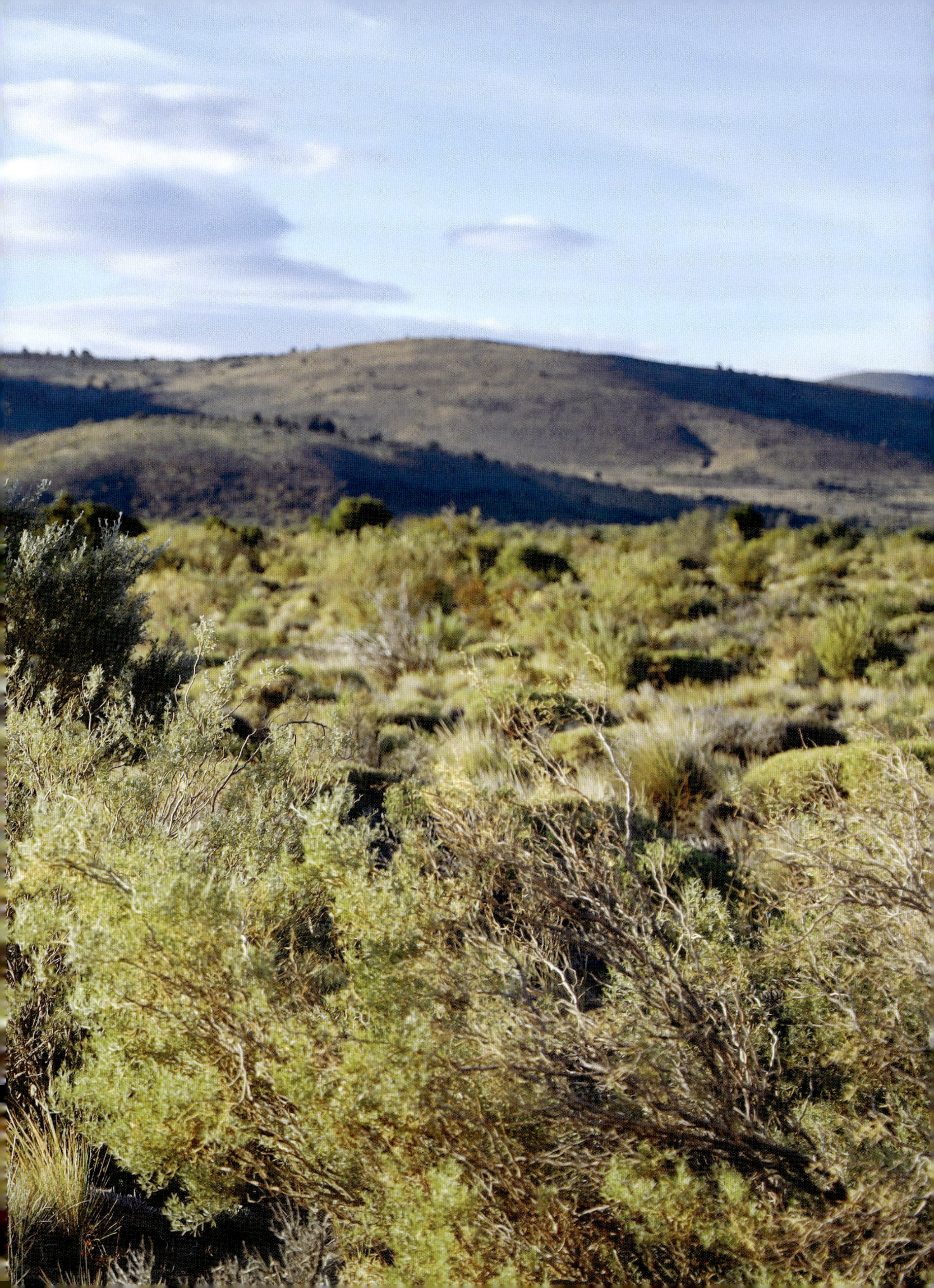

OPPOSITE, TOP A vivid chartreuse and silver mosaic of *Artemisia tridentata* (big sagebrush) and *Sarcobatus vermiculatus* (black greasewood) in the canyons of Dominguez-Escalante National Recreation Area, Colorado.

OPPOSITE, BELOW The heathlands of the British Isles have long been entwined with the twin emotions of attraction and repulsion and the complicated dance of magical and practical thinking. On the Isle of Skye, Scotland, the heath surrounds the waters of Sligachan Bridge. Legend has it that one can gain eternal beauty by these waters. Is the implication that the heath retains its stable, enduring forms by drinking it constantly?

The Grand Repeater

Even though teasing apart the individual components and interactions of shrublands can be challenging, humans are pattern-seekers, and something about shrubs en masse makes sense to us. Why do we find them appealing? What is it about these clumps, clusters and lines that make sense?

The modern domesticated shrubscape is often a tamer and more psychologically accessible place than its wild counterparts. A field of topiary, intricately knotted boxwood, starkly sheared hedges or neatly rounded shrub bubbles (shrubbles?) offer neat, tamed and civil forms and collections. This human urge to impose form, geometric and otherwise, may be rooted in our need to align ourselves with sustaining forces and to justify our choices of where to build our homes and care for ourselves and our kin.

Far from being fully unsettled and antagonistic places, shrublands have long been sources of food, water and shelter, and reading the different properties of shrubs in the landscape was crucial to the survival of early humans. They no doubt understood that larger and thicker vegetation coalesced around water sources, perhaps developing an appreciation for the aesthetics of contrasting species around water lines. They would have known the phenology of flowering and fruiting, depending on the fruits, nuts and berries of shrubs for survival. In the wild, finding rounded shrubs is not a sign of human hedging, but a sign of game; in shrublands with wild ungulates, it's not uncommon to find fields of browsed shrubs that look as if they have been sheared, dwarfed or miniaturized. Recognizing this phenomenon as an effect of animal presence, humans would have begun associating pruned shrubs with protein, a fitting history for the modern deprecatory nickname of green meatballs.

When we create shrubscapes we force a context. Depending on species and maintenance regimes, that context might reside in the realm of the unfamiliar and uncomfortable or that of the bountiful and reassuring. Shrubs can hide or reveal, be the thicket or clearing, create a line or the outline, stand alone or weave together. Learning to read the landscape, to read shrublands, may require reading many genres in many languages, but the stories are familiar. We have known them since the beginning of our time.

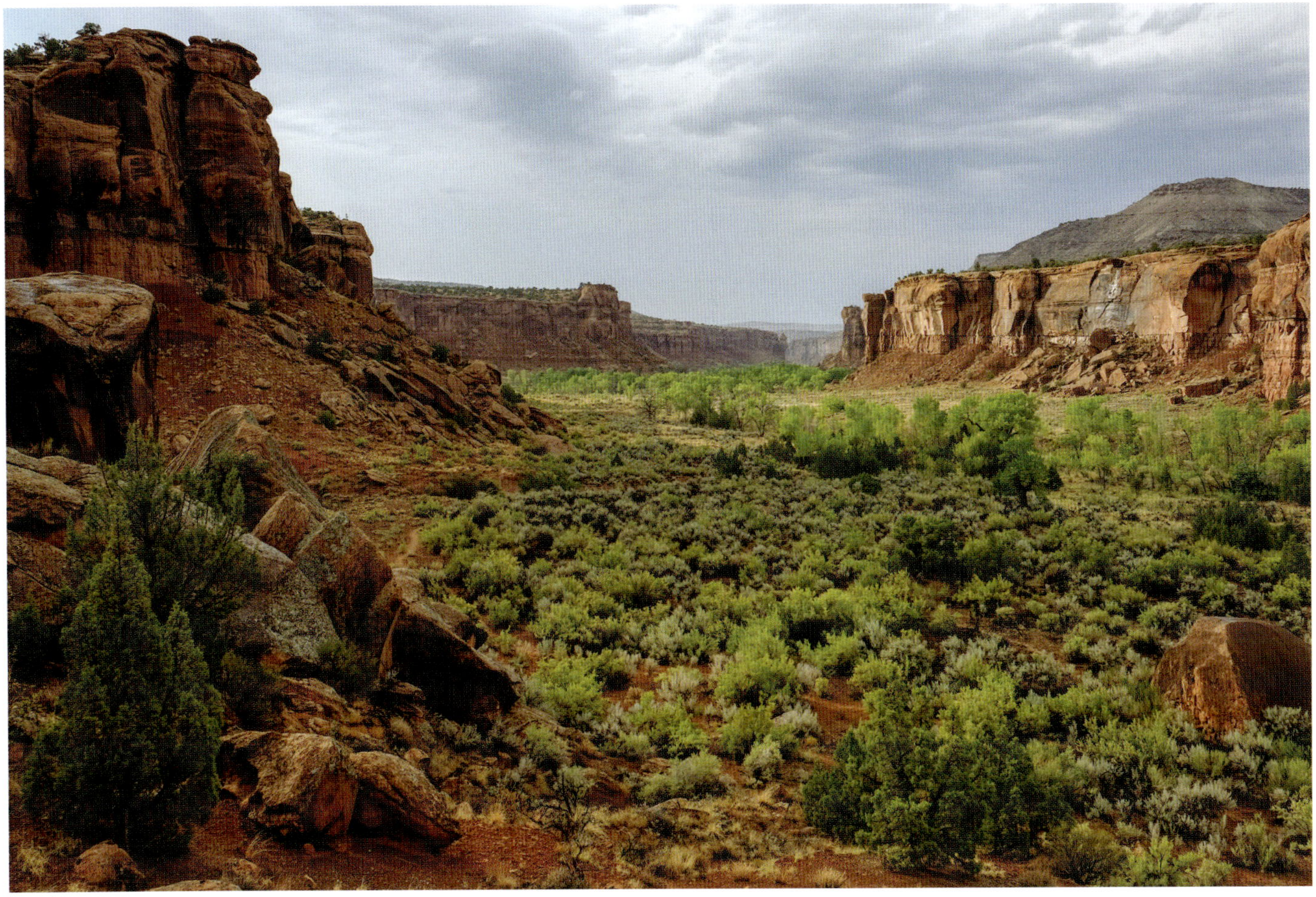

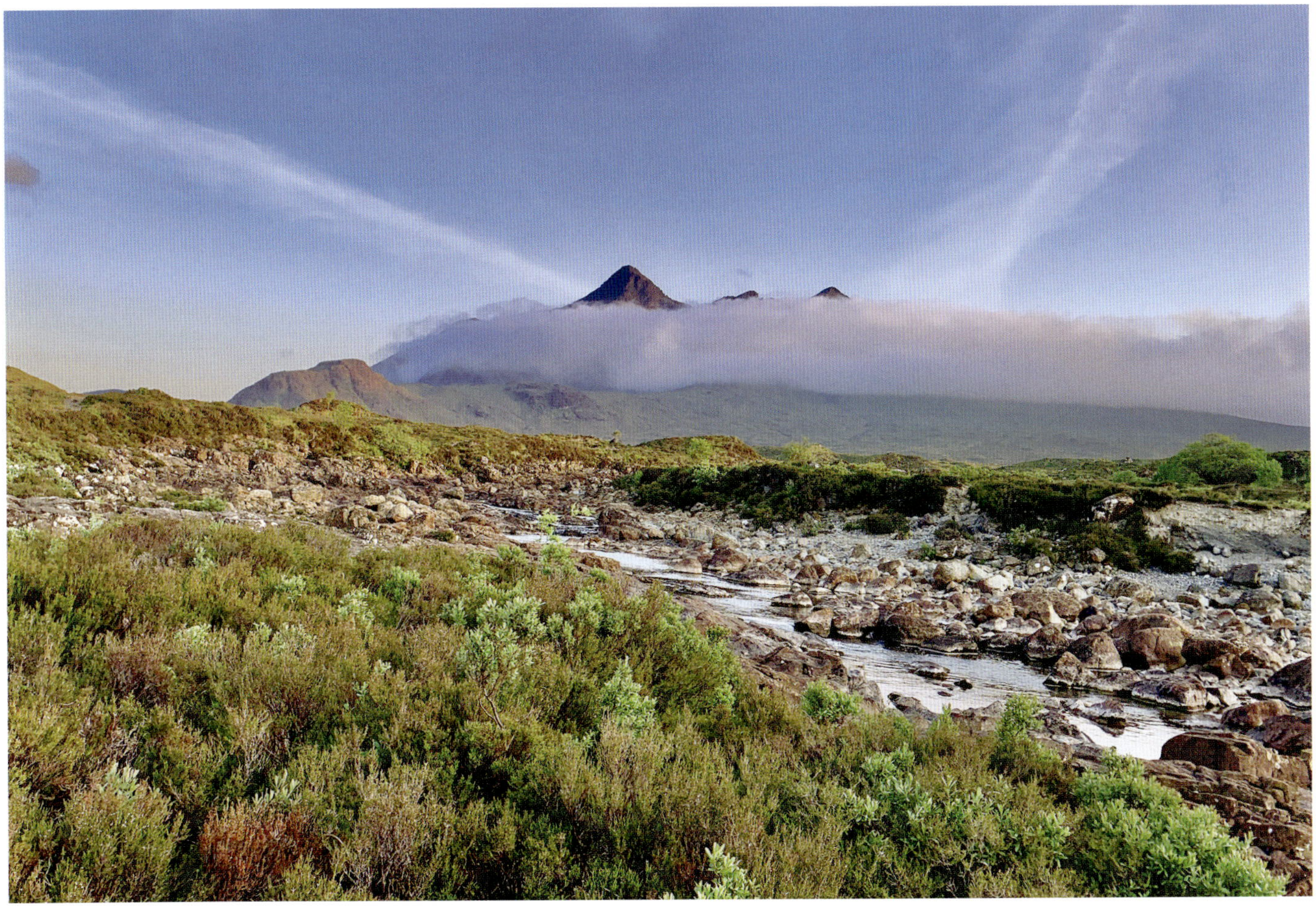

Harvest (2021)
ACRYLIC PAINT ON CANVAS 20.3cm x 25.4cm
Nicole Basilone

SEEING SHRUBLANDS 77

Neo-Expressionist Remixes

The patterns of wild systems are often so intricate that they appear unreadable, chaotic and unattainable. Visual abstractions, like the samples below, make it easier to read and extract a composition from them.

In the model shrublands that follow, the species components of each community are not listed in their entirety. The pictures are merely snapshots of a moment in time of a landscape that is constantly changing. These shrublands are composed of hundreds, if not thousands, of annual and perennial forbs, shrubs, trees, vines, fungi and lichen.

The following section presents inspections of model shrublands, or the major, environmentally-stable shrubland archetypes of the world. A landscape-scale photo of each shrubland is paired with a color-coded breakdown of the dominant visual elements in each. These abstractions highlight the spatial patterning that makes each landscape interesting. The rectilinear simplifications can be used as layouts to transpose the effect of these landscapes elsewhere, using whatever plant material is appropriate for your region.

In this landscape, just outside of Great Sand Dunes National Park in southern Colorado, the formations of *Artemisia tridentata* (big sagebrush), *Ericameria nauseosa* (rubber rabbitbrush), and *Krascheninnikovia lanata* (winterfat) merge in floating puffs among the open graminoid layer, mimicking the large forms of the clouds above them.

HEATH

Woven through our collective consciousness, heath is as thick and entangled as its own self-fulfilling landscape. Like all shrubs and shrublands, heath is more an impression than a definition. Ecologically speaking, heath is composed of shrubs growing in low nutrient areas. Heath substrates can be wet or dry, acidic, sandy and fast draining or hard and calcareous. Heath has become synonymous with the scrubby moors of the British Isles, but can be found on every continent except Antarctica, with exceptionally diverse heaths occurring in Australia and southern Africa.

Heath refers to plants from the family Ericaceae, and more specifically to the ericaceous genera *Epacris, Leucopogon, Cassiope, Daboecia, Phyllodoce, Hudsonia*, et al. However, not all heathland shrubs are ericaceous. The name heather is used commonly for the genera *Calluna* or *Erica*. Humans named Heather are imbued with the promise or hope that they will contain the beauty of the greater heath.

Heath, like most shrublands, is transient. It requires some level of disturbance in either regular or irregular cycles to prevent it from developing into forest, although heath that exists in less productive environments like the anaerobic, mummifying conditions of deep peatland are more stable. Heath is a wasteland. Heath is a butterfly.

Beyond even the deep lessons in ecological design that the Saco Heath Preserve offers, the boardwalk is itself a masterclass in materiality and trail-making. Even as an ecological relic, this is a joyous place and the pathway is a celebration, leading the explorer across long open stretches on boldly colorful boards that reflect the shifting hues of each season. Upon reaching evergreen blinds of *Picea mariana* (black spruce) and *Larix laricina* (tamarack), it dodges at acute angles towards the next stand, giving a sense of relief from the expanse and allowing one to experience the ecstasy of emergence again and again.

The often running and suckering nature of the shrubs in heathlands can create large homogeneous patches with complexly mixed heterogeneous edges. In the Saco Heath Preserve, *Chamaedaphne calyculata* (leatherleaf) separates the other shrubby masses, creating speciated islands of accretion with feathered coronas. In the home landscape, this could translate well for the controlling gardener who wishes to flirt with wildness, as it provides separate spaces for the main species while still allowing space for strange action; the calm eye at the center of the swirling storm.

The Saco Heath Preserve in southern Maine, USA, is a type of peatland known as a coalesced dome bog, which formed over thousands of years as decaying organic material filled neighboring ponds and eventually merged the two depressions together. Six meters (19½ ft) of peat lie beneath this braided fabric of space-time. But the heath doesn't stretch like a trampoline, it springs like an old mattress. It has the creak and crack of ribs. This is an old, old land that eats itself, Lovecraftian in its unknowability, and beautiful in its withdrawal. As far as the eye can see, stands of *Vaccinium corymbosum* (highbush blueberry) and punctuations of *Rhododendron canadense* (rhodora), *Rhododendron groenlandicum* (labrador tea), and *Kalmia angustifolia* (sheep laurel) are bound together by rivers of *Chamaedaphne calyculata* (leatherleaf). Interstitial plants add complexity and arrays of texture but rarely penetrate the upper shrub layers. The shrub canopy is almost completely closed; this world is absorbed in flora.

Kalmia angustifolia (sheep laurel), *Vaccinium corymbosum* (highbush blueberry), and *Rhododendron canadense* (rhodora) stacked among the inundated heath soils and sparse *Pinus strobus* (eastern white pine) trees

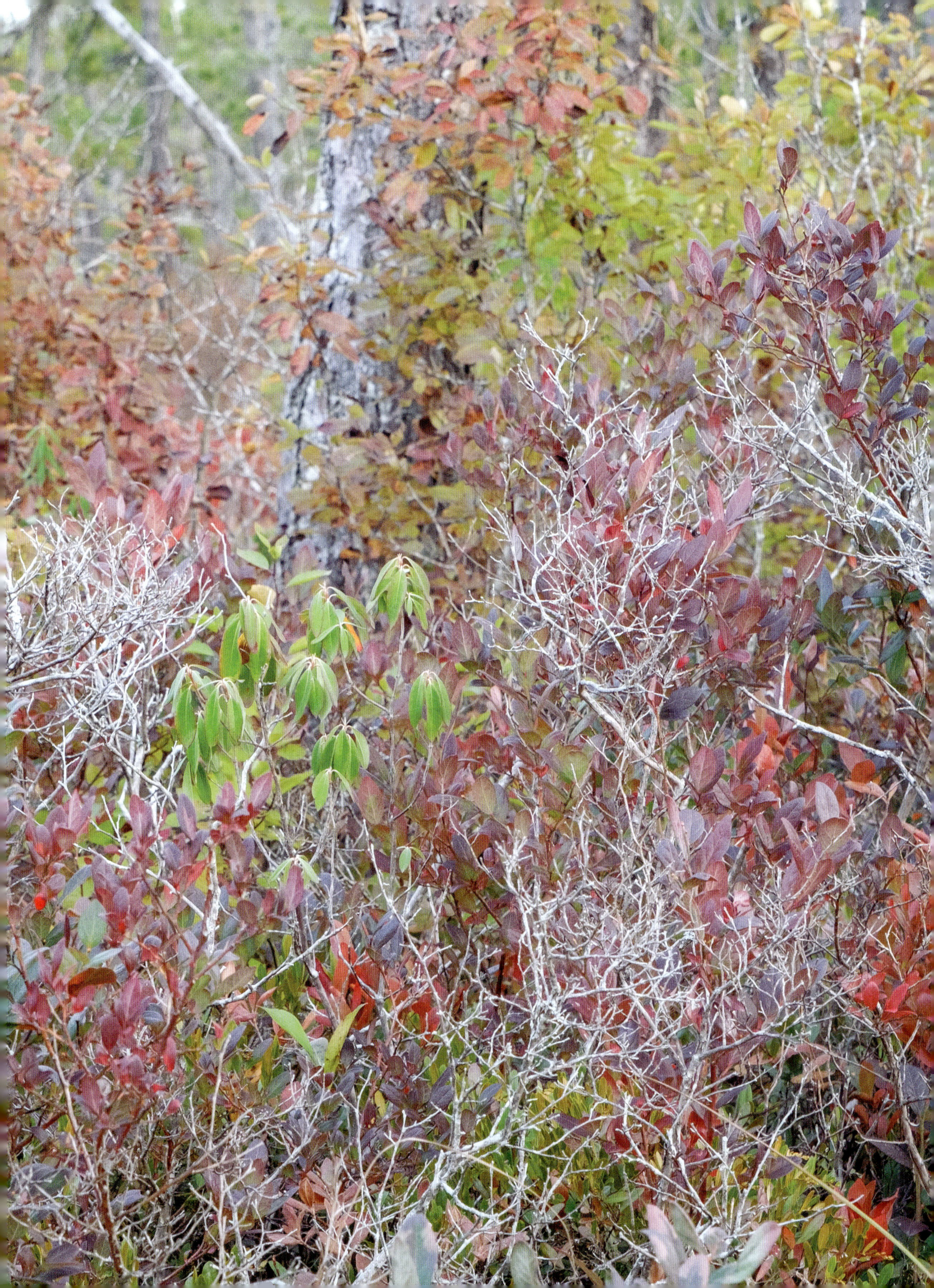

Kalmia angustifolia (sheep laurel) in seed

Rhododendron canadense (rhodora)

Arethusa bulbosa (dragon's mouth orchid)

Clubmosses (Lycopodaceae) are common inhabitants of heath shrublands.

LEFT *Ilex laevigata* (smooth winterberry)

BELOW Dense thickets of *Rhododendron canadense* (rhodora) meet the turbulent North Atlantic on the east coast of Newfoundland, Canada.

INLAND BARRENS

Some of the rarest shrublands on earth, inland barrens, hold innumerable lessons for growing shrubscapes in forested bioregions. They are most commonly found on inland dunes, relics from glacial ages where outwash and wind deposited large amounts of sand and silt across terrain mostly frozen and vegetation-sparse. The free-draining, nutrient-poor, mineral substrate creates drier and harsher conditions than an organically derived soil.

Surrounded by freeways, suburban homes, strip malls and parking lots, the Albany Pine Bush Preserve epitomizes the fringe and marginalized condition of modern shrublands. These sand dunes slamming into suburbia are more akin to the shrub meadows of the tallgrass prairie than they are to hardwood forests. The sandy soil creates a haven for remnant species from eastern balds, the Atlantic coast, and even the tallgrass prairies. This diversity creates a stunningly unique ecotone as these species mix with forest flora. They have, in a way, been protected by the providence of pines.

In areas with a tighter canopy, *Pinus rigida* (pitch pine) surmounts the scrub oaks, *Quercus ilicifolia* (bear oak) and *Quercus prinoides* (dwarf chinquapin oak), *Gaylussacia baccata* (black huckleberry) and a smattering of blueberries. In more open and recently disturbed areas, such as the Karner Barrens (opposite page), an explosion of species and morphologies fills the space. The deceptively named sweetfern (*Comptonia peregrina*), which is not a fern but a scented shrub in the Myricaceae family, is a major compositional element. The unique leaves, reminiscent of an Aspleniaceae fern, create a compelling textural break among the obtuse oaks and actual bracken fern, which is much looser and gracefully uninhibited among the shrub layer. The suckering *Sassafras albidum* (sassafras), acting in the fuzzy realm between small, suckering tree and large, colonizing shrub, pokes through the understory without intent to compete with the upper canopy.

As the accumulation of organic matter is almost unavoidable in wet climates, pine barrens tend to depend on fire to burn off duff and retain their open understory. Indigenous peoples used fire to steward pine barrens as rangeland. By preventing trees from creating dense canopies, a large diversity of fruiting shrubs and grasses could flourish. Forests are not always the question and trees are not always the answer.

TOP *Celastrus orbiculatus* (round-leaved bittersweet) with close relative *Celastrus scandens* (American bittersweet) and ABOVE *Symphyotrichum pilosum* (frost aster) all growing in the Albany Pine Bush Preserve, New York.

SEEING SHRUBLANDS

The key to legibility in semi-open, understory shrublands, like those found in inland barrens is a clear separation between the upper and lower canopies.

This community in the Albany Pine Bush Preserve is visually playful, with contrasting forms and textures, but is fully separate from the evergreens above.

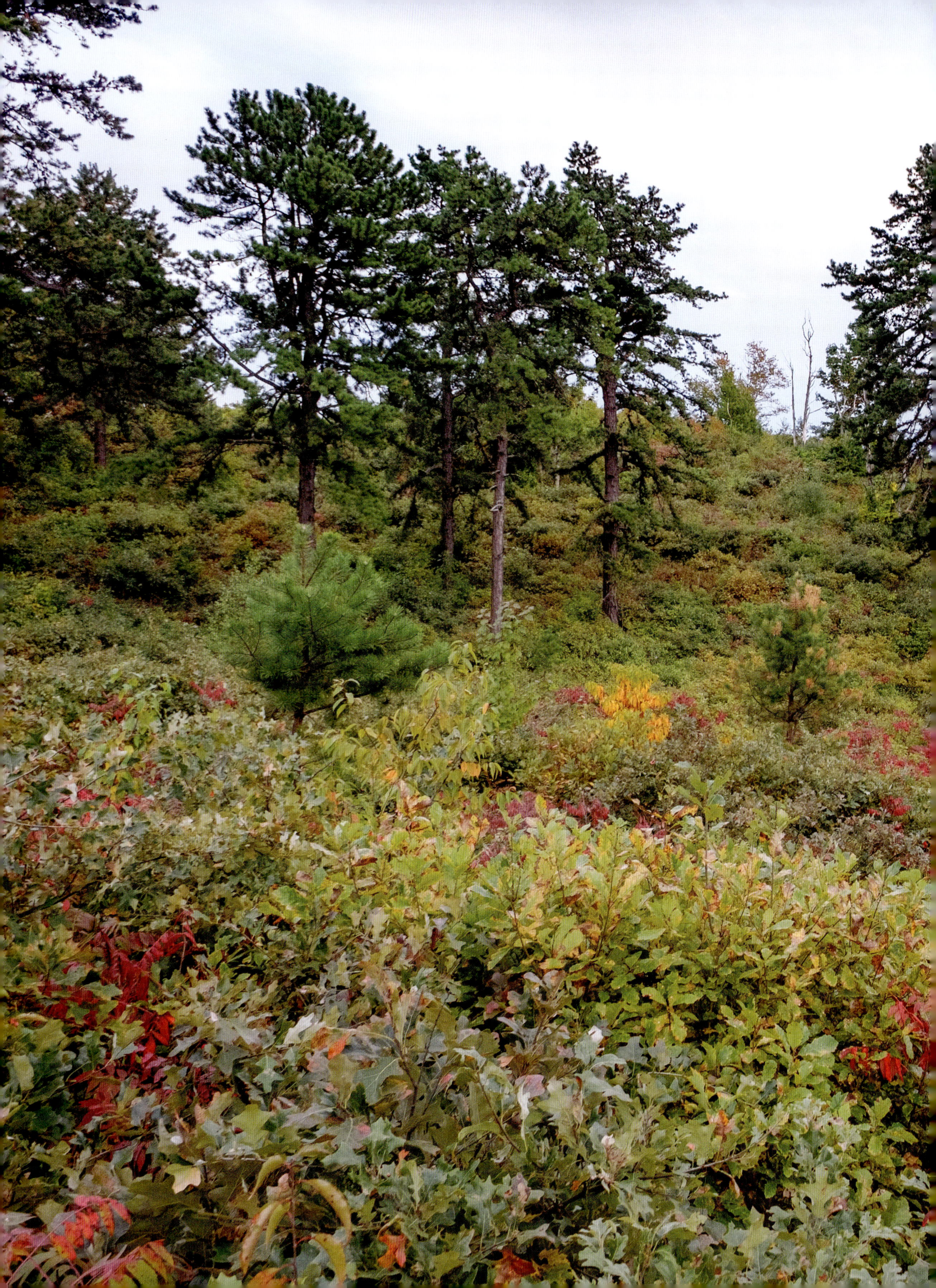

The plants beyond the pines: *Quercus prinoides* (dwarf chinquapin oak), *Rhus typhina* (staghorn sumac), *Prunus pensylvanica* (fire cherry) and *Sassafras albidum* (sassafras). The floristic compositions between the ridgetops, slopes and bowls of the dunes can vary dramatically, as warmer air flows over the ridges and cooler air descends, creating frost pockets in the bottomlands. Albany Pine Bush Preserve, New York.

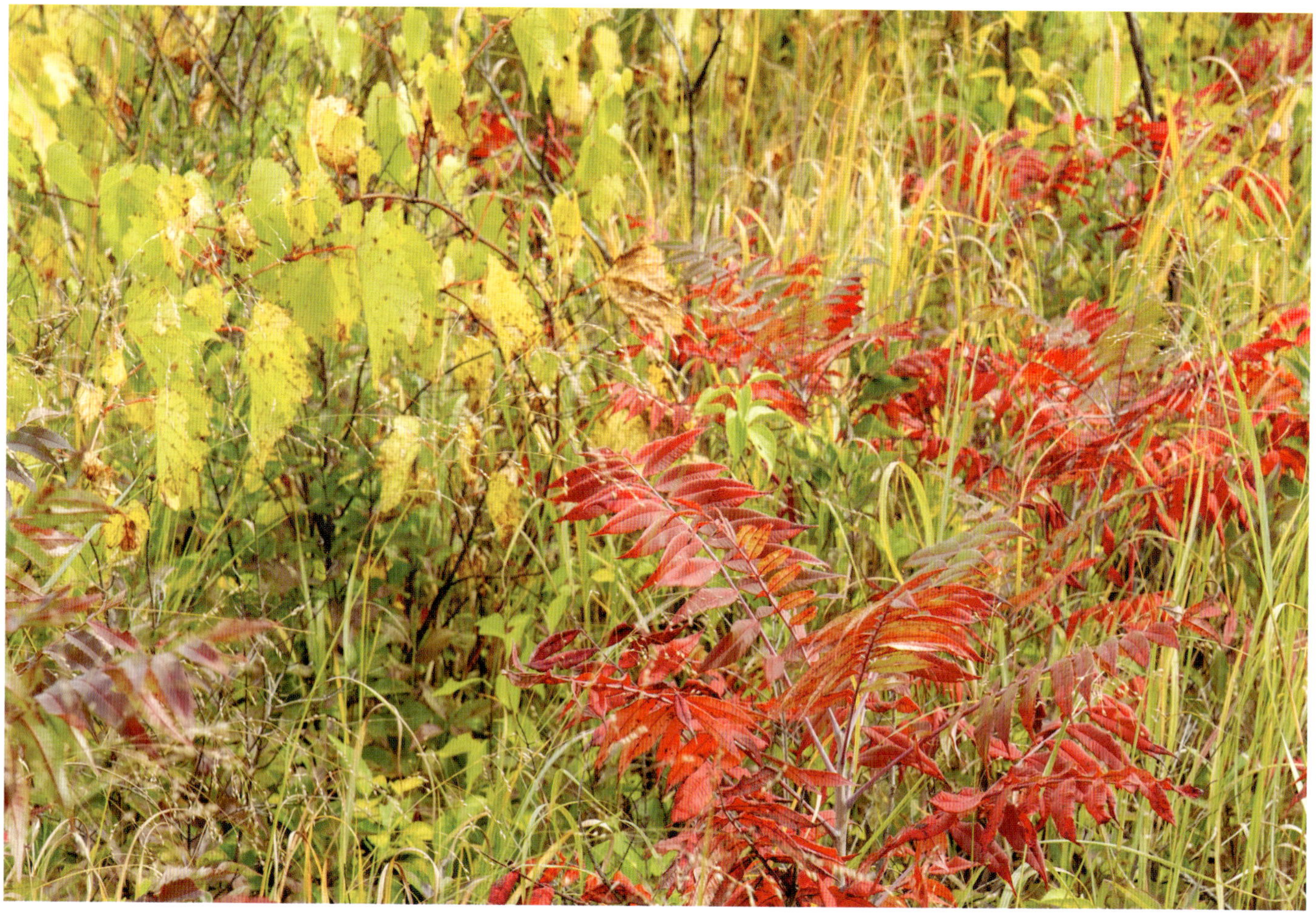

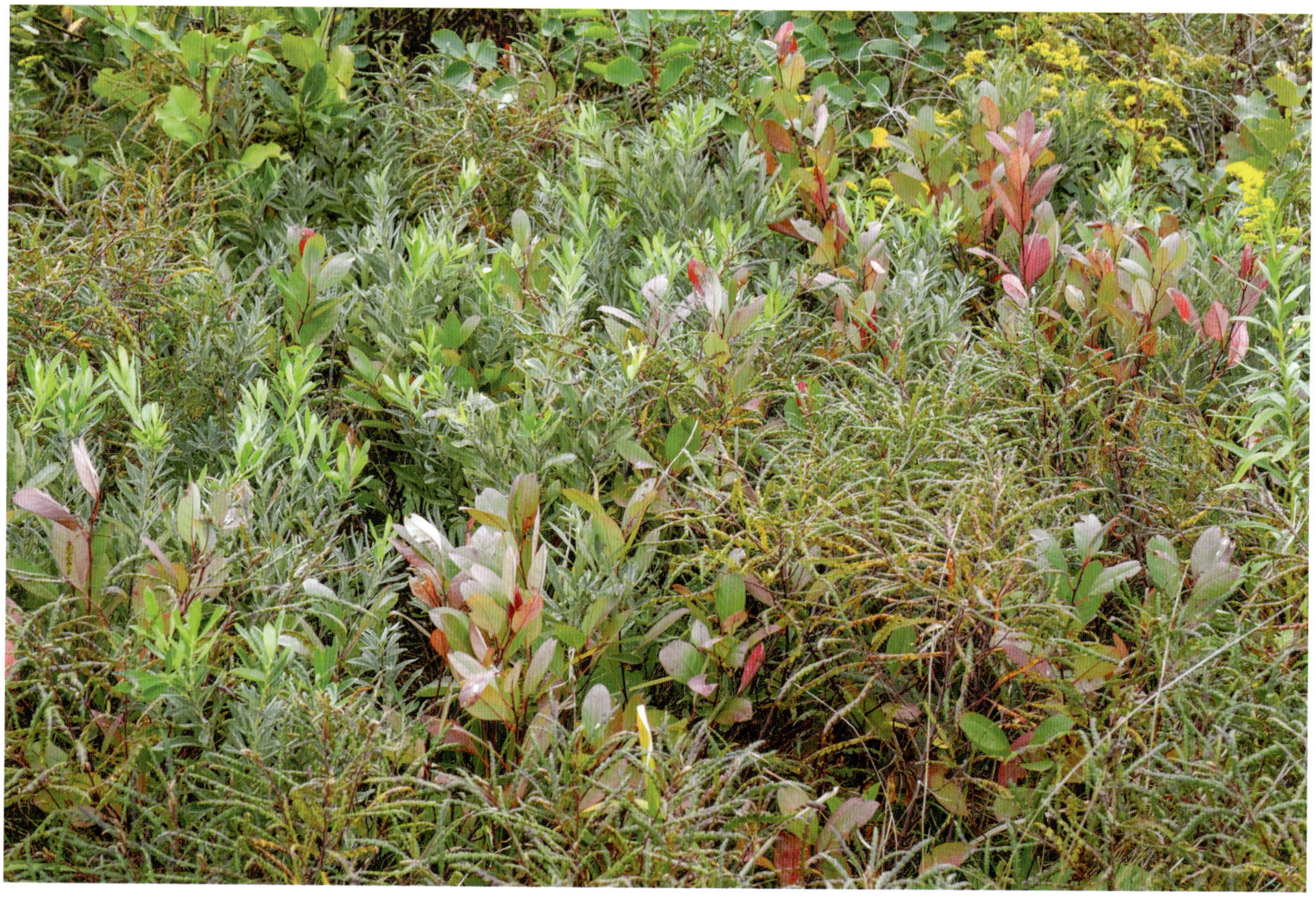

SEEING SHRUBLANDS

89

OPPOSITE, TOP *Rhus glabra* (smooth sumac) and *Vitis riparia* (riverbank grape); interplanting vines and shrubs, especially those that have complementary flowering or seasonal colors, can introduce exceptional dimensions in form, effect and architecture.

OPPOSITE, BELOW A gradient of textures, from the thin, crenulated leaf margins of *Comptonia peregrina* (sweetfern), through the lanceolate *Salix humilis* (prairie willow) to the elliptic *Prunus pumila* (sand cherry).

RIGHT *Ponds, bogs and swamps found within inland barrens contain diverse semi aquatic plant communities. The diminutive, carnivorous Drosera intermedia (spoonleaf sundew) is offered refuge in such places.*

BELOW *Monarda punctata* (spotted beebalm) plays in the interstitial layer of the Albany Pine Bush. Intermittent disturbance allows ruderal species to thrive for years, creating vibrant forb displays while shrubs regrow and recover stature.

BALDS

Balds occur on hilltops and mountain summits that are not cold or tall enough to support alpine plant communities and, due to free-draining substrates and historical conditions, resist encroachment from forests. Instead, balds host grasslands and shrublands, often acting as refuges for species that normally occur at much higher latitudes.

Balds have been grazed and browsed by herbivores for millennia. Megaherbivores, such as the mastodons of the Pleistocene, were succeeded by bison, elk and deer, which were then joined by domesticated livestock. This animal-action creates disturbance-based stable states and park-like expanses in an otherwise densely forested region.

On the balds, dense shrublands, shrub meadows and woody islands mix together, bleeding out from the edges of the forest on to exposed positions, running along ridges and peppering peaks. This is the place where old-time

Disturbance through extreme weather and wildfire is just as important in perpetuating the cycle of bald creation and maintenance as browsing and grazing. At the overlook for Graveyard Fields off Blue Ridge Parkway in North Carolina, the interpretive panel prose reads "Wind-thrown tree trunks covered with moss and spruce needles looked like a graveyard until destroyed by a fire in 1925."[22] The initial blowdown destroyed the tree canopy, allowing for the expansion of the existing shrub community, while the subsequent wildfire opened it even further, burning off smothering organic material and encouraging even more shrub suckering.

SEEING SHRUBLANDS   91

religion and ancient magic dissolve into each other; where belief is informed by experience. It's the land of Sparklehorse's haints, hollows, mist and rust.[23]

Pictured below is Blackbird Knob in the Dolly Sods Wilderness Area, Monongahela National Forest, West Virginia, USA, where highbush blueberry (*Vaccinium corymbosum*) flows over the crest like a torrent of molten lava breaking around mountain holly (*Ilex montana*), mountain laurel (*Kalmia latifolia*), and the parasol whitetop aster (*Doellingeria umbellata*).

Like other shrublands composed of mostly deciduous species, Blackbird Knob is a study in revelation and holds deep lessons for garden planning. Unlike desert scrub, which mostly depends on seasonal flowering to create additive effects, this bald's most dramatic moments come through senescence and dissipation. The lush greens slide into various warm tones with species specific pigments holding peak vibrancy at different times. As the leaves drop, or fade, the deep evergreens and upright, broom-like bundles of naked stems hold the winter scene. Using this model, we can consider the culmination of garden interest that occurs during dormant seasons, which may radically alter how we approach layout.

FOLLOWING SPREAD The Blackbird Knob, a highly diverse open heath shrubland in the Dolly Sods Wilderness area of the Allegheny Mountains, West Virginia, with *Kalmia latifolia* (mountain laurel), *Picea rubens* (red spruce), *Vaccinium angustifolium* (lowbush blueberry), *Vaccinium corymbosum* (highbush blueberry), *Acer pennsylvanica* (striped maple), *Sorbus americana* (American mountain ash), *Acer rubrum* (red maple) and *Rhododendron viscosum* (swamp azalea)

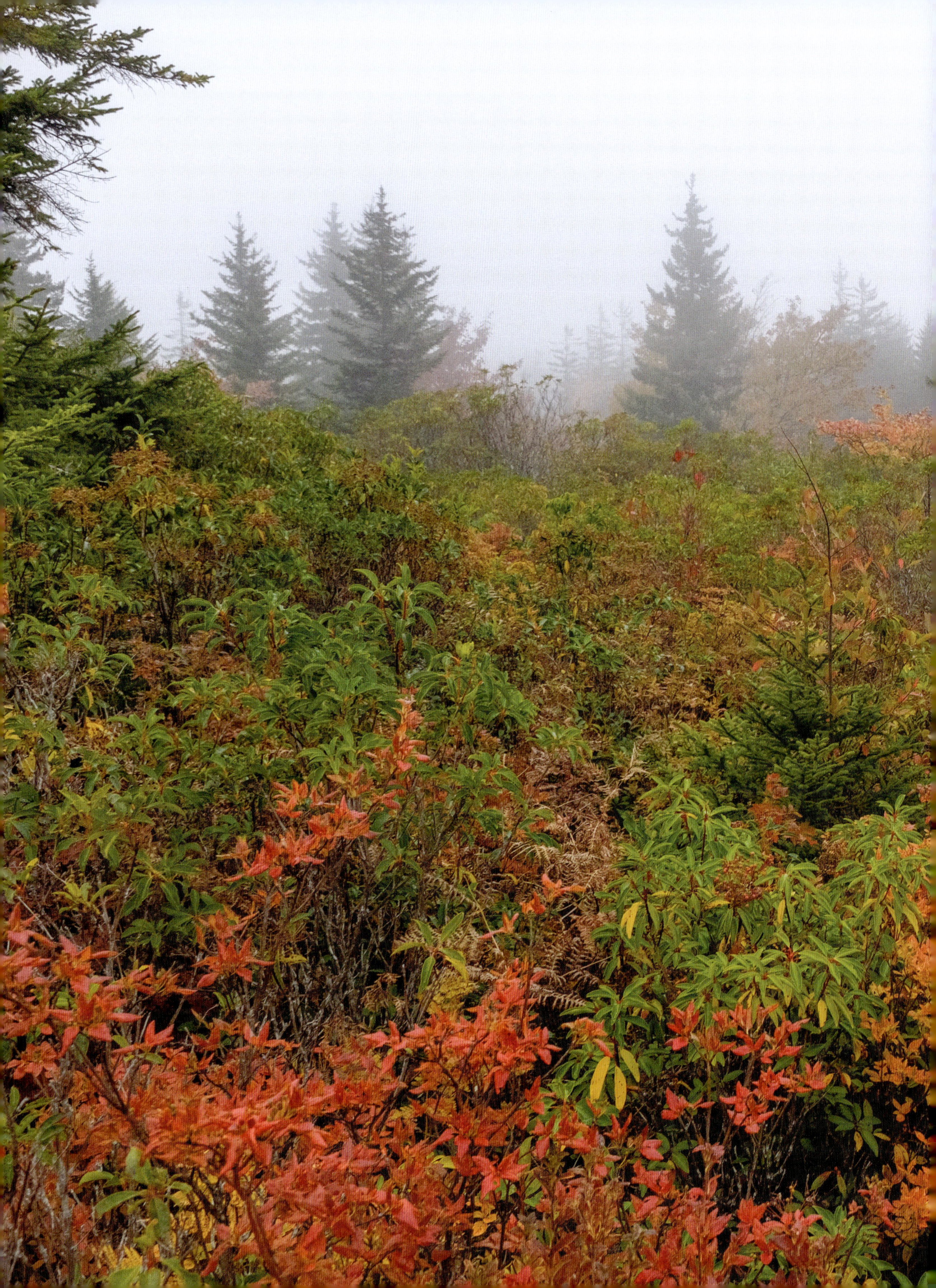

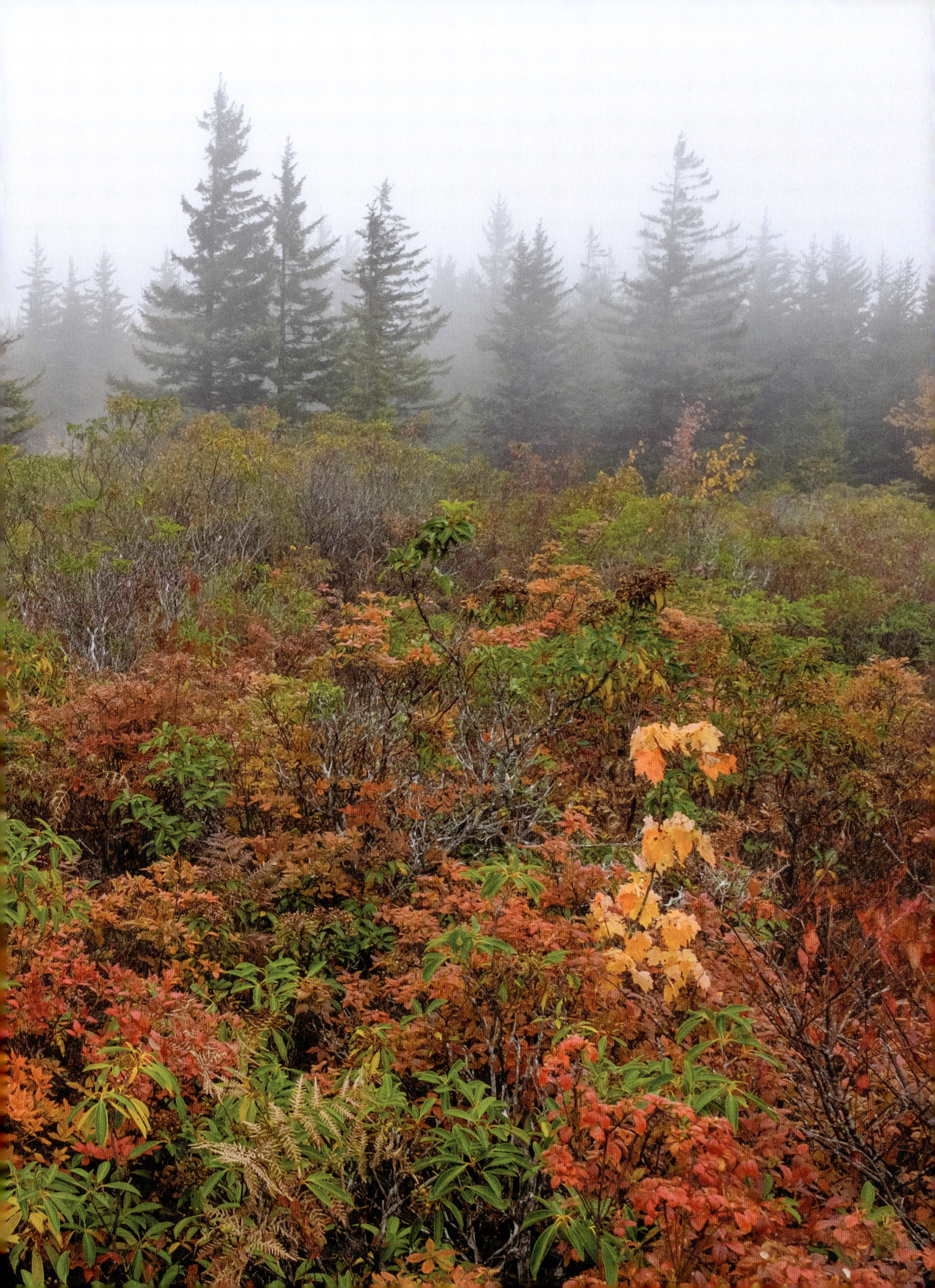

The musky, mildewed pungence of decay hits hard in the rain-shrouded mountains and valleys. Monongahela National Forest, West Virginia.

The phenomenon of shrubs and non-vascular plants colonizing the quick-draining, acidic and mineral outcroppings on balds leads to incredible compositions and stark juxtapositions of shrubs forced to push high above the thick bryophytic carpet.

Rhododendron catawbiense (mountain rosebay) grows as a solid phalanx on open balds among the *Picea rubens* (red spruce) and *Abies fraseri* (Fraser fir) at the Roan Mountain Rhododendron Gardens in North Carolina. Although this is a natural area, calling it a garden recognizes the human influence on the space over the millennia.

SHRUB-STEPPE

Shrub-steppes are perhaps the largest and most expansive shrublands on the planet having major footholds in North America, Patagonian Argentina, Central Asia and Southern Africa. Steppes are semi-arid bioregions subject to extremely hot summers and cold winters with low precipitation and mineral soils dictated by presiding mountain ranges. As a result, steppe plants have evolved to be exceptionally tough and resilient.

Steppes are transitional regions that connect mountains to plains and forests to deserts. Although visually they are largely defined by large monotonous swaths of shrubs and grasses, they contain great multitudes of biodiversity. Even within large areas dominated by just a few species, small changes in the landscape, often geological or hydrological, can spur variations in microclimates and species composition.

Hedysarum boreale (northern sweetvetch) and *Opuntia* species (prickly pear) flush with spring moisture amidst *Artemisia tridentata* (big sagebrush) rangeland near Monticello, Utah.

SEEING SHRUBLANDS 97

In this open landscape near Moab, Utah, shrubs are seemingly the only life forms that exist. This type of high-stress, open system is an excellent model for our urban environments, full of harsh conditions that quickly change based on building orientation and soil conditions, and perfect for incorporating lots of ruderal and low-competition interstitial species to dance and play among the persistent shrub layer.

In the Moab shrublands pictured above (top), *Sarcobatus vermiculatus* (black greasewood) provides the light green contrast. This slightly spiny, succulent amaranth is as gnarly as barbed wire and as unforgiving as the surrounding sandstone. The dark green punctuations of *Juniperus osteosperma* (Utah juniper) provide height as they drift through the composition and the familiar silver of *Artemisia tridentata* (big sagebrush) fill out the space. In the back, *Populus deltoides* (eastern cottonwood) and *Fraxinus anomala* (single-leaf ash) and *Tamarix ramosissima* (salt cedar) follow a drainage line.

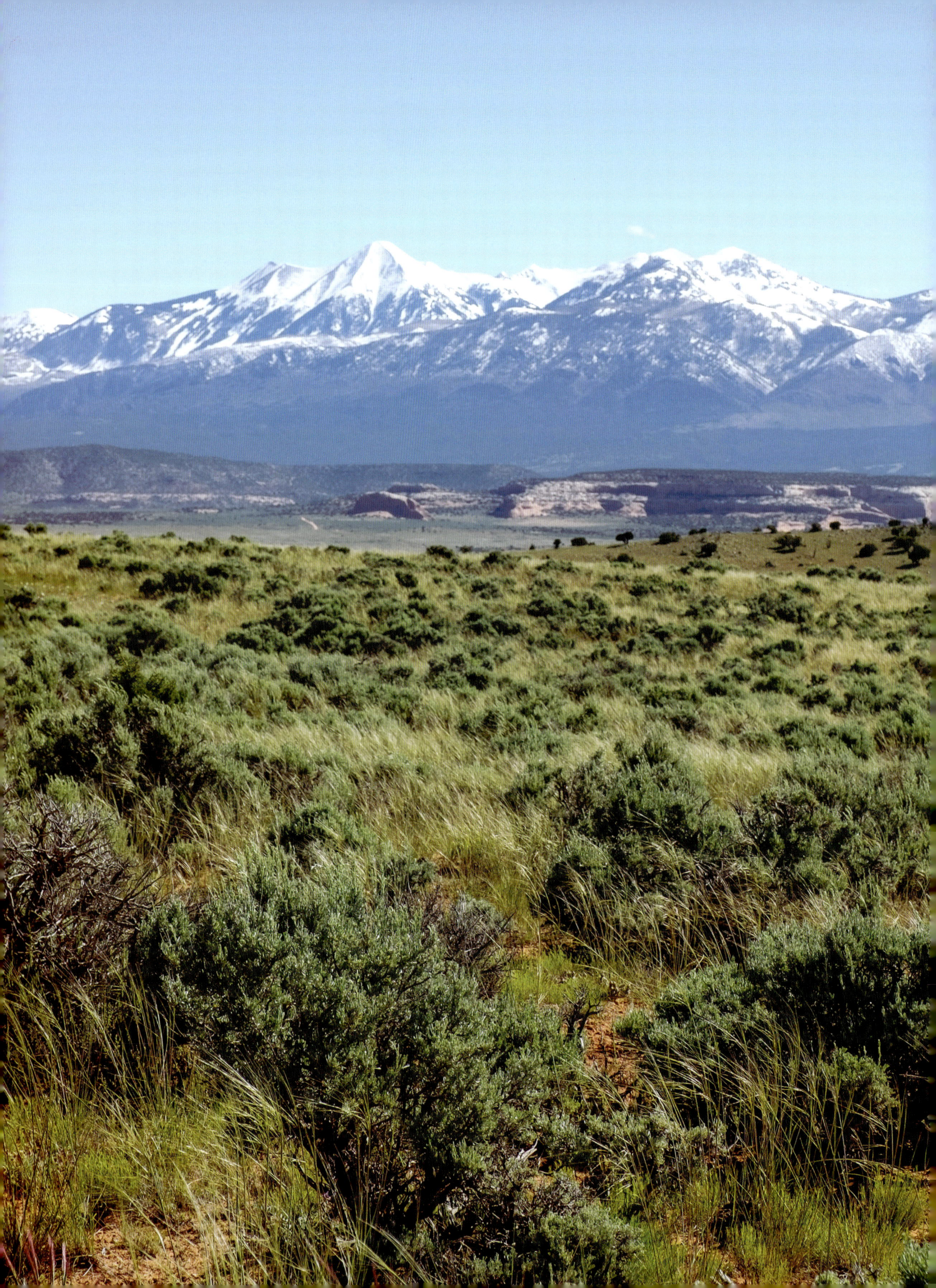

Structurally, shrublands offer longevity and consistency. A shrub-based design in the style can retain much of its form season-to-season even as graminoid and herbaceous layers swell and break against them. The durability and lifespan of shrubs means that with minimal influence a shrubscape can persist for decades, even centuries. Even with the herbaceous layer largely absent from this shrub-steppe outside of Canyonlands National Park, Utah *Artemisia tridentata* (big sagebrush) and *Hesperostipa comata* (needle-and-thread grass) offer a compelling template for garden design.

Many of the shrubs found in shrub-steppes, including the genera *Sarcobatus* (greasewood), *Atriplex* (saltbush), and *Baccharis* (baccharises) are halophytes, meaning that they can survive in soils high in dissolved mineral salts. Identifying and learning to work with the plants in these communities is critical for designing dynamic urban ecosystems in our increasingly polluted cities, roadways and yards.

SEEING SHRUBLANDS 101

Sclerocactus brevispinus (fishhook cactus). Cacti are a ubiquitous element in the vast shrub-steppe of North America, often establishing under the shelter of shrub canopies.

BELOW Crepuscular flowers of *Oenothera pallida* (pale evening primrose) open as the searing daytime heat fades.

Castilleja scabrida (rough paintbrush) parasitizes the tough woody plants of the shrub-steppe, helping to maintain plant species diversity over time by dampening their competitive dominance.

Calochortus nuttallii (sego lily). Unlike shrubs which mostly tolerate drought and other adverse environmental conditions, geophytes like this sego lily emerge during favorable spring weather and avoid the harshest months in dormancy.

Lupinus argenteus (silvery lupine) blending with *Artemisia tridentata* (big sagebrush) below the Wind River Range in the Bridger Wilderness, Wyoming. This area, part of the Great Sagebrush Sea, is quintessential shrub-steppe, stretching across rolling plains as far as the eye can see, interrupted only by mountains or canyons.

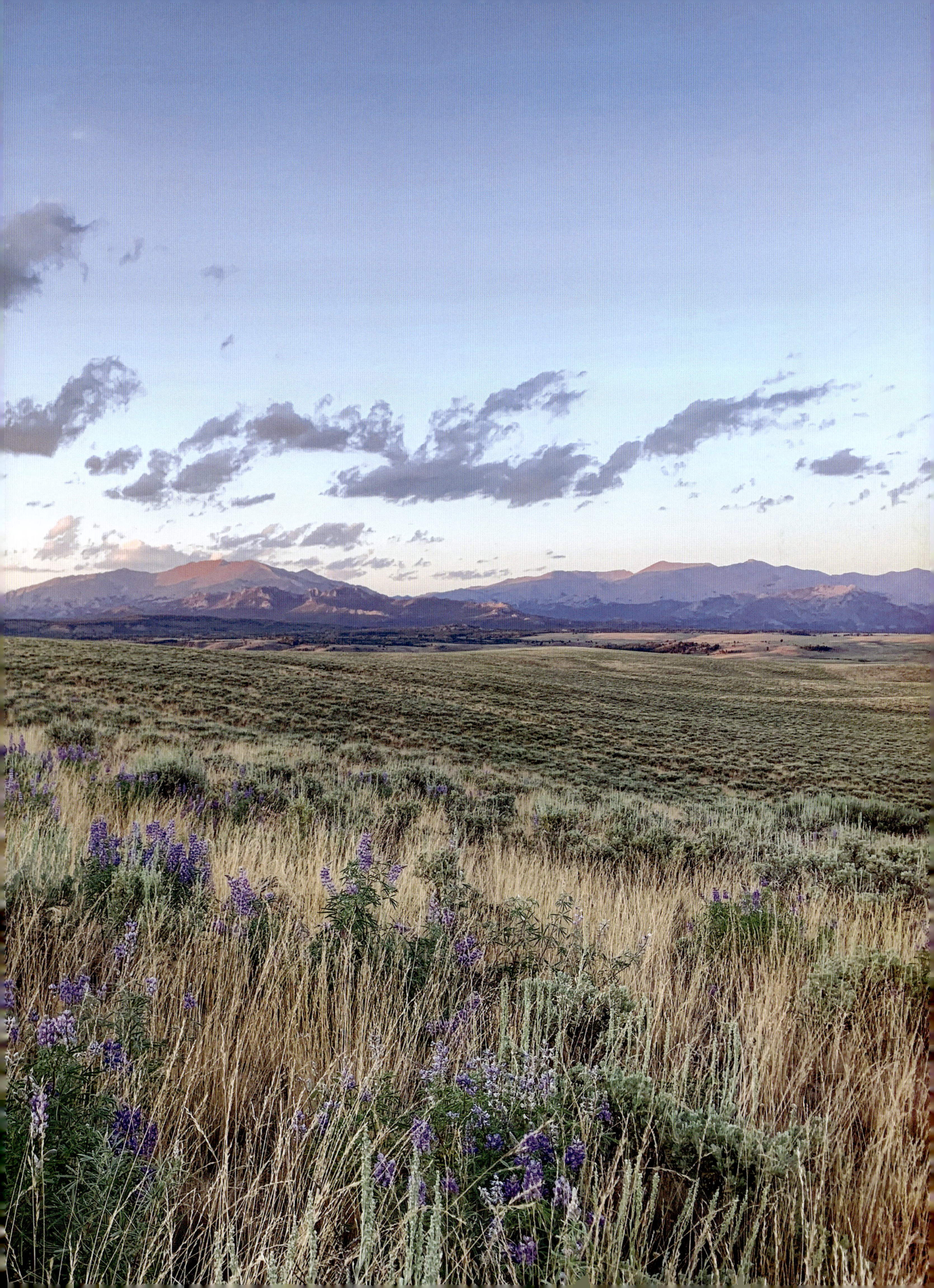

DRY MONTANE SHRUBLANDS

The dry montane regions contain some of the most diverse shrublands in the world. These communities occur anywhere that steppe or desert bioregions transition into cooler, higher elevation conditions, or where rain shadows cause leeward droughts, creating a confluence of flora, flourishing and testing the limits of their own expansion.

The foothill shrublands of the Rocky Mountains change rapidly, based on aspect, slope and elevation across the rolling ravines and peaks of the landscape. On eastern-facing slopes, in the rain shadows of the high peaks, heterogeneous shrub communities connect shortgrass steppe and montane forest, blending dense thickets of aromatic and sclerophyllous shrubs with more open, park-like coniferous expanses. The scene is repeated on the western slopes, where the shrublands are just out of reach of windward mountain runoff, with the seemingly infinite shrublands of the Great Basin pulling the desert-steppe into the high reaches of the mountains.

At montane elevations, where tree canopy coverage is absent, due to disturbance, sparse substrate or xeric conditions, patches of shrubland hold open court. These communities are often composed of several interwoven

The petran, a unique dry montane shrubland often called the Rocky Mountain oak chaparral, fragmentally blushing its way into autumn. The wide spectrum of genetic variability within a population of *Quercus gambelii* (Gambel oak) is in full display as neighboring clone clusters show differing pigment concentrations and chlorophyll breakdown rates.

SEEING SHRUBLANDS 105

The drifts of dry montane shrubs in this Rocky Mountain scene feel like ancient continents being pulled apart by slow, almost imperceptible forces. The simple, repeated combination of big sagebrush (*Artemisia tridentata*) and rubber rabbitbrush (*Ericameria nauseosa*), is a lesson in continuity. Even when disconnected by a complex interstitial plant community, the scene is clearly connected — like puzzle pieces scattered across a table.

shrubby species full of grasses and forbs. Big sagebrush (*Artemisia tridentata*) and rubber rabbitbrush (*Ericameria nauseosa*) pictured above are common cohabitants in this landscape, playing off each other with unmistakably different forms. The heavy, black trunks of the sagebrush silently writhe and offer plumulaceous studies of foliage and flowers. They call to mind feathery depictions of dinosaurs, loong dragons and bonsai. En masse, they flash across the mountains. The rabbitbrush does not display such continuity or posture, but rather insists its presence through a constant

FOLLOWING SPREAD Spring snowmelt and seasonal storms can adorn dry montane systems with a profusion of blooms. At the edge of a dark forest, continuous bands of *Artemisia tridentata* ssp. *vaseyana* (mountain big sagebrush) punctuated with the upright pale yellow-flowered *Eriogonum umbellatum* (sulphurflower buckwheat) and airy pink *Geranium viscosissimum* (sticky geranium) in the Gore Range near Silverthorne, Colorado.

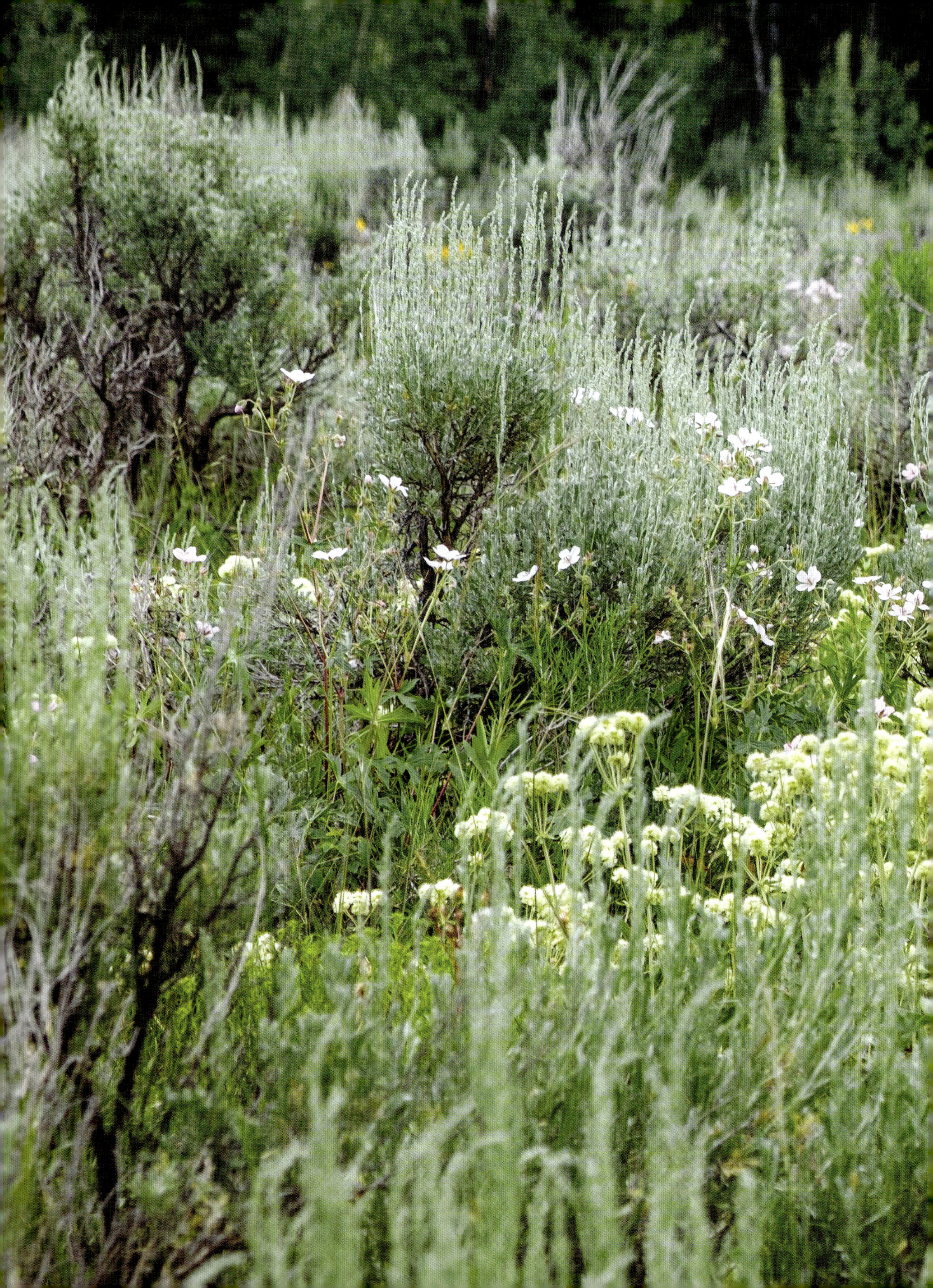

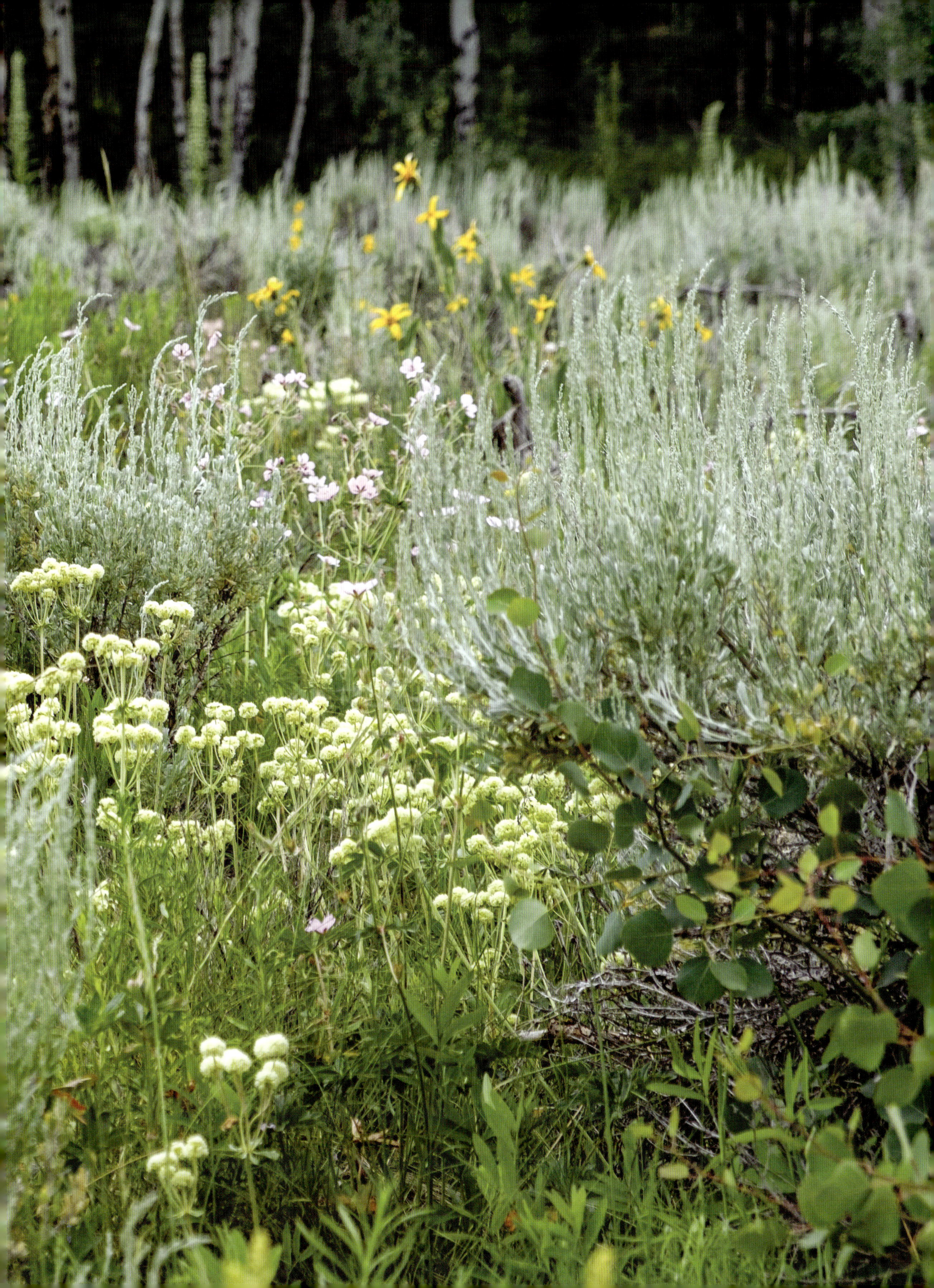

While many shrubby species may drift from lower elevations into the montane (or vice versa), providing a continuous visual connection, the interstitial species will shift and offer cues about the new environmental conditions. This profusion of *Wyethia amplexicaulis* (mule-ears) is typical for higher elevation sagebrush shrubland, but at lower, hotter elevations, it will be much sparser.

interest, offering diversity in size, shape and color. The epicuticular wax coating on the leaves and stems is delightfully variable, causing a spectrum of colors within communities ranging from almost lime green to pure white. The two responses to form and function by these two plants are equally adept in a demanding place.

The silvers of these landscapes are themselves classic clouds; echoes from above in the remnants of light lodged in the dark pine understory.

SEEING SHRUBLANDS 109

FAR LEFT The megaforb *Frasera speciosa* (monument plant) can be found punching through the interstitial layers of montane shrublands and meadows throughout the American West.

LEFT The emergence of the light-catching, feather-tailed seedheads of *Cercocarpus montanus* (mountain mahogany) is an annual spectacle that sets the Rocky Mountains aglow.

LEFT *Calochortus gunnisonii* (Gunnison's Mariposa lily) floats on grassy stems among hemiparasitic *Orthocarpus luteus* (yellow owl's-clover) in Summit County, Colorado. Strange ecologies, for example the hemiparasitism of *Orthocarpus*, typify shrublands and result in unexpected feedbacks that promote species coexistence.

WET MONTANE SHRUBLAND

On the windward sides of mountains, ample precipitation and snowmelt create a drippy, slippy, saturated world. These are the genesis points of our watersheds. Rivers, streams, creeks, lakes, bogs and seeps dot these landscapes, surrounded by dense and lush flora. The shrublands of the wet montane benefit from elevation, substrate and disturbance, all of which limit forest growth and allow large areas of shrub colonization to occur.

In tropical regions, wet montane shrublands push layer upon layer of ever denser foliage as the plants themselves become covered in moss, algae, lichen and even other vascular plants. In cold temperate regions, winter temperatures slow life to a creep and offer a pause to growth and a vista through. Denuded forms of plants dominate the landscape for the better part of the year. Flushes of foliage and flowers are brief, but the necroarchitecture of shrubs is ever-present and striking during the defoliated moments. Many shrubby species, for example willow and dogwood, have bark rich in anthocyanins, carotenoids and other secondary metabolic compounds that give their stems and trunks extraordinary winter colors, which often darken and texture with age.

ABOVE Strata of shrubs and moisture-loving forbs in Routt National Forest, Colorado.

RIGHT The herbaceous layers of this scene typify diversity driven by topography, the small dips and undulations causing moisture gradients that support different flora. Whereas *Agastache urticifolia* (horse mint) and *Erigeron elatior* (tall fleabane) compose most of the meadow, a dip in the middle of this path causes *Veratrum californicum* (corn lily) to cut through the center. Even without a moisture gradient on a site, you can plan and plant a garden taking cues from these awesome dynamics at Crested Butte, Colorado. These are the conversations that we don't have enough of, the ones that we wait for, wish for, the ones we cannot force. Because of these, we lie awake, replay and dissect. These are the gang vocals and pile-ons that we rehearse in our heads and hope we can experience again.

SEEING SHRUBLANDS

This whirlpool of color in the Rocky Mountains practically churns, playing between the realms of contrivance and chaos. The yellows, greens, reds and silvers of this shrubland are dizzying. Contrastingly flamboyant and bombastic color schemes tend to not be used in naturalistic design, living more in the space of traditional garden borders which feature highly bred and selected plants. However, recognizing that insane bombardments of color can be found in natural systems permits us to invite and include exuberantly colorful plants back into wild systems.

In the scene pictured above at Steamboat Springs, Colorado golden-yellow *Salix monticola* (mountain willow) crests out of a moist seep, flanked by the redder tones of *Salix wolfii* (Wolf's willow) and the dulling gray of *Salix geyeriana* (Geyer's willow). The strong upright of *Populus tremuloides* (quaking aspen) breaks the scene well before the horizon.

Wet montane shrublands are typified by thick shrubby growth, or undergrowth where stands of trees are present.

TOP, RIGHT *Ilex verticillata* (winterberry) in a stand of *Larix laricina* (tamarack) in Hiawatha National Forest, Michigan.

BOTTOM, RIGHT The marmalade-colored fruit of *Sorbus scopulina* (western mountain ash) punching through the bracken fern.

OPPOSITE PAGE *Salix* (willow), shaped and braided by winds and browsing.

FOLLOWING SPREAD Wet montane shrublands also support rich herbaceous plant communities. Here, *Delphinium barbeyi* (subalpine larkspur) and *Castilleja miniata* (giant red paintbrush) weave through thickets of *Salix brachycarpa* (barren-ground willow) that cling to the wet mountainside. Maroon Bells-Snowmass Wilderness, Colorado.

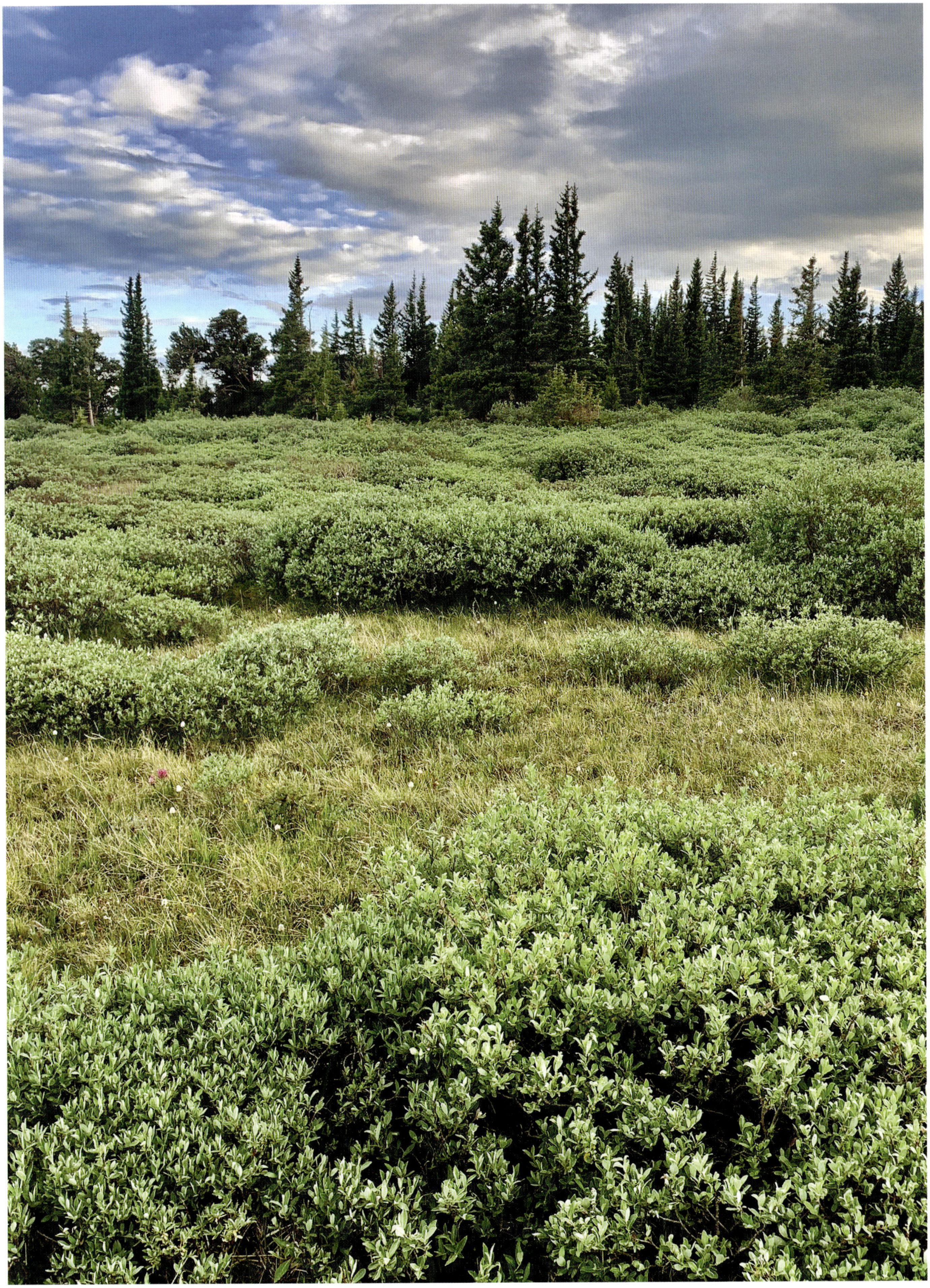

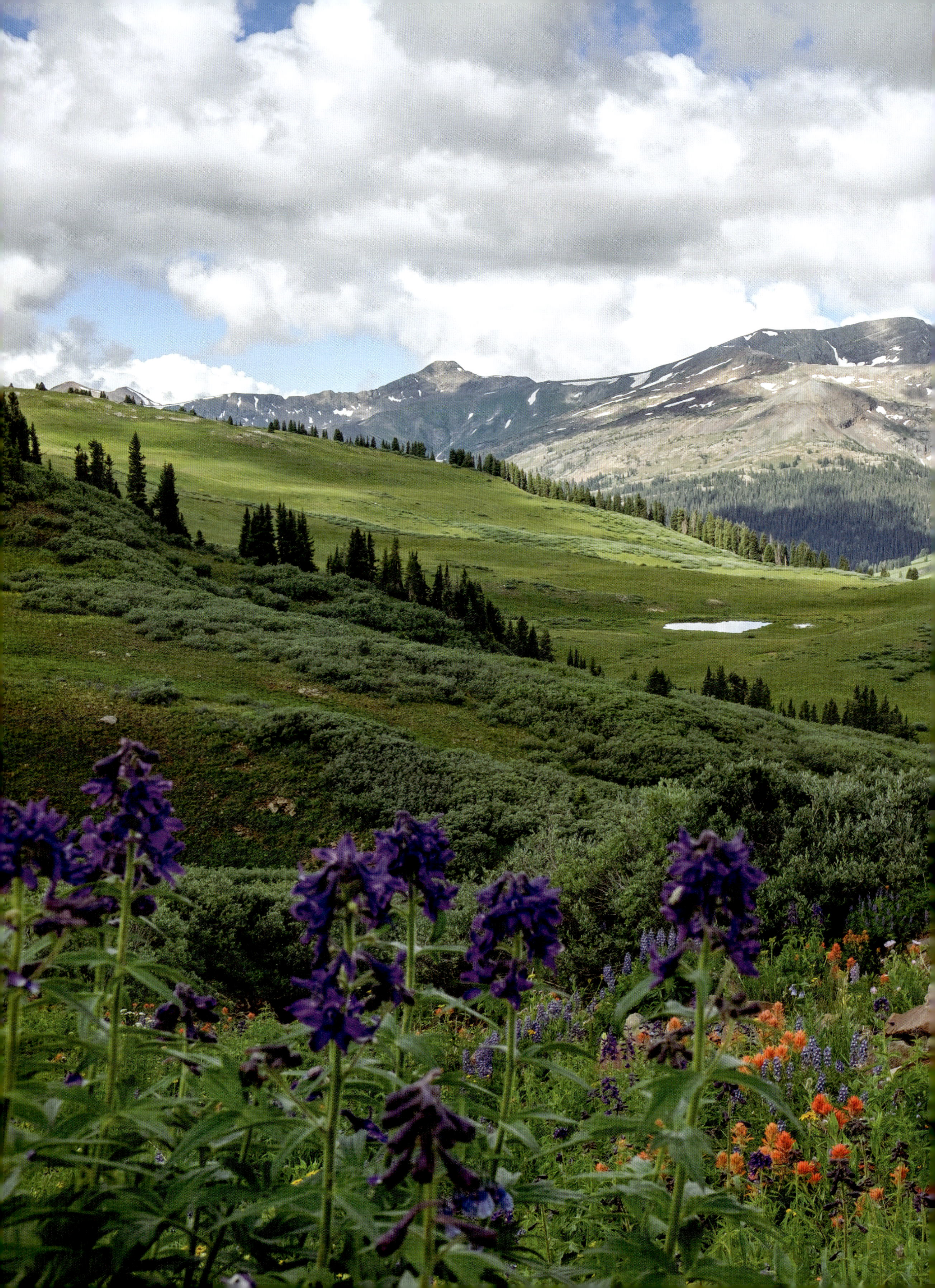

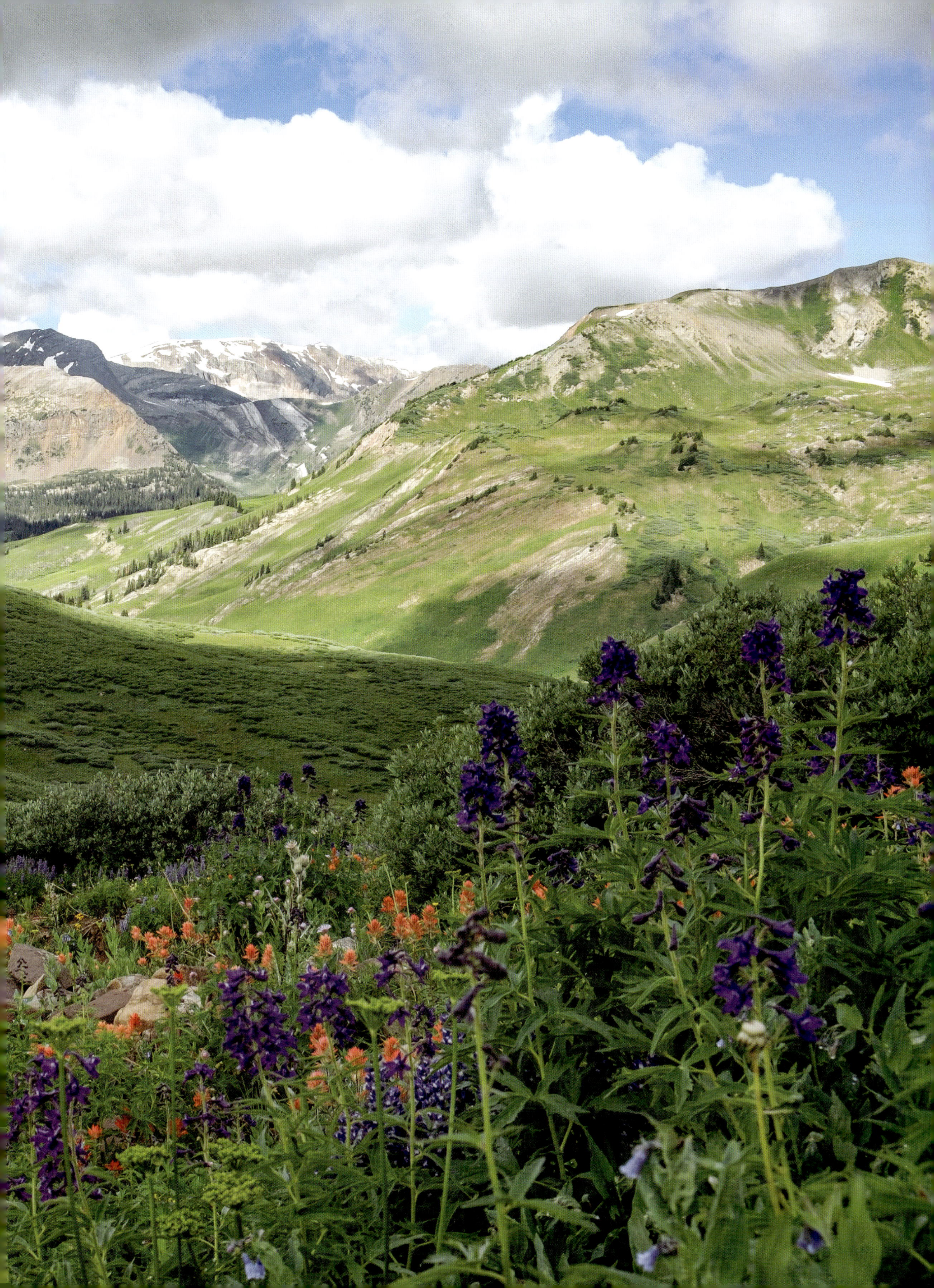

DESERT SCRUB

To declare the desert a peaceful place is not quite correct. The desert is resolved. The same is true of the desert dwellers, who are resolved to the daily swings of activity, consumption and emotion that correspond with extreme temperature, the desire for shade and water, and the recognition that when the complex and beautiful outside world is not accessible then the inner world must do.

The Chihuahuan desert is a "landlocked type of state,"[24] encompassing more than 500,000 square kilometers (193,051 square miles) in northern Mexico and the southwestern United States. Its huge area includes extensive mountain ranges, which create biodiverse sky islands and areas of biological refuge and drive the aridity of the desert below.

Eye-scraping textures interlace this upland desert shrubscape. Bold architectural forms of *Opuntia engelmannii* (desert prickly pear) and *Dasylirion leiophyllum* (smooth-leaf sotol) ground a milieu of diaphanous herbs and subshrubs including *Gutierrezia sarothrae* (broom snakeweed) and perennial bunchgrasses near the Chisos Mountains, Texas.

SEEING SHRUBLANDS   117

Exuberance and rest. Mass and void. Finding the balance and tension between positive and negative space is crucial in life. In this desert scene the solid paddles of the prickly pear offer visual brakes, catching and holding the eye, while the erupting, lanky forms of the ocotillo release it back into the fine-leaved haziness of the full composition. Depending on their frequency and surrounding plant communities, the stable forms of shrubs can act as either points of interest and excitement or areas of rest and respite.

The shrublands and succulent scrub of the Chihuahuan Desert (above) are austere in function but playful in form. Scabbing along the coalesced alluvial fans of bajadas and the shallow, rocky soils of the washouts, ocotillo (*Fouquieria splendens*) and large paddled prickly pear (*Opuntia engelmannii*) stand in stark contrast to each other and the rest of the landscape. This is the loud-quiet-loud dynamic of the American West that alternative rock was built upon; the feeling of traveling for hours across an endless plain before crashing into a mesa or diving your mind into a canyon.

FOLLOWING SPREAD *Rhus virens* (evergreen sumac), *Dasylirion leiophyllum* (smooth-leaf sotol), and *Opuntia engelmannii* (desert prickly pear) provide an evergreen backdrop as defoliated winter shrublands drape over the shoulders of the Chisos Mountains in south Texas. Vegetation here is rich and layered, despite receiving fewer than 30cm (12in) of precipitation annually.

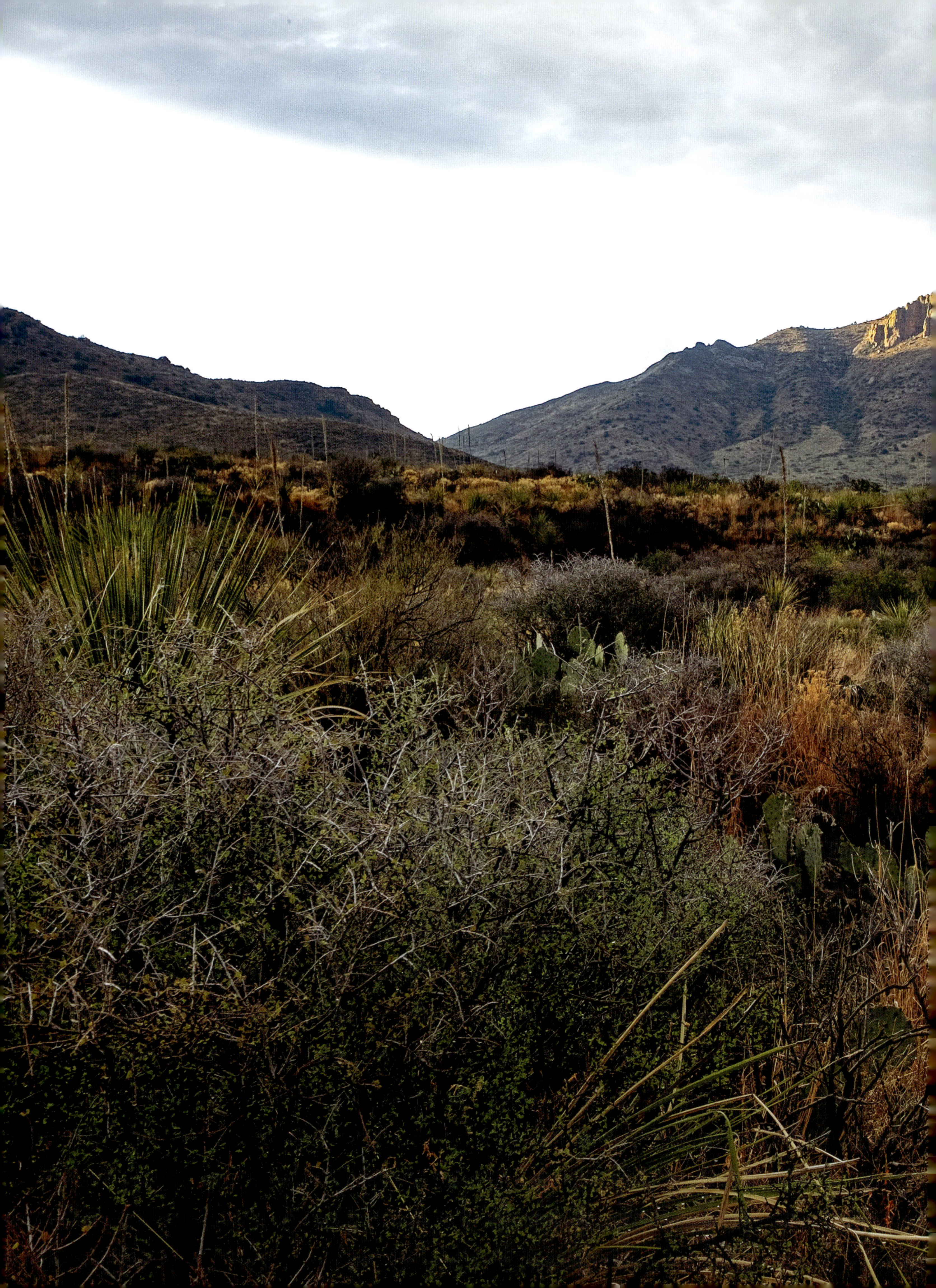

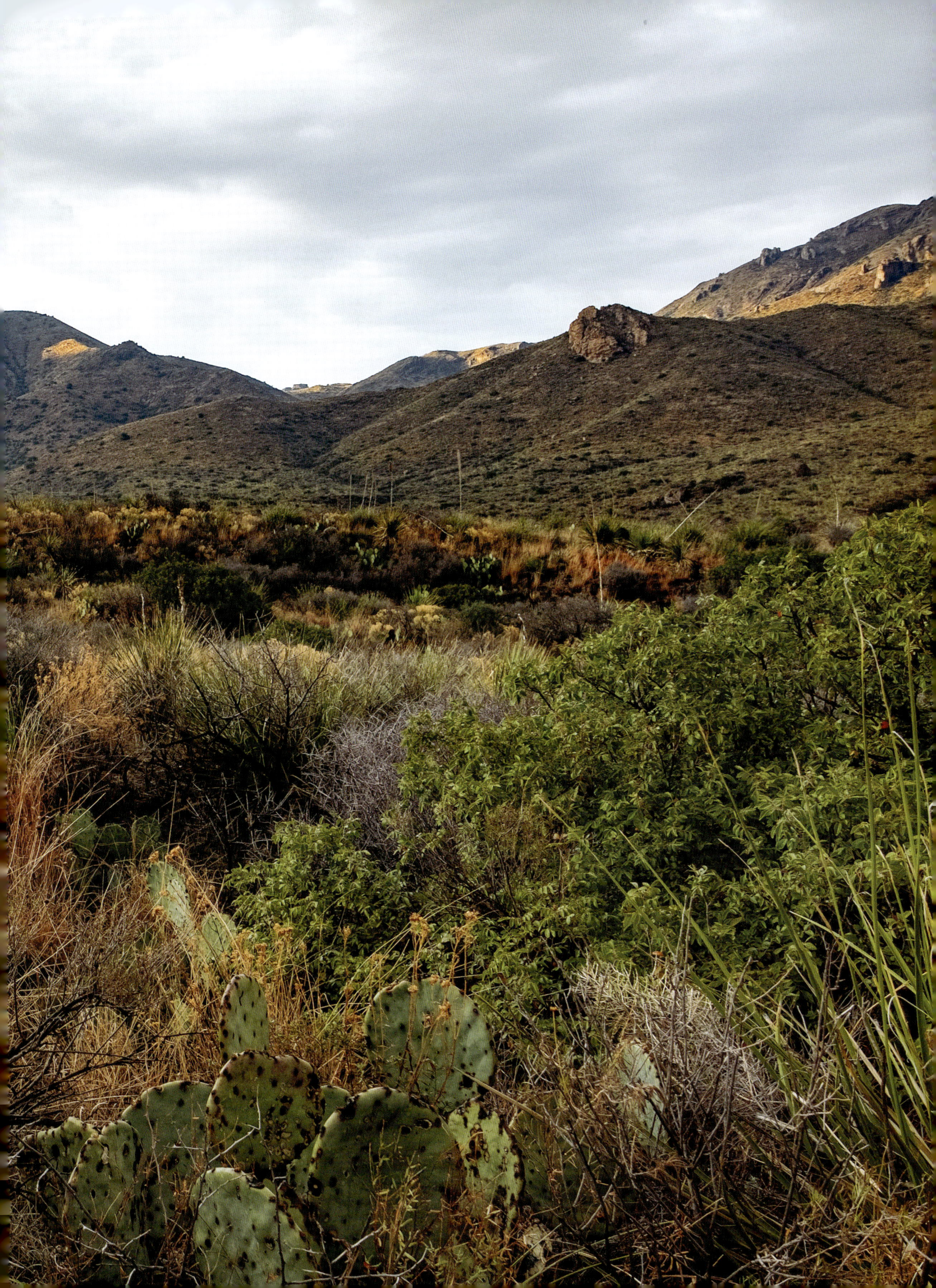

BELOW Floriferous *Dalea foliosa* (leafy prairie clover) crop up from rock fissures with *Opuntia engelmannii* (desert prickly pear) in Big Bend National Park, Texas.

SEEING SHRUBLANDS

Delicateness, exuberance and danger are all contained within the desert scrub flora.

LEFT *Myriopteris* sp. (lip fern)
MIDDLE *Larrea tridentata* (creosote bush)
BELOW *Yucca faxoniana* (giant dagger)

Late winter moisture brings heavy blooms to the California chaparral. Vast stands of white *Ceanothus cuneatus* (buckbrush) flowers form a contrast against maroon cliffs and follow the curve of the land. Sespe Wilderness, Los Padres National Forest, California.

CHAPARRAL

Shrublands have been pushed to the uninhabitable margins of human civilization and nowhere is this more noticeable than in the mixed Mediterranean and chaparral biomes of the world, where if land cannot be developed, it's either grazed or left alone. These shrubs are defensive and unforgiving, fortified with hard leaves, thick branches and dense architecture armed with thorns, spines and flamboyant biochemistry. Regardless, it remains one of the most beautiful and inspiring shrublands on this planet.

In this dense chaparral, chamise (*Adenostoma fasciculatum*), leads the scene with other shrubs taking supporting roles. The gravity of the leading element seems to attract the next heaviest, creating rifts populated by the remaining pieces. These patterns move like ripples of energy across the landscape.

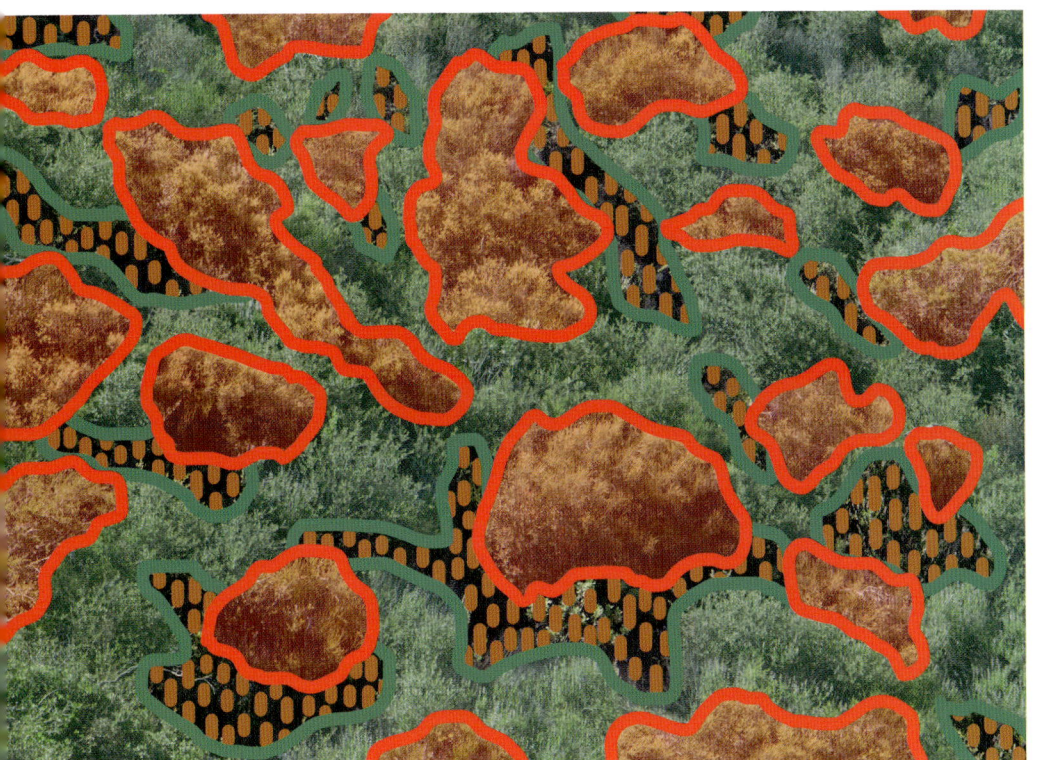

In the mixed chaparral of Angeles National Forest (above), *Adenostoma fasciculatum* (chamise) is queen with delicate white flowers and foliage reminiscent of rosemary. Its grace and boldness is the uncomplicated hook that cuts through the heavy riffs of *Eriogonum fasciculatum* (California buckwheat) and *Salvia mellifera* (black sage); the three-part botanical equivalent to Bad Religion harmonizing "When the hills of Los Angeles are burning."[25] Strewn throughout, as individuals and their own clustered micro

FOLLOWING SPREAD Manzanita chaparral along Blue Canyon Trail in Los Padres National Forest, California. Although chaparral is adapted to frequent fire disturbance, these forces are stochastic and temporally irregular. Longer disturbance intervals allows for the development of branching architecture in *Arctostaphylos* (manzanita) and dense infilling of *Heteromeles arbutifolia* (toyon) and *Frangula californica* (coffeeberry). The gaps in vegetation seem to have a gravitational pull and are rife with a sense of mystery.

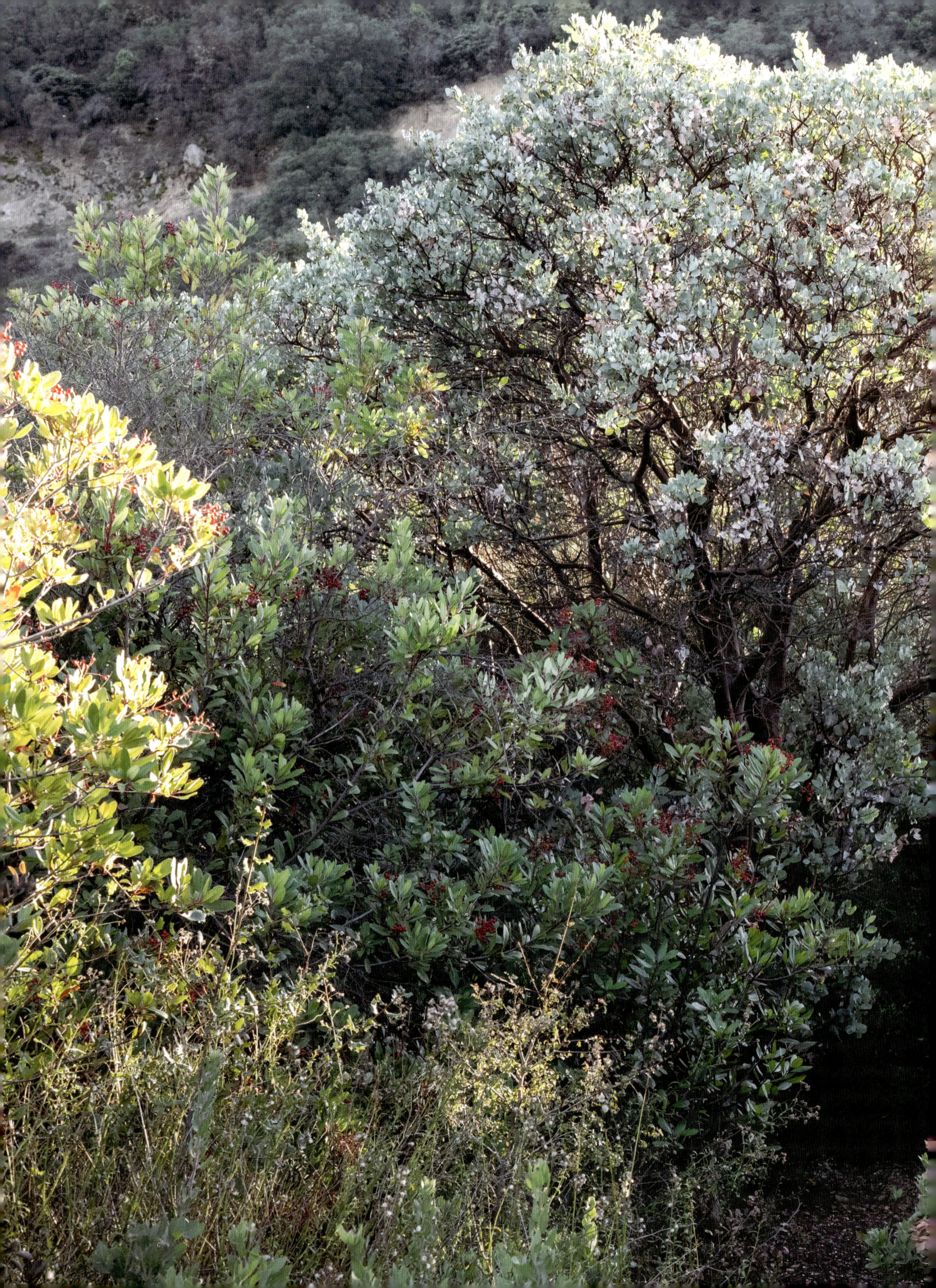

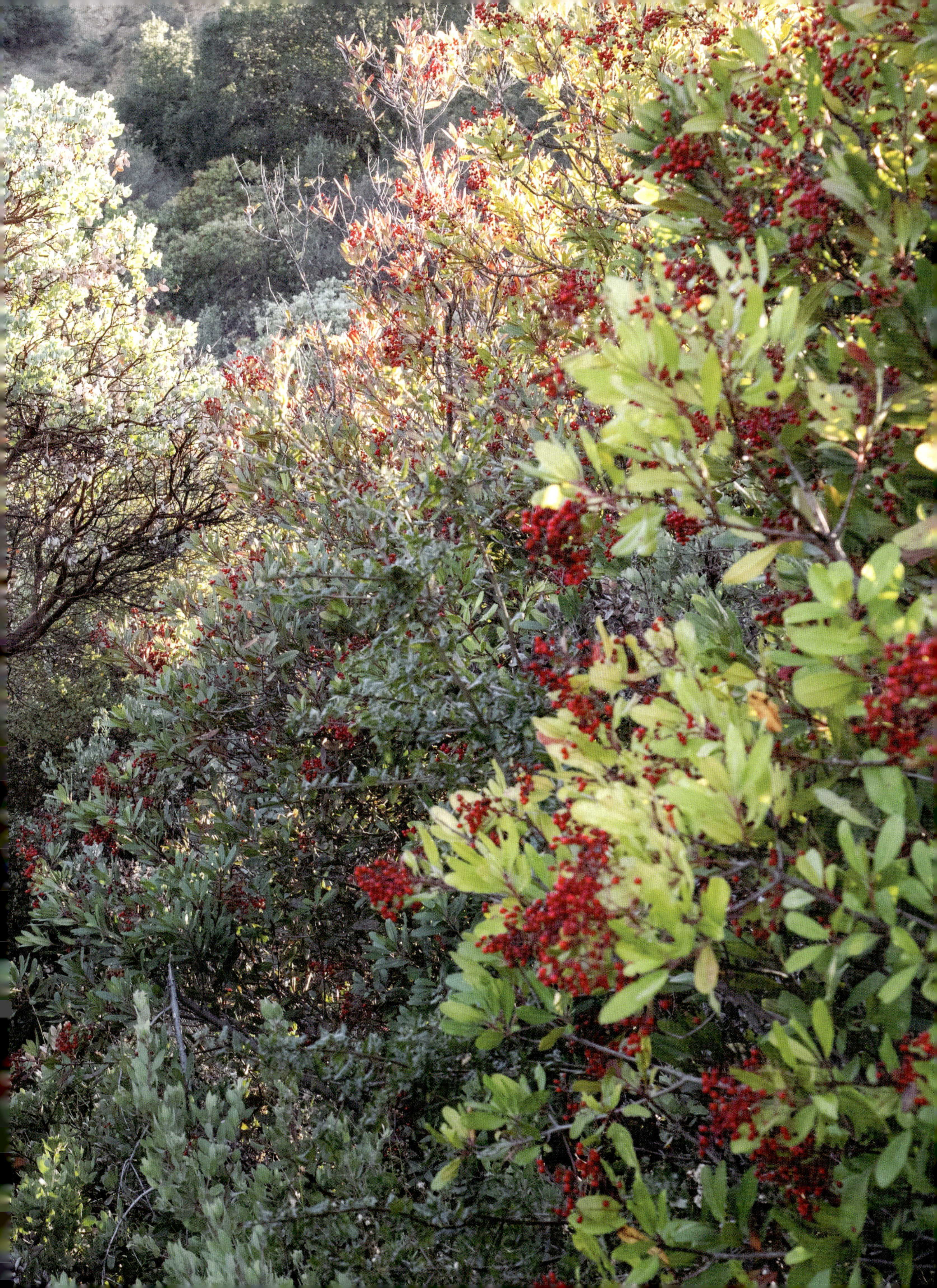

groups, are *Heteromeles arbutifolia* (toyon), *Ceanothus leucodermis* (chaparral whitethorn) and *Ceanothus cuneatus* (buckbrush). In areas of fire disturbance, the astringently sweet smell of *Cytisus scoparius* (Scotch broom) fills the air and mingles with the fruity patchouli fragrance of *Fremontodendron californicum* (California flannelbush). The result attracts thousands of bees and their therapeutic resonant drones.

The composition of chaparral is incredibly variable and can change rapidly, depending on slope, aspect, elevation, microclimate and fire frequency, making the landscape incredibly dynamic. Thus, each patch of chaparral is usually distinguished and named by its dominant shrubby genera, such as ceanothus chaparral, chamise chaparral, and scrub oak chaparral, while mixed chaparral is exactly that – a mixture of genera and species that form a tight union, binding together the acute and arid lands.

Moments in bloom and fruit from California mixed chaparral

ABOVE, CLOCKWISE FROM LEFT *Prunus ilicifolia* (hollyleaf cherry), *Fremontodendron californicum* (California flannelbush), *Marah macrocarpa* (chilicothe), *Hesperoyucca whipplei* (Lord's candle), *Solanum xanti* (chaparral nightshade)

OPPOSITE Mixed chaparral with *Ceanothus megacarpus* (bigpod ceanothus) in full bloom in California, looking as if the shrubs themselves were the source of the light.

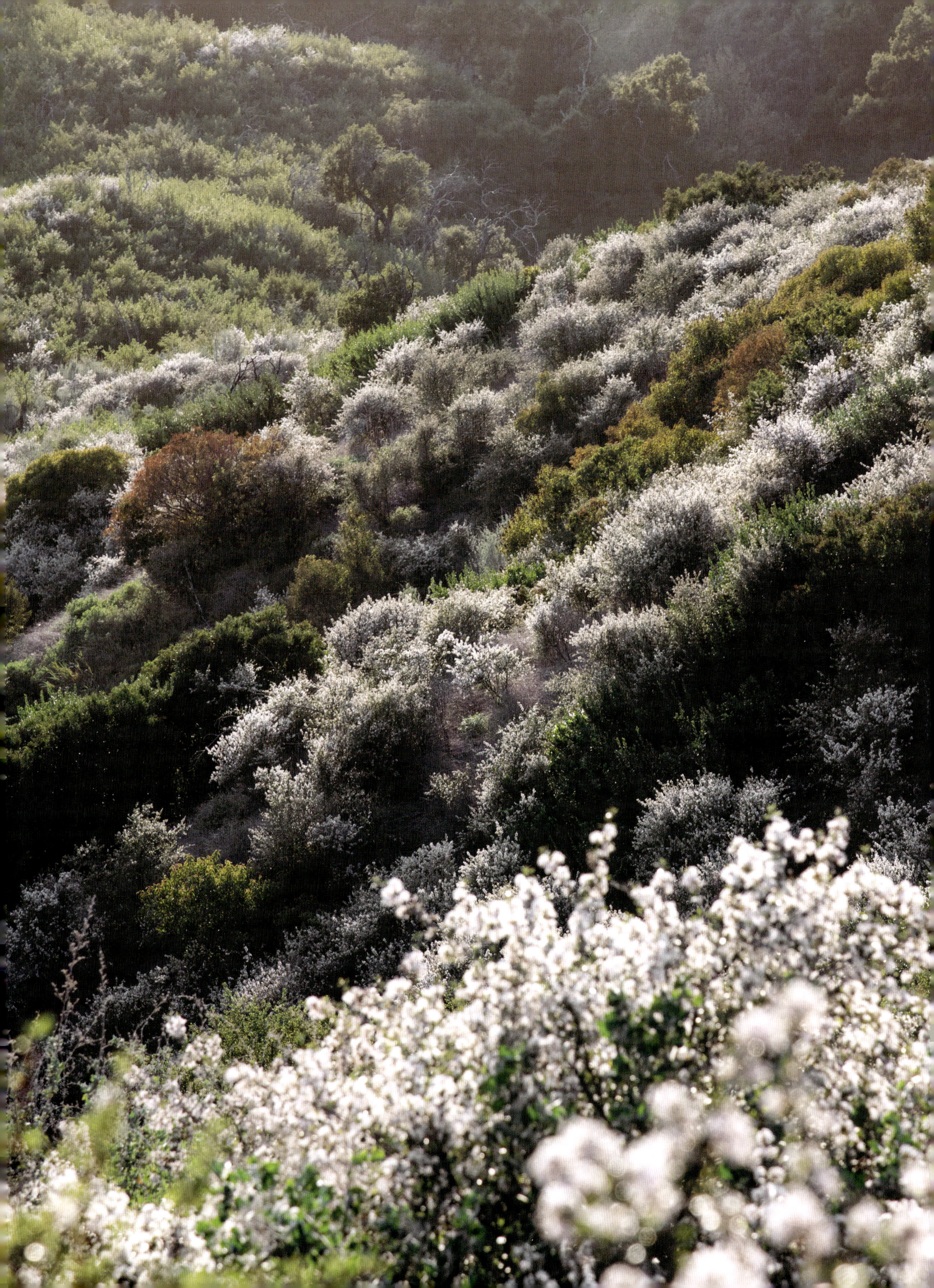

Soft textures of coastal sage scrub set against the dramatic backdrop of the Big Sur coastline in California. Undulating bands of *Ceanothus thyrsiflorus* (blueblossom) meshed with domes of *Ericameria ericoides* (mock heather) and *Baccharis pilularis* (coyote brush) give the vegetation an impenetrable appearance.

COASTAL SCRUB

Whether coastlines rise quickly from the oceans, barring all access if not for coves, tributaries and the trails of humans, or if the land gradually and gently slopes to the sea, coastal scrub reigns supreme. These shrubs take on forms that are dwarfed and tortured by the sandy soils, saline waters and blasting winds, creating dense mats of vegetation stitched together by forbs, succulents and grasses that, in spite of the conditions, never quit. These plant communities are exceptionally resilient and stable, often running for hundreds of kilometers/miles along coastlines.

The shrublands of Fort Ord Dunes State Park in Monterey Bay (opposite page) are reclaiming precious habitat formerly occupied by a military

SEEING SHRUBLANDS 129

Shrubs of similar stature, but with contrasting colors and textures, can be thickly interplanted to create a knotted, organic tapestry. In these compositions it can be hard to tell where one shrub begins and another ends, or where one lives and the other dies. Here, the forms offered in death can be just as triumphant as those achieved in life.

training facility. Where the army hid munitions in bunkers, the windswept forms of the coyote brush (*Baccharis pilularis*) mimic the carved sands of the dunes, creating new organic bunkers across the beach and protecting insects, birds, and lizards. In the face of abuse and abandonment, this is the best-case scenario. The progressive gradient from green to silver is most arresting in this foliar collage. The bright green coyote brush slices thinly from the back to midground (and holds its foamy white flowers high above the shrubby seaside), while the slightly tomentose leaves of seacliff

ABOVE The silver pipe cleaner inflorescences of *Artemisia pycnocephala* (coastal sagewort) rise through a mesh of annual grasses and forbs among the dominant shrubby forms of *Baccharis pilularis* (coyote brush) and *Ericameria ericoides* (mock heather). The wavy forms of the dense shrubs and conifers reveal the direction of persistent coastal winds. Fort Ord Dunes State Park, Monterey Bay, California, USA.

OPPOSITE The red foliage of *Carpobrotus edulis* (sour fig) burning through coastal forms of *Artemisia californica* (California sagebrush) on the Big Sur coast of California. Several species of ice plants from southern Africa are now ubiquitous along the California coastline. Although their ecological effects are debatable, they unquestionably add a striking visual element to coastal communities.

buckwheat (*Eriogonum parvifolium*) shift the entire scene to olive (except when its white pom-pom blooms fade to pink and rust deeper and deeper). The silver seaside wooly sunflower (*Eriophyllum staechadifolium*) provides the major contrast, cooling the entire hillside to the hues of sea and sky (until its sunshine yellow flowers shift it to that of sun and sand). The defoliated and grayed-out deadwood structures, mostly present in the stands of the seacliff buckwheat and coyote brush, offer long tears, silences, and moments of darkness in an otherwise very bright and active space.

These ever-present mats are the epitome of a model for a low-maintenance garden, especially when interplanted with forbs or succulents such as seaside daisy (*Erigeron glaucus*), California aster (*Corethrogyne filaginifolia* syn. *Lessingia filaginifolia*) or California poppy (*Eschscholzia californica*) to add spasms of flowers that disappear into the seamlines of the eternal quilt of shrubs.

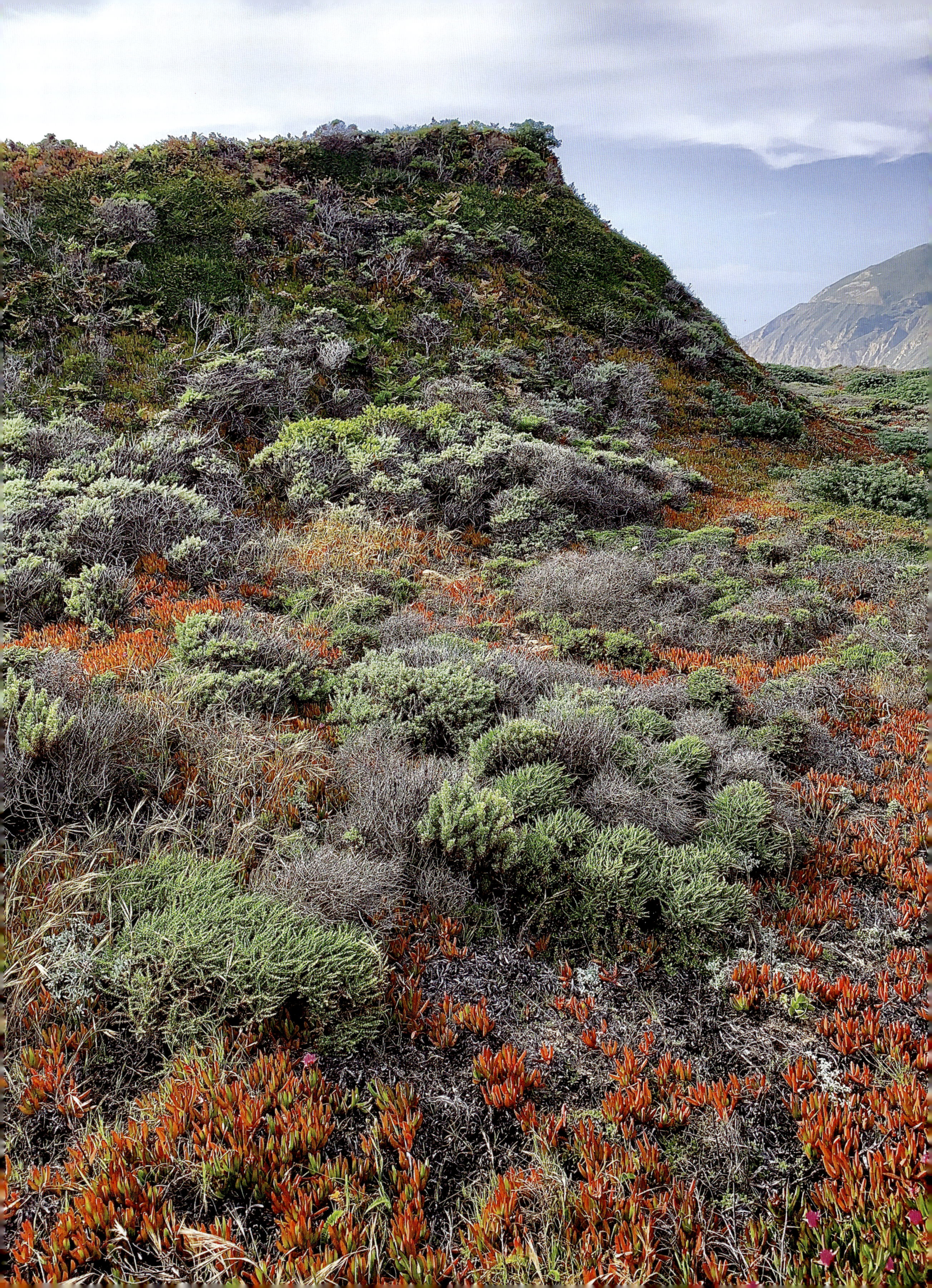

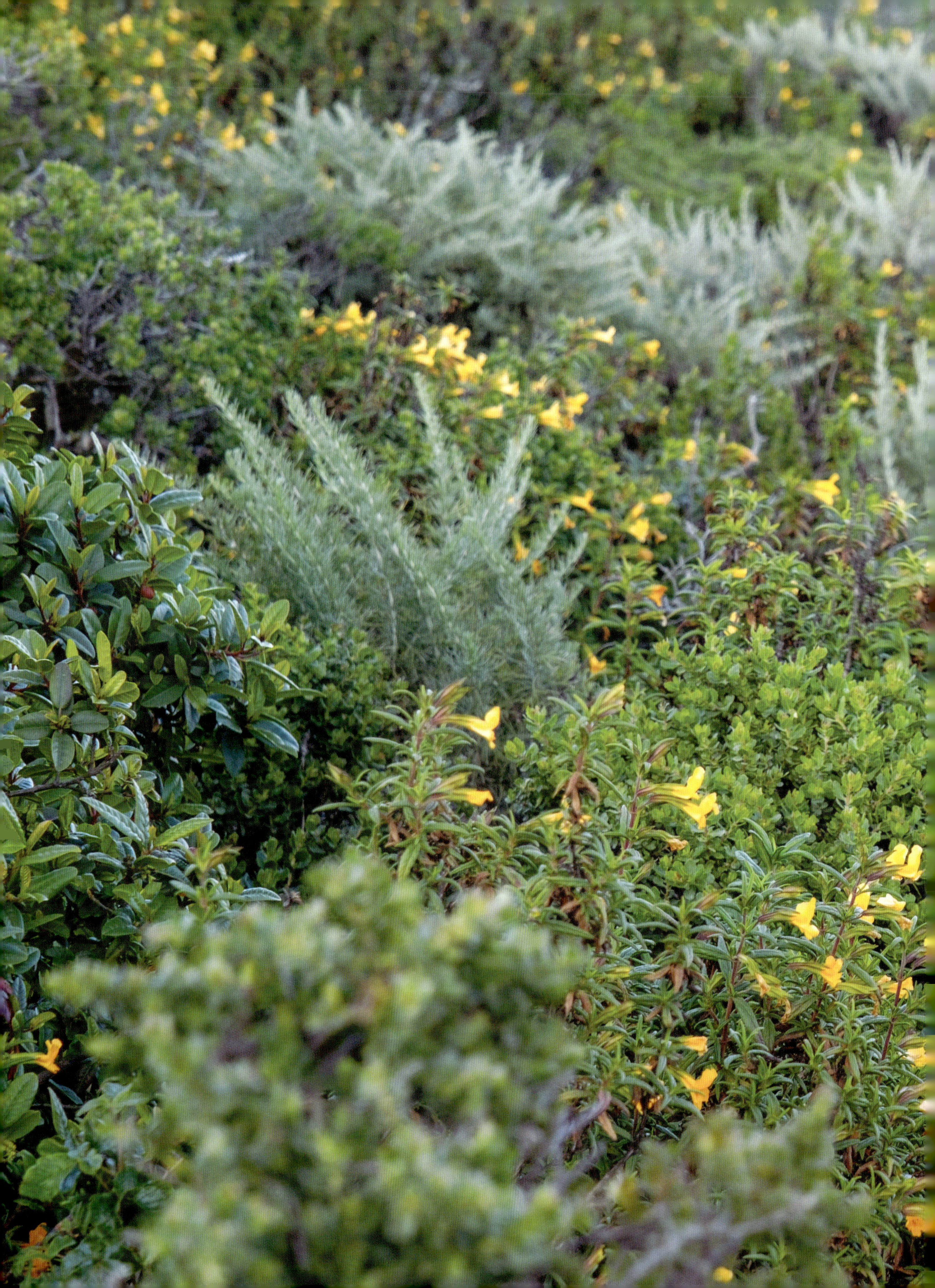

Neon orange *Diplacus aurantiacus* (sticky monkey-flower) and silver sprays of *Artemisia californica* (California sagebrush) punctuate the subtler vegetative textures of *Frangula californica* (coffeeberry) and *Baccharis pilularis* (coyote brush) in this dwarfed expression of coastal sage scrub at San Bruno Mountain State & County Park, California.

Alternative Shrublands

Shrublands exist in a continuum of environmental spaces throughout the world: salty, sandy coastlines, dense forest understories, the rich edges of agricultural fields, wide-open steppes, the ebb and swell of waterways. They defensively homestead the alpine, defy desert desolation and even find purchase in the urban façade. At varying scales, shrub-rich plant communities can be found almost anywhere, fitting almost every type of ecological niche and adapted to almost any environmental condition. Due to contrasting geologies, hydrologies, microclimates and disturbances, our diverse bioregions contain multitudes apart from the simplifications of their overarching classifications – for example, the grassland contains more than just endless fields of rippling blades, also hosting riparian forests and chasmophytic shrublands. The forests are not just shaded realms of towering hardwoods; their transitional edges abound in highly competitive shrub

BELOW In the Moorland Mosaic walk in Wombat Moor, a sparse woodland of *Eucalyptus coccifera* (Tasmanian snow gum) presides over a ground layer of stunted shrubs and forbs. *Astelia alpina* (pineapple grass) and *Gleichenia alpina* (alpine coral-fern) mix with the low shrubs *Microcachrys tetragona* (strawberry pine) and *Leptospermum rupestre* (prostrate tea-tree). Mount Field National Park, Tasmania, Australia.

thickets and flowering herbaceous meadows can be found where the canopy has opened. More than a blending at ecotonal edges, this phenomenon is a nestling of remnant or emergent ecologies where conditions subvert the dominant paradigm. Where we seek to create shrubscapes, identifying these transgressive moments and applying them to our gardens can help us equal the power of shrublands.

Every bioregion, habitat and climate has specific conditions that push their corresponding plant communities to develop shared adaptations and tolerances. Plants are fluid creatures with an almost unmatched will to survive, specializing and speciating to their environment across a spectrum of extremes. Understanding their life histories, their kin and their places of origin on this planet is critical to designing all naturalistic gardens that seek to take advantage of these adaptations.

BELOW **The mat-forming daisy *Raoulia hectorii* (Hector's cushion daisy), and *Donatia novae-zelandiae* (New Zealand cushion) in the Mackenzie region of New Zealand.**

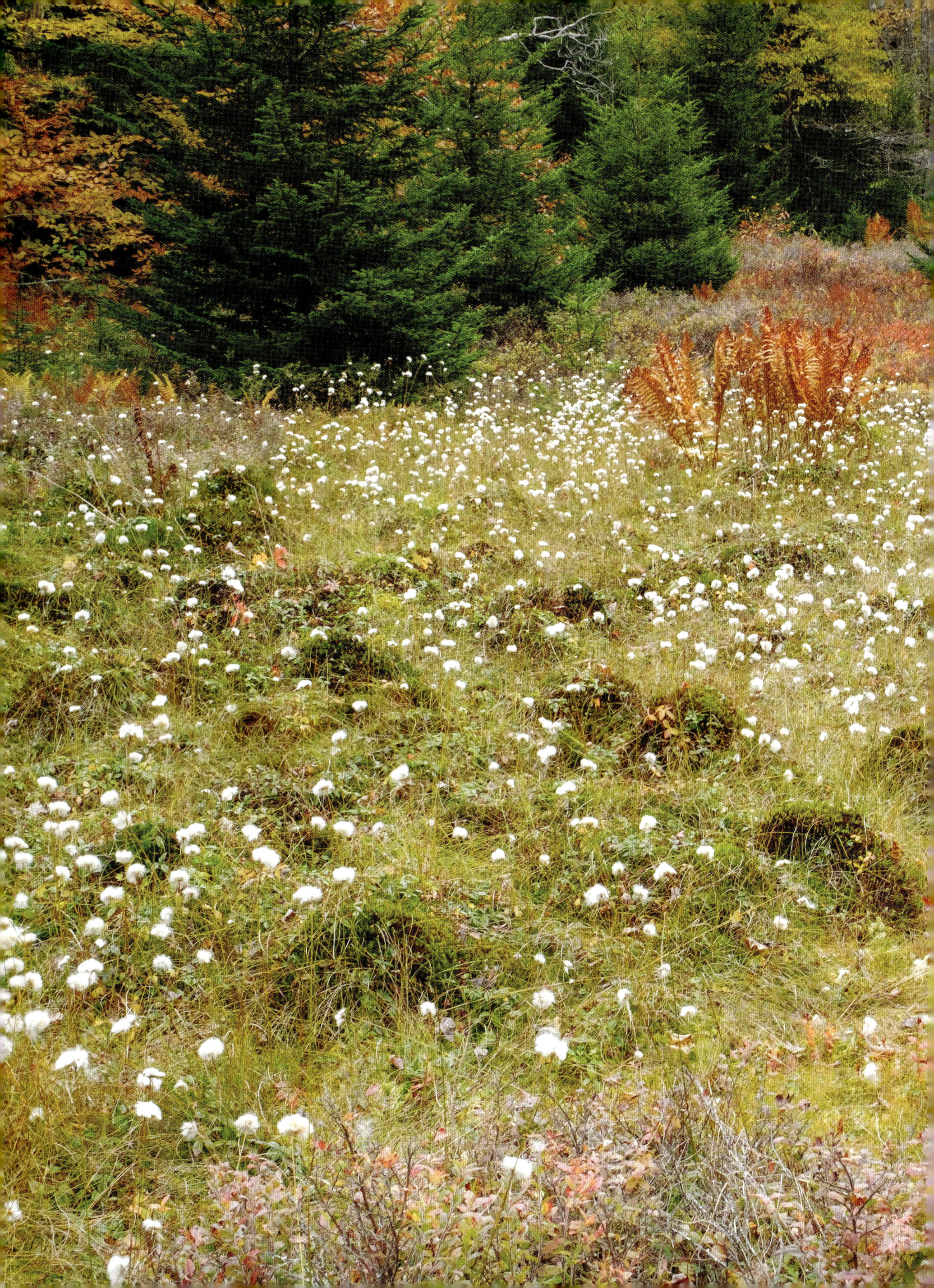

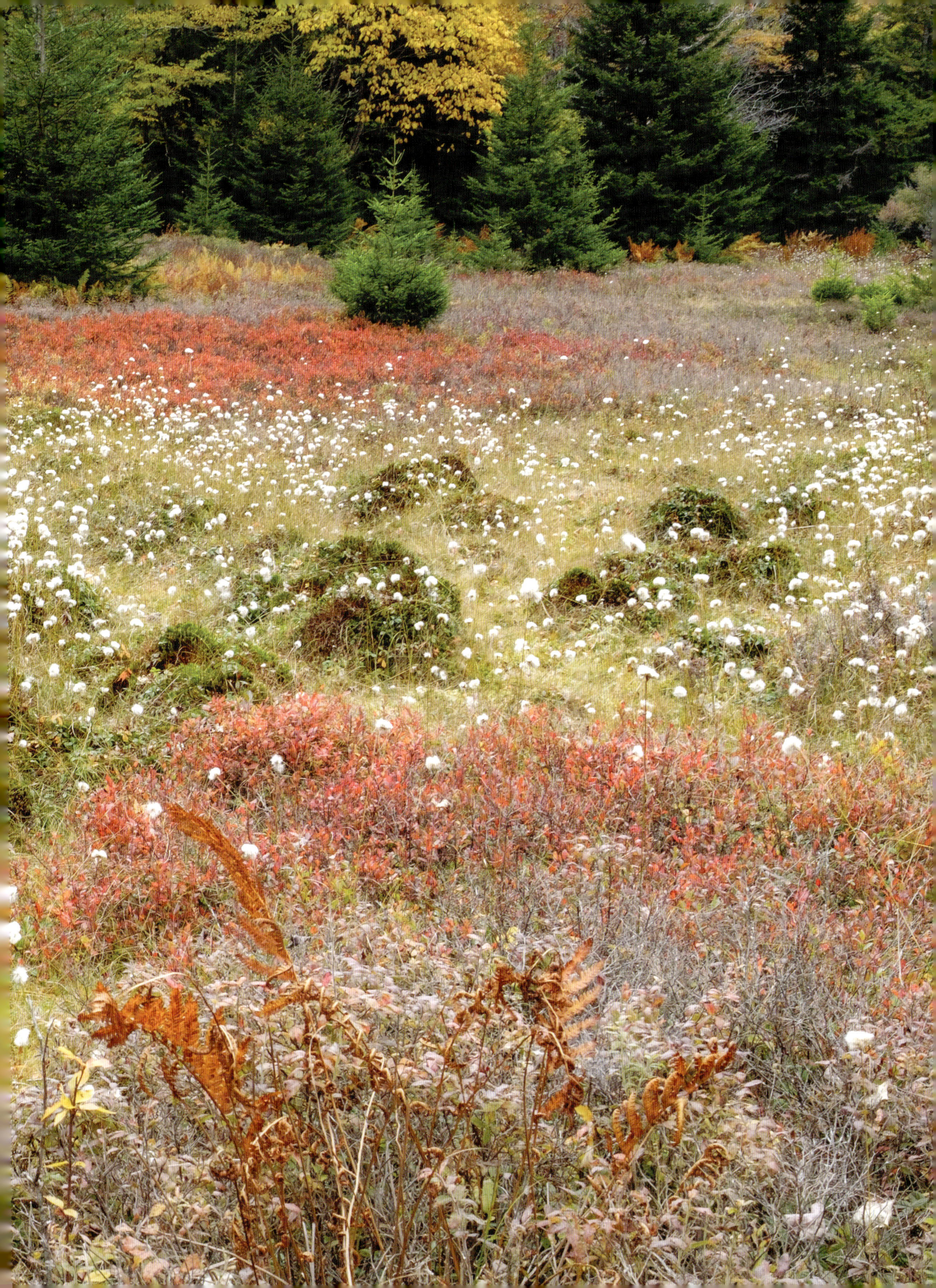

PREVIOUS SPREAD **This sphagnum glade minefield in Monongahela National Forest, West Virginia, greeted us with hummocks of** *Vaccinium macrocarpon* **(cranberry),** *Rubus hispidus* **(swamp dewberry) and a warning of unexploded ordnance. The floating smoky seedheads of** *Eriophorum virginicum* **(tawny cottongrass) and incendiary autumn color imply detonation.**

OPPOSITE **Prepetrified flora clinging to a cliff's edge in the brutal conditions of Petrified Forest National Park, Arizona – possibly becoming Petrified Shrubland National Park in another epoch.**

Shrub Love Coast to Coast

Using the conterminous United States as proof of concept that shrublands are everywhere, we begin thinking east to west, starting in the heathlands, blueberry patches and cranberry bogs of New England and moving through the edges of what were once great hardwood forests to encounter juniper, holly, the northern spicebush, and an impressive diversity of dogwood. The clearings in the woods, once remnants of game fires or homesteads and now almost exclusively maintained by utility companies, hold viburnum, chokeberry, sumac and serviceberry, among many others. Further south, sandy communities of beach plums and groundseltree give way to the light-punctured, mystical rhododendron and mountain laurel realms of the Appalachians. Where the Piedmont hits the deep south, some of the most enviable shrublands occur. Mountain witch alder, American beautyberry, buckeyes, honeycup, Virginia sweetspire and oakleaf hydrangea mix with the saw palmetto and needle palm scrub of the southern coastal plains. Heading into the midwest, woven throughout the memories of mesic tallgrass and mixed-grass prairies are thickets of wild plums and raspberries, New Jersey tea, prairie crabapple, prairie willow and elderberry.

At this point, our circuitous rambling faces a more definite latitudinal choose-your-own-shrubventure. To the south, the great diversity of shrub oaks in the scrublands of Oklahoma and Texas blend into the Trans-Pecos and Chihuahuan Deserts with their creosote bush, mesquite, ocotillo, fourwing saltbush, junipers and succulent scrub of yucca, agave and prickly pear. To the north, the cold steppes of the Dakotas, support rich pockets of silver buffaloberry, fire cherry, hazelnut and American plum. Straight ahead, the great American steppe, the Rocky Mountains and the Great Basin. In the exaggerated and nuanced geologies of the American west, life zones change quickly and dramatically, offering new shrubland communities with every slight increase in elevation or change of aspect. Rabbitbrush, sandsage, leadplant, sand cherry, skunkbush sumac and winterfat are scattered throughout the shortgrass steppe. Dozens of species of willows can also be found weaving through the scant but precious rivers, tracing their lines through every life zone and across the West.

As the plains rise into the mountains, rabbitbrush mixes with big sagebrush, antelope bitterbrush, mountain mahogany, mountain spray and maple. In the subalpine, krummholz junipers, firs and spruce intermingle with mountain ash, shrubby cinquefoil and twinberry. In the true alpine, tight cushions and mycelial-like expanses of sub-shrubs such

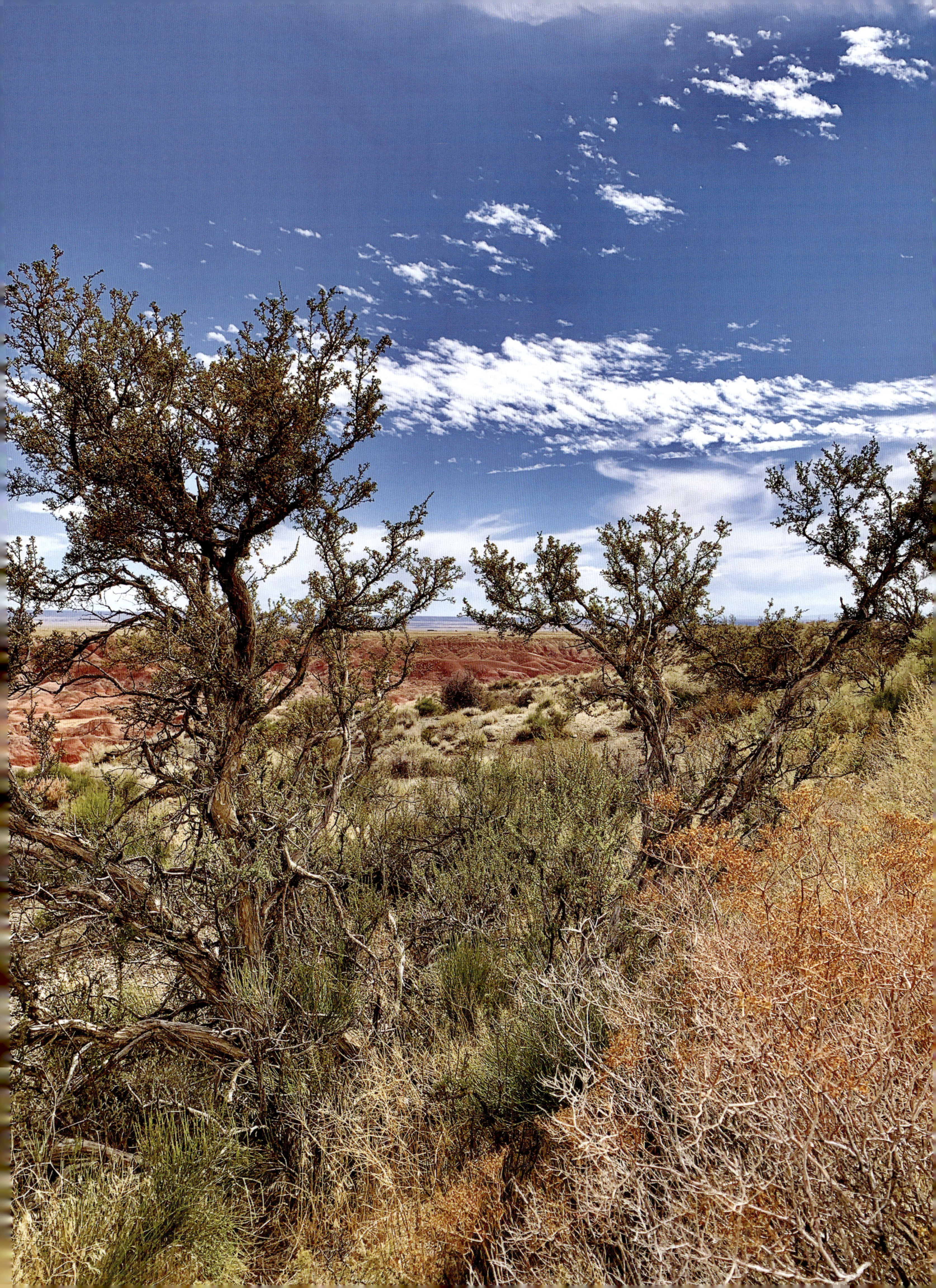

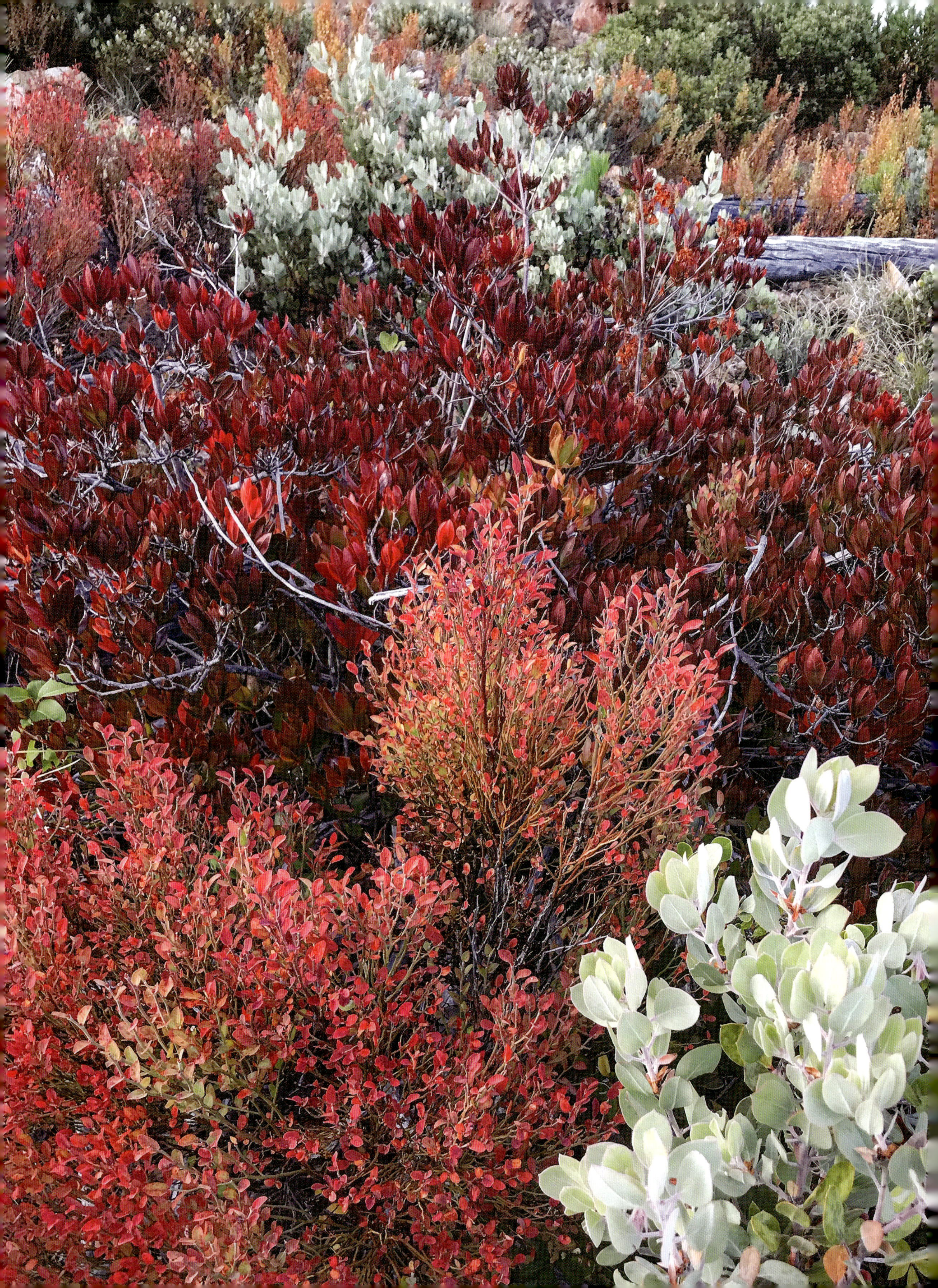

as currant, kinnikinnik, willow, bilberry and mountain dryad mix with tight hummocks. Beyond the Rockies, sagebrush rules the Great Basin, with blackbrush, horsebrush, greasewood, jointfir, shadscale, fernbush and greenleaf manzanita occupying different niches. The Cascades hold a huge diversity of habitats and associated shrubs: chamise, oak, manzanita, California lilac, poison oak, and salal fill the woodlands and chaparral, mixing with the buckwheat, toyon, black sage, deerweed of the chaparral and coastal scrub. Heading to the cooler, wetter world of the Pacific northwest, snowberry, vine maple and black hawthorn entwine with myriad edible brambles, hazelnuts and grape hollies.

That narrative (fraught with gross generalizations, glossings over, and a gigabytes worth of omissions) could happen through almost any place on earth.

OPPOSITE *Vaccinium deliciosum* (Cascade blueberry), *Rhododendron occidentale* (western azalea), *Arctostaphylos canescens* (hoary manzanita) and dwarf forms of *Notholithocarpus densiflorus* var. *echinoides* (bush tanoak) and *Umbellularia californica* (California bay laurel) on the serpentine soils of Oregon's Siskiyou Mountains, Josephine County, Oregon.

BELOW *Solidago roanesnsis* (Roan Mountain goldenrod) and *Rubus canadensis* (smooth blackberry) ramble through grassy interstitial spaces and between shrubby islands of blood red *Vaccinium angustifolium* (lowbush blueberry) on Carver's Gap in Pisgah-Cherokee National Forest, North Carolina.

Blasted by wind, coastal dune communities remain rounded and compact. Here, accumulated deadwood on *Ericameria ericoides* (mock heather) adds a layered and sculptural quality to the scene, while *Eriogonum latifolium* (seaside buckwheat) threads through the interstitial space with rusty faded inflorescences.

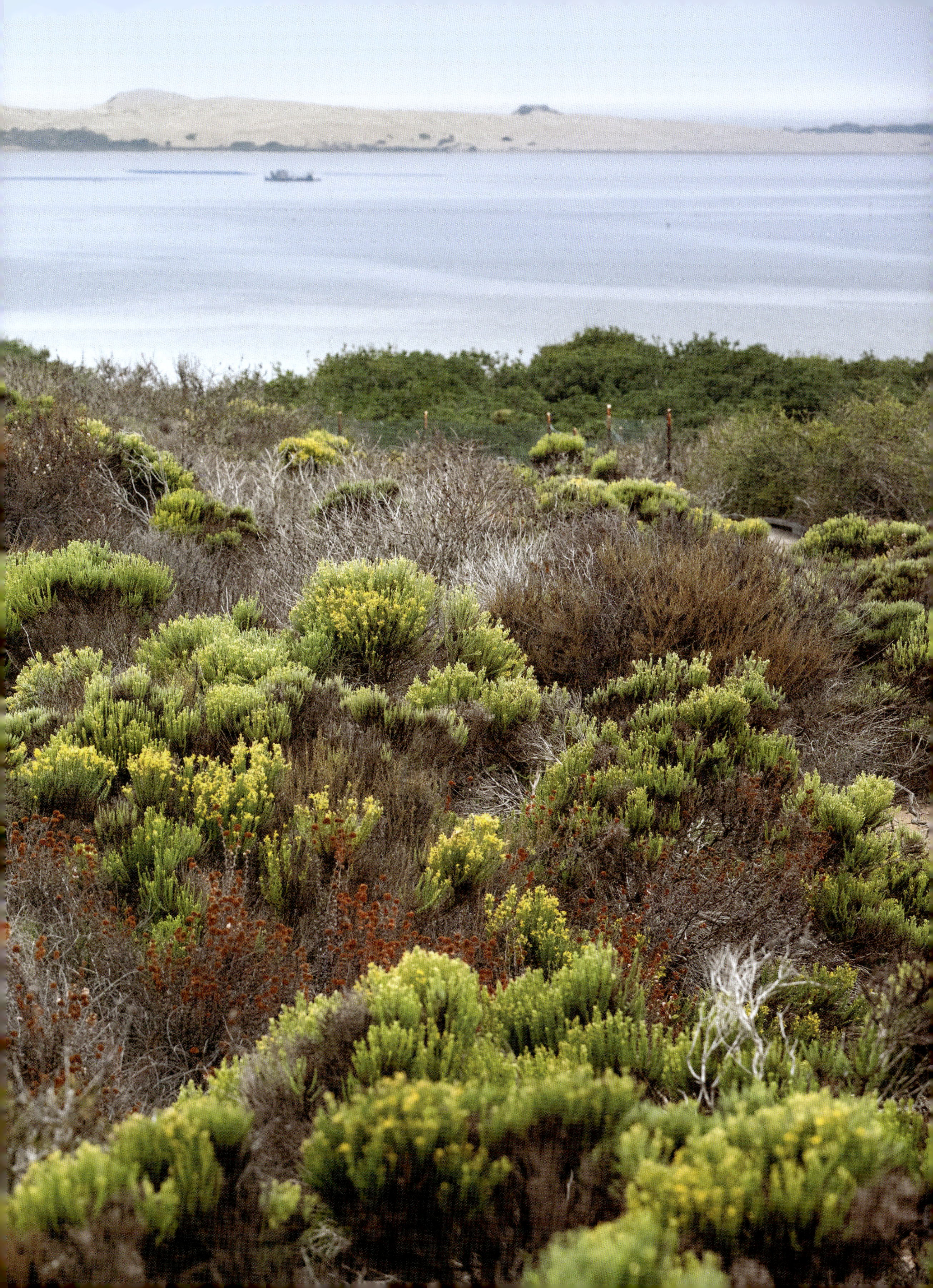

A dry prairie remnant that escaped agricultural development in Rock Creek State Park, Iowa, rich with mixed woody vegetation. Silver masses of *Salix humilis* (prairie willow) pour light into a mysterious woodland edge habitat of *Corylus americana* (American hazelnut), *Cornus racemosa* (gray dogwood) and *Amorpha canescens* (leadplant).

THE DISTURBED

In *The Mushroom at the End of the World*, Anna Lowenhaupt Tsing asks if we could create "disturbance-based ecologies in which many species sometimes live together without either harmony or conquest."[26] Disturbances such as burning, browsing, trampling and mowing keep landscapes in transitional states. Humans are very good at disturbing things and have kept much of the earth in disturbance-based transitional states for most of our history. We are chaotic rearrangers of information and multitudes of flora and fauna have evolved to thrive in these conditions. Accepting and encouraging disturbance-based ecologies is a necessity for preserving and working with shrublands, and can be used to our advantage to create more directed, time-saving, and compassionate stewardship plans for our gardens.

The growth habits of many shrubs reflect the disturbance responses of certain shrublands. The majority of shrubs have evolved in disturbance-based habitats prone to fire and heavy browsing by animals and tend to reshoot readily from underground growth points or from swollen caudices. These energy stores allow them to compete with other fast-growing species by quickly pushing flushes of young growth to newly opened canopies. Others may not be as tolerant to major traumas, but may have produced seeds that germinate only after the mature vegetation is removed.

Eriodictyon californicum (California yerba santa) dreamily light-paints the hillsides with lilac purple post-fire blooms while the rest of the landscape is still in snags. Dry Lakes Ridge Botanical Area, Los Padres National Forest, California.

RIGHT The fall-line sandhills xeric plant communities of South Carolina are defined by deep sands with varying levels of productivity supporting a loose, plantation-like arrangement of *Pinus palustris* (longleaf pine) with an almost constant understory of interlocked scrub oaks transitioning through the spectrum of burned-out open clearings, bone-dry dappled shade and saturated pocosin bottomlands. Here, longleaf pine seedlings emerge through *Quercus laevis* (turkey oak), *Schizachyrium scoparium* (little bluestem) and *Eupatorium capillifolium* (dogfennel).

BELOW *Umbellularia californica*, the California bay laurel, resprouting from its own charred spires, just a few months after being ravaged by the Cave Fire outside Santa Barbara, California.

OPPOSITE PAGE Regular mowing with heavy duty brush cutters keeps the vegetation beneath this powerline in the state of an early successional shrubland. Without regular disturbance, the wet temperate climate of Seattle would quickly push this plant community towards a forest. Tiger Mountain State Forest, Washington.

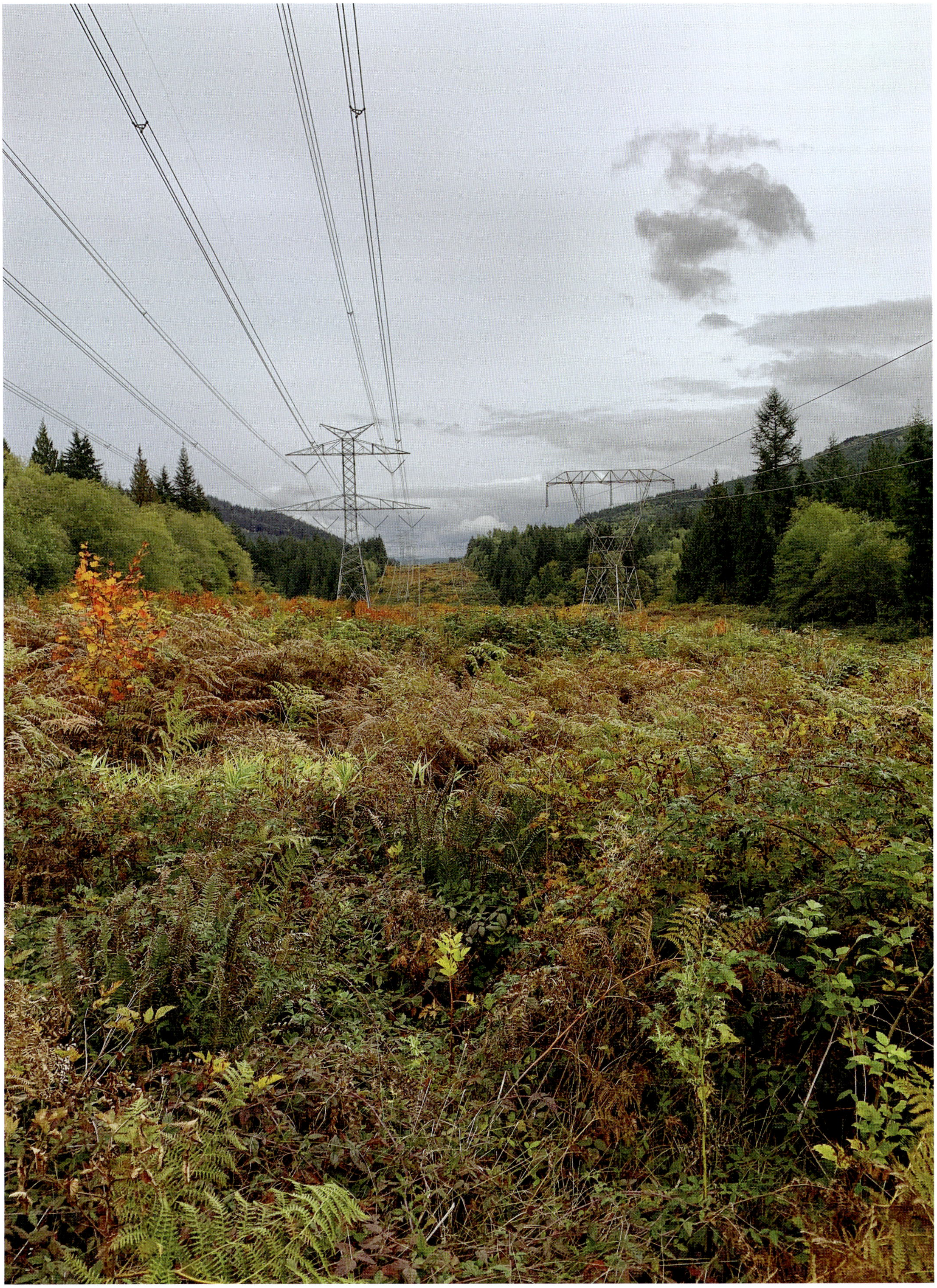

THIS AIN'T NO MEADOW

In areas with frequent fire cycles or when grazing and browsing pressure is constant, shrubs tend to grow in balance with grasses and forbs, occupying a similar niche to herbaceous perennials. Since these disturbance events tend to favor the graminoid layer, shrubs take on more juvenile forms, as shoots or whips running through meadows, and only occasionally making islands of intergrown woody mass. In a system where humans are controlling the frequency of disturbance, the shrubby layer can grow together for years before coppicing or burning, allowing the composition to shift significantly before hitting the reset button back towards slightly shrubby.

This ain't no meadow with shrubs. It also isn't a shrubland with grasses. The species in these habitats (shrub-meadows or shrub-prairies) are equally matched competitive species that are as settled as they are uncomfortable – but while competition for light is high, competition for water resources is often not. Unlike grasses, which despite their deep root systems most commonly draw water from the top 30cm (12in) of soil, shrubs draw water from anywhere between 45cm (18in) and 3m (10ft), making them resilient and complementary partners in ecosystem creation.[27]

This shrub-meadow community in the chopped sand dunes of Sheyenne National Grassland, North Dakota, is visually dominated by *Rhus glabra* (smooth sumac), *Amorpha canescens* (leadplant) and *Schizachyrium scoparium* (little bluestem).

SEEING SHRUBLANDS 149

Differences in disturbance produce different plant compositions.

LEFT A post-burn mesh of *Amorpha canescens* (leadplant), *Echinacea pallida* (pale purple coneflower), and *Achillea millefolium* (yarrow) reads as an herbaceous meadow.

BELOW With a lack of disturbance, *Amorpha canescens* (leadplant) and *Sorghastrum nutans* (yellow prairie grass) has become visually dominant, overshadowing the forb layer, which lays in wait for less competitive times.

ABOVE *Coccoloba uvifera*, or the seagrape, is an edible fruit-bearing shrub in the buckwheat family that grows on beaches and coastal dunes throughout the tropical Americas.

CHILDREN OF DUNES

Shrubs and shrublands often occur in areas where the substrate is too mineral, well-draining, unproductive, or unstable to support larger plant life. Beach and inland dunes, sand and gravel deposits, and areas where the topsoil has eroded are full of shrub diversity. On wide open dunes, shrubs act as refugia, creating microclimates and windbreaks, stabilizing surfaces and depositing organic matter.

The coverage and density of dune shrublands varies dramatically with regional precipitation, since dune communities can occur anywhere from the wet maritime to the deep desert. The visual relationship between plant material and substrate that's revealed by sporadic blowouts or patterned spareness is an ever-present and important piece in understanding the hard stories of hard places. To accept the aesthetic appeal of these places we must embrace the sand and the stone that surround them.

In a world of skyscraper wind tunnels, concrete rubble substrates, and environmental contaminants, dune plant communities are critical partners in developing diverse and adaptable living infrastructure. They are the plants for the anthropogenic apocalypse, the ones that will populate our toughest spaces and add surprise to our planned environments.

ABOVE *Iva imbricata* (dune marsh-elder) is naturally distributed on the North American Atlantic coastline from Cuba to Virginia, USA. Its power to stabilize dunes is legendary and it's often the plant found growing closest to the tide-line.

RIGHT The veritable candy dish of a heath shrubland in flower, seen here on the sandy beaches of Fitzgerald River National Park, Western Australia.

ABOVE The red pea flowers of *Templetonia retusa* (coral bush) scattered across a coastal heath sand dune on the Eyre Peninsula in Coffin Bay National Park, South Australia.

RIGHT *Quercus welshii* (Tucker oak), a scrub oak in the sand shinnery ecosystem whose masses accumulate sand and create inland dunes as they grow. Navajo Nation.

SEEING SHRUBLANDS　　　153

TOP, LEFT As in all dry regions, the appearance of vibrant colors is dependent on water. Seasonal or even multi-year weather patterns dictate the hues and tones of these plants, which more often assume earthier colors that allow the inherent darkness in their masses to leak out from the center. Here *Cereus* cacti take advantage of the shelter offered by these shrubby masses to survive their precarious adolescence.

ABOVE *Myrica cerifera* (southern waxmyrtle) is found on the coastlines, coastal plains and adjacent low-lying areas from northern New Jersey to Texas.

CENTRE, LEFT Buns of *Hudsonia tomentosa* (woolly beach-heather) speckling a backdune at the Cape Cod National Seashore, Massachusetts. This species doesn't tolerate high competition and requires periodic disturbance of its environment, making the ever-changing surface of the dunes perfect for its establishment. Ironically, it is very sensitive to direct disturbance and doesn't tolerate trampling or heavy saltspray.

BOTTOM, LEFT Wireless shrubs transmitting transatlantic texts of triumph over telegraph towers; *Rhus copallinum* (winged sumac) and *Quercus ilicifolia* (bear oak) preside over the former site of the Marconi Wireless Station in the Cape Cod National Seashore, Massachusetts. *Myrica pensylvanica* (northern bayberry), *Rubus* (raspberry), *Prunus maritima* (beach plum), and *Arctostaphylos uva-ursi* (kinnikinnick) round out the offerings.

RIGHT The fully armed *Oplopanax horridus* (devil's club) stalks through the understory of ancient, moss-draped conifers and vine maples (*Acer circinatum*) of the Pacific northwest. Olympic National Park, Washington.

OPPOSITE, CLOCKWISE FROM TOP LEFT
Typically not an understory shrub, *Rhus aromatica* (fragrant sumac) survives here as a remnant of open prairie shrublands. It punctuates open areas of the *Quercus velutina* (black oak) and *Quercus rubra* (northern red oak) canopy with bright autumn color in Woodman Hollow State Preserve, Iowa.

Chrysolepis sempervirens (bush chinquapin) thrives in pools of light through an open canopy of *Pseudotsuga menziesii* (Douglas fir), *Calocedrus decurrens* (California incense-cedar), and *Pinus ponderosa* (ponderosa pine). A shifting amalgam of ecological interactions results in a constantly changing composition and assemblage of understory species.

Gaylussacia baccata, the black huckleberry, mingles in the understory with bracken fern on the edge of a heath in the Saco Heath Preserve, Maine.

Quercus laevis (turkey oak) in a disorientingly even band of *Pinus palustris* (longleaf pine) in the Carolina Sandhills National Wildlife Refuge, South Carolina.

Chamaebatia foliolosa (known as kit-kit-dizze by the Miwok tribe of northern California) rapidly occupies open-forest habitat after wildfires in the Sierra Nevada mountains of California. Its resinous foliage bathes the forest understory in a pungent fragrance reminiscent of sagebrush.

The range of *Paxistima myrsinites* (mountainlover) extends through the North American Rocky Mountain, Pacific and Sierran forests, often mixing with *Vaccinium* (blueberry) to cover large swaths of the duffy understory of coniferous forests.

SHRUBS OF DARKNESS

In the shady understory of forests, a suite of shrubs has evolved to tolerate filtered and reflected light conditions. Late in successional cycles when grasses and other forbs have been outcompeted, these shrubs create low-diversity but ultimately very stable plant communities. Many of these species flower early in the growing season, taking advantage of energy collected before the tree canopy leafs out and when the angle of the sun is still low on the horizon. Additionally, clonal stands are connected via underground networks of roots, rhizomes and mycorrhizae, sharing net energy and creating resiliency.

Ericaceous and rosaceous shrubs are the most dominant families in these landscapes with a huge diversity in genera and species, which is not surprising. These shrubs are often fruit-bearing and have been cultivated and encouraged to inhabit this niche for millennia by human and non-human animals. Consistent browsing and burning has given many of these systems an open-canopied, park-like feel, with mature trees seemingly evenly staggered throughout the expansive landscapes.

Visually, these goth shrublands read as homogenous, unified systems. The monocultural, monochromatic sweeps tightly interweave several species into shimmering, high-texture tapestries with subtle contrasts of leaf shape and color.

SEEING SHRUBLANDS 155

BELOW The moisture gradients of a coastal wetland on the North American Atlantic coast; grasses and *Baccharis halimifolia* (groundseltree) in the wetter zones give way to natural dead hedges of *Juniperus virginiana* (southern red cedar) on the ridges.

SWAMP THINGS

The heath, the pocosin, the carr, the sweetwater. The fange, the mire, the bog. The multiverse of shrub swamps is almost endless, as hydrologically inundated areas across the globe play host to deeply adaptable, diverse and difficult-to-access shrublands.

Shrub swamps are some of the most uncomfortable and perilous places that humans explore and inhabit. Biotic and abiotic forces are primordial and

ABOVE A pocosin is a type of shrub wetland found in the American south with deep sandy, acidic soils that harbor a huge diversity of shrub species, many of which have been tapped for use in horticulture and many more that hold huge potential for application in shrubscapes. In this scene in the Carolina Sandhills National Wildlife Refuge, South Carolina, we encountered *Ilex coriacea* (big gallberry), *Oxydendrum arboreum* (sourwood), *Persea palustris* (swamp bay), *Ilex glabra* (inkberry), *Rhododendron viscosum* (swamp azalea), *Cyrilla racemiflora* (swamp titi), *Clethra alnifolia* (sweet pepperbush), *Lyonia mariana* (staggerbush), *Magnolia virginiana* (sweetbay magnolia), *Toxicodendron vernix* (poison sumac), and *Rhus copallinum* (winged sumac).

Flora of the swampy areas of the New Jersey Pine Barrens, Franklin Parker Preserve, New Jersey.

ABOVE, CLOCKWISE FROM TOP LEFT *Clethra alnifolia* (sweet pepperbush) in seed

Ilex coriacea (big gallberry).

Callicarpa americana (American beautyberry).

The thick-leaved *Lyonia mariana* (staggerbush) growing on the edge of a flooded former cranberry bog.

constant. Mosquitos, leeches, snakes, spiders, prehistoric reptiles, tangled, ankle-breaking root masses, oppressive humidity, swiftly running water, tidal swells, and deep, rotting pits of organic matter are inevitabilities. This is the wet primordial soup of the world. The pulse of the green. The origin of life. The risk is worth the reward. Many of the shrubs found in these swamps are already cultivated and celebrated in our landscapes and there are many more still to be tapped for that purpose.

Interpreting and emulating a shrub swamp requires understanding the varied growing conditions and regionality of these habitats. Some shrubs grow directly in deep, still water with their roots anchored in anaerobic muck, and some on hummocks of organic matter that allow their crowns to breathe. Some grow in rich organic matter and others in deeply saturated and aerated gravel beds. Notwithstanding, the rule of no rules reigns supreme. Most of the shrubs in these often transitional shrublands merely tolerate these conditions and a shrub-swamp-inspired shrubscape can be grown in a more traditional garden bed.

LEFT **The brilliant autumnal color and form of *Cyrilla racemiflora* (swamp titi) in the pocosin of the Carolina Sandhills National Wildlife Refuge, South Carolina, USA.**

TOP ***Borrichia frutescens* (bushy seaside tansy), a halophyte found commonly on the North American Gulf and southeastern Atlantic coasts, is extremely tolerant of both saturated and droughty soils. Pea Island National Wildlife Refuge, North Carolina, USA.**

ABOVE ***Cephalanthus occidentalis* (common buttonbush) growing near the interdunal ponds of Nags Head Woods Preserve, North Carolina, USA.**

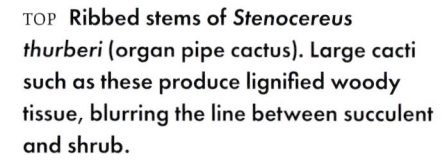

TOP Ribbed stems of *Stenocereus thurberi* (organ pipe cactus). Large cacti such as these produce lignified woody tissue, blurring the line between succulent and shrub.

ABOVE Gregarious *Echinocactus grusonii* (golden barrel cactus) tessellation.

MAIN IMAGE Cartoonish forms of *Carnegiea gigantea* (saguaro), *Fouquieria splendens* (ocotillo), and *Stenocereus thurberi* (organ pipe cactus) morph this shrubland of *Encelia farinosa* (brittlebush), *Simmondsia chinensis* (jojoba), and *Parkinsonia florida* (blue palo verde) into an otherworldly landscape.

PRICKS AND PINHEADS

Thornscrub trades in pain. It requires a blood sacrifice. An intimate exchange. The animal leaves its ever-traveling skin, fur, plasma and platelets in the immortal landscape and in return the plant gives thorns, spines and glochids to the interloping soft bodies. This environment is natural analog to the S&M fantasy of Clive Barker's *Hellraiser*: "Explorers in the further regions of experience. Demons to some. Angels to others."[28]

The charismatic layer of thornscrub, or succulent scrub, has two main components, succulents and shrubs, living interwoven, blurring the lines between each other. The succulents take on multi-stemmed, ranging, shrub-like forms mimicking the visual patterns and rhythms of shrublands at the landscape level and the weight and feel of shrubs at the organismic level. The shrubs in turn grow thorns and spines, succulent stems and leaves, and offer brilliant flowers and tumescent fruits to ensure their survival.

The aesthetics of the thorn scrub are some of the densest and most deeply veiled of all shrublands. Each creature is dancing in its own tortured reality. Turgid cacti and euphorbia (spurge) erupt into candelabra or flail across the sky. Beguiling branches shoot out at all angles, while tesselated divaricate growth expands to swallow the surrounding chaos, ignoring the concept of personal space and creating the shroud of life that so many depend on in harsh environments.

TOP The hollow stipular spines of *Vachellia collinsii* (bull horn acacia) play a part in the mutualistic relationship between ants and acacias.

ABOVE *Psittacanthus calyculatus* (parrot flower) is a mistletoe that takes the form of a hemiparasitic shrub, attaching to a number of broad-leaved and conifer species and rambling through their canopies.

An overstory of *Aloidendron dichotomum* (quiver tree) in Kamiesberg, South Africa, with an understory of *Euphorbia* (spurge) and dormant shrubs.

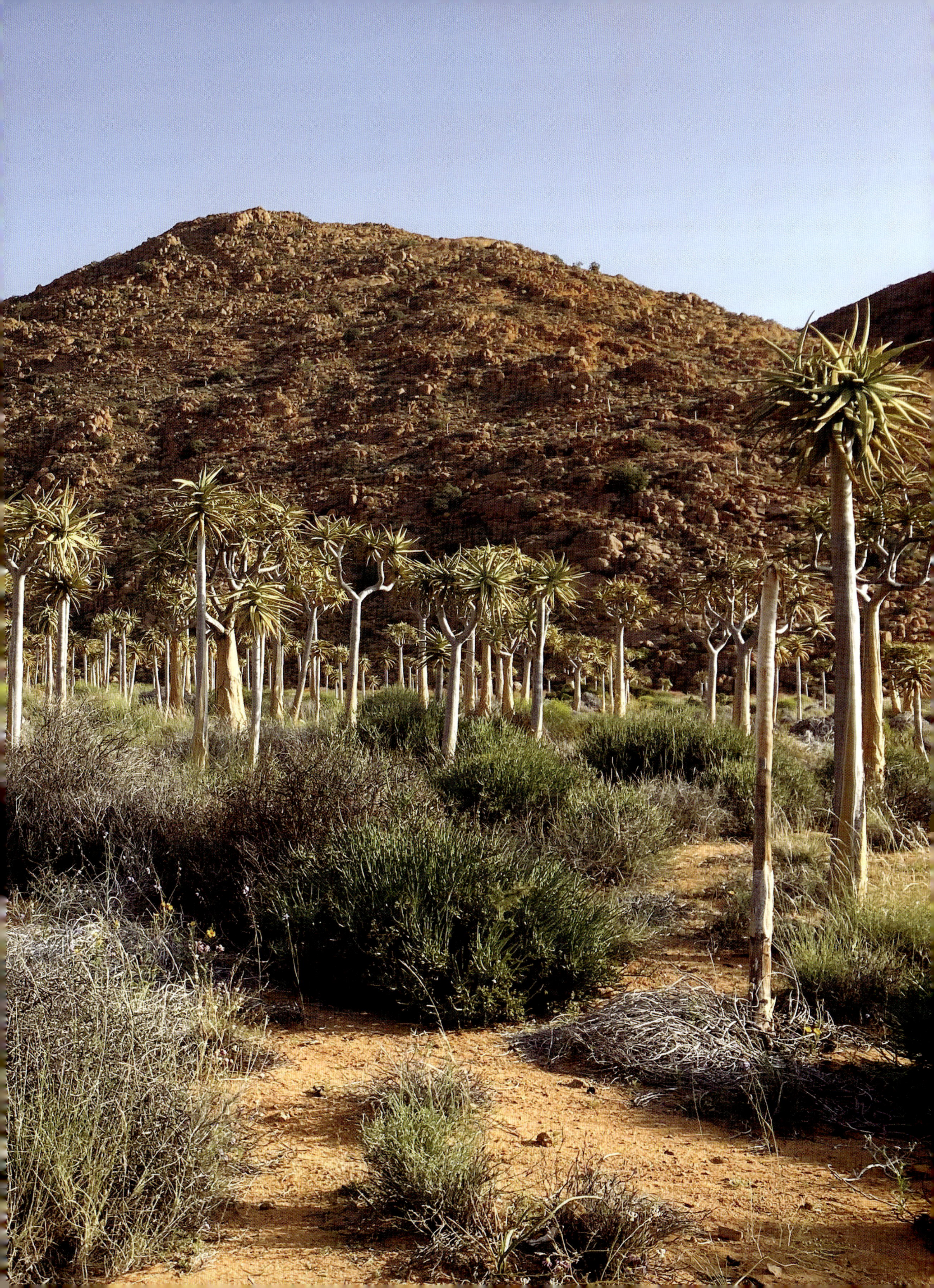

RIGHT Shrubs, two ways. Mat-forming, cespitose shrubs benefiting from the nurse plant protection of taller scrub in Patagonia, Argentina.

BELOW A *Hudsonia ericoides* (pine barren false heather) microshrubland in the Franklin Parker Preserve, New Jersey, growing with *Amphicarpum amphicarpon* (blue maidencane), *Schizachyrium scoparium* (little bluestem), *Panicum virgatum* (switchgrass), *Aristida tuberculosa* (seaside three-awn), *Carex pensylvanica* (Pennsylvania sedge) and *Polygonella articulata* (coast jointweed). The disturbed surface of this inland dune has been stabilized by a form of west cryptobiotic soil crust composed of tar lichen, thorn lichen, false reindeer lichen and species of *Polytrichum* (haircap moss), allowing for the establishment of the vascular plant layer.

OPPOSITE *Kalmia procumbens* (alpine azalea) carpets the tundra of Denali National Park and Preserve, Alaska.

NANOSCRUB

Some shrublands rise only a few centimeters or inches from the earth. Prostrate or diminutive shrubs hiding in duff, intermingling with graminoids or living on the edges of their much larger kin can go unrecognized, passed over or trampled. Despite their size, these shrubs can still create extensive colonies, harbor huge amounts of diversity and serve the same aesthetic functions as a larger anthro-scaled shrubland. "It's a hard world for little things."[29]

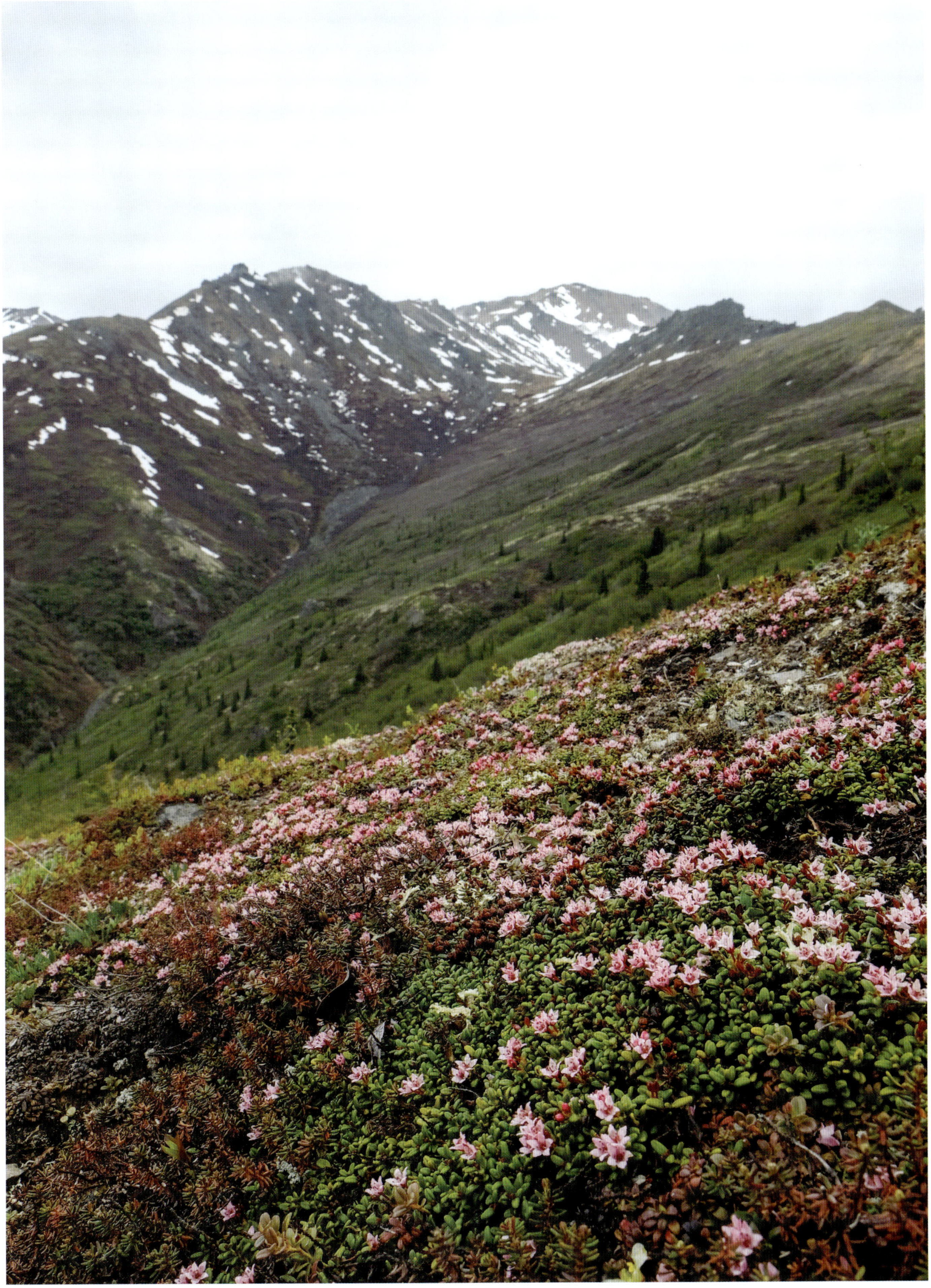

TOP LEFT *Cornus canadensis* (creeping dogwood) in a nest of *Harrimanella hypnoides* (moss-plant) and *Sibbaldia procumbens* (creeping sibbaldia).

TOP RIGHT *Andromeda polifolia* (bog rosemary).

ABOVE LEFT *Salix petrophila* (rock willow).

ABOVE RIGHT *Vaccinium macrocarpon* (cranberry) and *Rubus hispidus* (swamp dewberry) in a sphagnum moss bog.

Calling it nanoscrub might be an overstatement, but small shrubs make small shrublands and recognizing environments through the lens of shifting scales can help us grasp a diverse dimensionality in how we build and experience our landscapes. Obvious applications of these shrubland systems would be in crevice, miniature or fairy gardens. More nuanced implementations could greatly extend the depth of layers in a garden, creating stacks on stacks of shrubs that challenge arrangement hierarchies.

BELOW, LEFT *Pyxidanthera barbulata* (littleleaf pixiemoss) masquerading as a bryophyte in Franklin Parker Preserve, New Jersey.

BELOW, RIGHT *Gaultheria procumbens* – the famous eastern teaberry known for its sweet, mint-like taste.

BOTTOM, RIGHT *Astraeus hygrometricus*, the barometer earthstar fungus.

BIODOMES

Cushion plants are environmental engineers that create their own moderate microclimates by regulating temperature and moisture levels beneath their canopies. They occur in extreme environments and, like nanoscrub, are simply shrubs at scale. These diminutive, tap-rooted plants take on rounded forms resembling buns, cushions or mats with woody, multi-stemmed growth. Although they appear as mossy or lichenous ripples on the landscape, they are shrubs. And bunneries, communities of cushion plants, are shrublands.

Pin-sharp mounds of *Acantholimon albertii* (prickly thrift) in the western Tien Shan Mountains of Kazakhstan.

LEFT Cushions of *Azorella prolifera* (neneo) protruding and proceeding across the Patagonian landscape. These communities feel like a primordial and periodic congregation of animals drawn together by forces unseen. They deserve their own herd term: could they be called pods and reclaim the botanical origins of the designation?

BELOW *Azorella* (mulinum) and *Nardophyllum* (nardo) mega-cushions display only minute differences, one slightly larger, darker in color and shaggier, the other more compact, lighter and smoother. This is minimalism, omission, suggestion. There is power in this subtlety that is lost in more disparate scenes.

We can use cushion plants as the gateway for thinking about shruboids, or things that resemble shrubs but are not often considered as such. Are certain perennial or annual forbs with shruboid growth patterns actually shrubs in different environmental conditions? Does a shrub need to make wood or can it be ephemeral? We should always inspect our need to classify organisms as human impulses, not biological truths, especially when our classification only serves to inhibit deeper knowledge about other creatures. Convergent evolution has shown that plants respond to planetary conditions with similar adaptations. Are these survival responses limited to just the plant kingdom? Is a coral reef a zoological shrubland building stone instead of wood? What would it mean to create a shrubland with other partners?

A steppe bunnery in Pawnee National Grasslands, Colorado

SEEING SHRUBLANDS

RIGHT *Euphorbia acanthothamnos* (Greek spiny spurge) in the Hymettus Mountains, Greece

BELOW The low, acanthamnoid shrub *Astragalus angustifolius* (Cretan hedgehog-heath); the chickenwire-like mesh of thorns and branches is a common feature of Mediterranean scrub, providing browsing protection and condensation of mist. Crete, Greece.

TOP, LEFT Bimodal distribution of woodland and forest; flowering *Amelanchier alnifolia* (western serviceberry) and chartreuse leaves of *Quercus gambelii* (Gambel oak) cascade down a hillside against a backdrop of *Picea engelmannii* (Engelmann spruce) in the La Sal Mountains in eastern Utah.

TOP, RIGHT A *Picea engelmannii* (Engelmann spruce) krummholz – a German term meaning twisted or bent wood – and here the harsh environmental conditions of the subalpine life zone cause just that. Trees growing here are forced to assume strange shapes, and their usual upright growth instead becomes rambling shrubby masses of spires and lateral growth. Horseshoe Mountain, Pike National Forest, Colorado.

RIGHT The mottled autumnal colors of the shrub layer in Graveyard Fields with *Vaccinium corymbosum* (highbush blueberry) and *Hypericum densiflorum* (bushy St. John's wort) running through the *Prunus pennsylvanica* (fire cherry) in Pisgah National Forest, North Carolina.

WHAT DO YOU CONSIDER A TREE?

Could some forests actually be shrublands? Forests consisting of mostly smaller, multi-stemmed trees or transitional communities where forests and shrublands begin to blend together are often referred to as woodlands. Woodlands can be fairly stable in their composition due to a homogeneity of dominant species and stressful environmental conditions, like those found in scrub oak woodlands, or they can be ever-changing places kept in constant ecological succession because of disturbances. These transitional states, like a complex early seral forest, host dense mixtures of recovering and resprouting trees, shrubs and herbaceous plants which engulf the timber and snags of the previous community. For decades, the function and visual impact between trees and shrubs, and forests and shrublands, can remain virtually the same. We're not forest bathing here, we're scrubbing up. This poses two questions: can a shrub be perceived and can a shrub be made?

TOP, LEFT Old-growth maritime chaparral at the Burton Mesa Ecological Reserve in Lompoc, California, with manzanita trunks more twisted than the magical pathway they line.

TOP, RIGHT *Populus tremuloides* (quaking aspen) bisect a hillside of *Quercus gambelii* (Gambel oak) in Mt Sneffels Wilderness, Colorado. Gambel oaks lie on a spectrum form, from singular trees to multi-stemmed gregarious shrubs, depending on their genotype and environment.

LEFT *Amelanchier alnifolia* (western serviceberry) systematically fracturing and occupying the understory of *Populus tremuloides* (quaking aspen) in the Beartooth Mountains, Wyoming.

While some plants have genetics conducive to the classic definition of a shrub, by using horticultural techniques a tree can be made bushier. Hedging, pruning, coppicing, pollarding and grafting can force a tree to develop multiple trunks, suckers and watersprouts. Stem training, topiary and pruning can build mass, creating shrubby states. These effects occur naturally, as well. The environmental effects of nutrient scarcity and environmental extremes create the krummholz of subalpine elevations and the tuckamore of coastal regions transforming tree-like species into twisted, persistently shrubby forms. Is a multi-stemmed tree really a tree? Is a suckering, clonal tree not a single organism? Could the entirety of Pando, the Trembling Giant, *Populus tremuloides* (quaking aspen) of Utah, made up of over 40,000 connected trunks, be simply a colossal shrub?

These are handcrafted, bespoke shrubs – transfunctional shrubs.

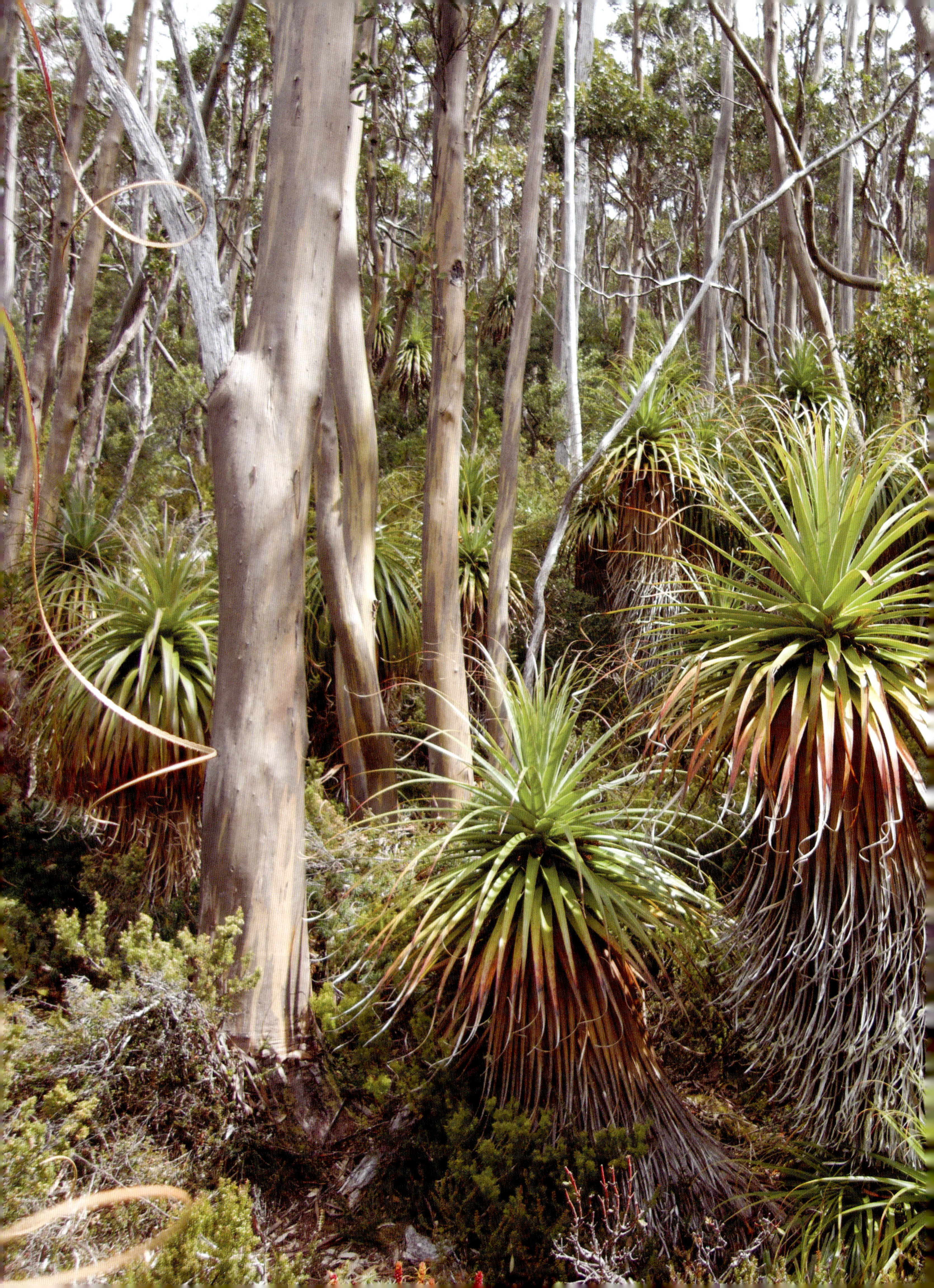

An open *Eucalyptus* (gum tree) forest with an understory layer of proteaceous and ericaceous shrubs including the Tasmanian endemic *Richea pandanifolia* (pandani) in Mt Field National Park, Tasmania, Australia.

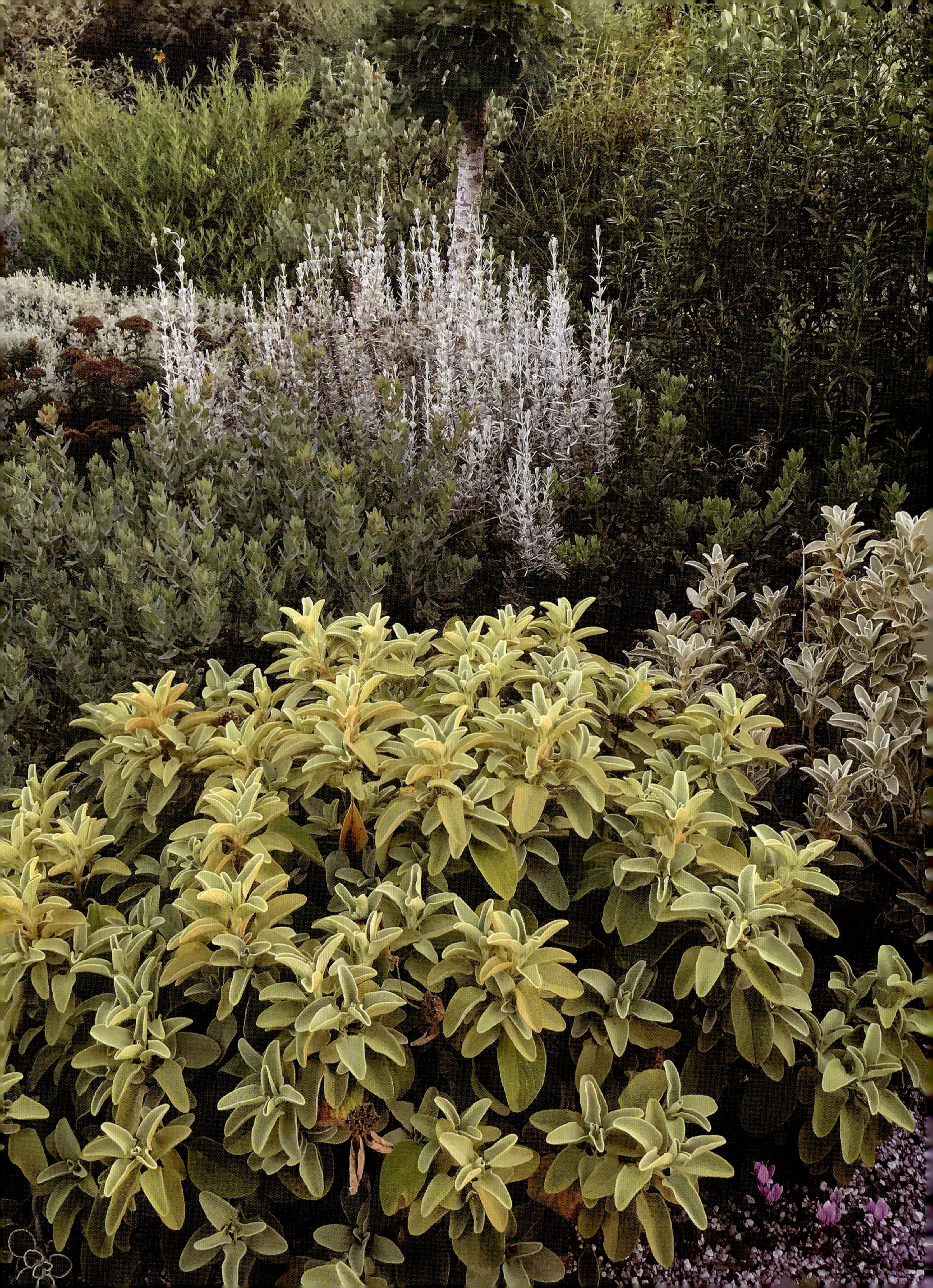

3

The Med Bed, a mixed planting of Mediterranean shrubs at Rancho Cistus on Sauvie Island, Oregon, by Sean Hogan and Preston Pew with *Phlomis chrysophylla* (golden-leaved Jerusalem sage), *Phlomis viscosa* (viscid Jerusalem sage), *Arctostaphylos pajaroensis* 'Jade Diamond' (Jade Diamond Pajaro manzanita) and *Lavandula stoechas* 'Silver Anouk' (Silver Anouk French lavender)

MAKING SHRUBSCAPES

"What is become of Bushy?"

William Shakespeare, Richard II, Act 3, Scene 2

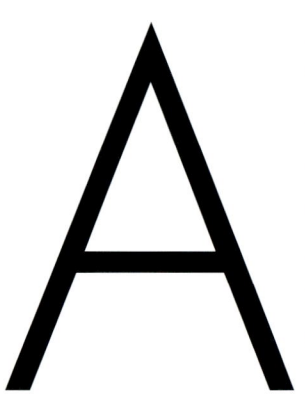

A GARDEN IS A CONSTELLATION OF IDEAS. Gardening is world-making. It should not be easy with simple, linear ideas or outcomes. When emulating shrublands and making shrubscapes we must open our eyes and practice humility. As with most garden endeavors based on wild systems, everything we're trying to do has been done before, better than we could ever imagine, on timescales and against adversity that we cannot perceive. We can never create something in its entirety, we can only observe and hope to start something based on those observations.

Model Shrubscapes

Replicating a natural landscape is impossible and will not produce a garden with a satisfying or feasible future. We need places that are their own places, not just like other places. We need things that are their own things, not just like other things. Our greatest achievement will be to set an interesting process in motion.

Digital Shrublands (2022–2023). Digital shrubscapes created by Stable Diffusion's text-to-image modeling software. Captioned by the prompts that created them.

A wild and glowing, dense and dangerous scrubland thicket garden

A shrubland of flowering shrubs illuminated by a moody sky

Flowering shrubland shrouded in light

MAKING SHRUBSCAPES

A shrubscape of exuberance and caution at Ruth Bancroft Garden & Nursery, California

In the Polanco neighborhood of Mexico City, an eccentric commercial shrubscape mixes tropical, subtropical and temperate shrubs, forbs and trees including *Hebe speciosa* (titirangi), *Vitex trifolia* (simpleaf chastetree), and *Thaumatophyllum bipinnatifidum* (tree philodendron). This hellstrip is an absolute rampage that shifts dramatically from angle to angle.

Before the blooms of spring, the exuberant forms and flowers of cool-season shrubs such as *Salvia apiana* (white sage) writhe from the mesh.

The highly textural *Artemisia californica* (California sagebrush), *Salvia apiana* (white sage), and *Rhus integrifolia* (lemonade berry) seen through a screen of *Ceanothus integerrimus* var. *macrothyrsus* (deerbrush).

The LA WAVE (Est 2017)

DESIGNERS: *Kevin Philip Williams and Frank Antonoff*
LOCATION: *South Central, Los Angeles, California, USA*

The LA WAVE, a privately owned, urban shrubscape is a reimagination of the intersections of southern Californian coastal sage scrub and mixed chaparral. Established in pure sand through a combination of seeding and planting using the methods laid out by James Hitchmough in *Sowing Beauty*[30], early spring flushes of herbaceous wildflowers and annual grasses ripple around the heavy heads of shrubs that fade to hues of olive and gold in the heat and drought of summer.

MAKING SHRUBSCAPES

Chaotic textures challenge the idea of readability in the landscape. This isn't a symphony, it's hardcore punk.

Lower stature interstitial shrub *Arctostaphylos pumila* (sandmat manzanita) mixing with *Symphyotrichum chilense* (Pacific aster) and *Muhlenbergia dubia* (pine muhly)

A hardcore punk ethos is central to the LA WAVE. In a neighborhood still dominated by a Post-War,[31] turfgrass and foundation planting landscape, the concentrated wildness of shrubs barely contained by the surrounding concrete is a rage of anti-establishment non-conformity. The plants surge around the yard, unbound by their original placements, embodying NO CONTROL and challenging cars and pedestrians to pay attention.

Where does this second-wave, anthropogenic chaparralscape live in the scheme of naturalistic design? Maybe this wave is more of an ensō. A feedback loop from early times that obliterates and accumulates with each pass; an iconoclastic ecosystem. This is shrub-wave. This is shrubcore.

ABOVE *Yucca rostrata* (beaked yucca) in a sweep of *Ericameria nauseosa* (rubber rabbitbrush) and *Salvia reptans* 'Autumn Sapphire™' (West Texas grass sage)

RIGHT An interstitial mass of *Agastache rupestris* (licorice mint), *Catananche caerulea* (Cupid's dart), *Salvia reptans* 'Autumn Sapphire™' (West Texas grass sage), *Monarda punctata* (spotted beebalm), *Solidago speciosa* (showy goldenrod) and *Muhlenbergia reverchonii* 'P011S' (Undaunted® Ruby Muhly Grass)

SummerHome Garden (Est 2020)

DESIGNERS: *Kevin Philip Williams, Sonya Anderson and Lisa Negri*
LOCATION: *Denver, Colorado, USA.*

SummerHome Garden was created as an act of defiance. Owner and visionary Lisa Negri saw the monster of overdevelopment swallowing the psychic and physical green space of her neighborhood through the replacement of bungalows by yardless mini-mansions. When the opportunity arose, Lisa bought the house next to her own and collapsed it into its own basement, creating a gap in the relentless cityscape and a void for life. No Spiritual Surrender[32]. That void became SummerHome Garden, now a privately owned, publicly accessible pocket park.

The plantings of SummerHome Garden take inspiration from the places where the shrublands of the North American shortgrass steppe collide with those of the desert southwest. *Ericameria nauseosa* (rubber rabbitbrush), *Artemisia filifolia* (sand sagebrush), *Atriplex canescens* (fourwing saltbush), *Fallugia paradoxa* (póñil), and *Krascheninnikovia lanata* (winterfat) are the dominant shrubs with *Salvia yangii* (Russian sage), *Cercocarpus ledifolius* (curl-leaf mountain mahogany), *Prunus pumila* var. *besseyi* 'P011S' PAWNEE BUTTES® (sand cherry), *Salvia pachyphylla* (Mojave sage), *Chilopsis linearis* (desert willow), and *Lycium pallidum* (pale wolfberry) playing minor roles. The shrubland base is interplanted with graminoids and forbs. The airy pink

LEFT SummerHome Garden was built as a gift to the local community, both human and non-human.

LEFT *Muhlenbergia reverchonii* 'P011S' (Undaunted® Ruby Muhly Grass) in a haze screening *Atriplex canescens* (fourwing saltbush) with the pre-bloom buds of *Ericameria nauseosa* (rubber rabbitbrush)

plumes of *Aristida purpurea* (purple three-awn) and *Muhlenbergia reverchonii* 'PUND01S' (UNDAUNTED® Ruby Muhly) warm the cool tones of *Andropogon hallii* (sand bluestem) and *Helictotrichon sempervirens* (blue oat grass). Tying the interstitial spaces together is a thick mesh of seeded species including *Linum lewisii* (blue flax), *Monarda punctata* (spotted beebalm), *Ipomopsis rubra* (Texas plume), *Eschscholzia californica* 'Purple Gleam' (purple gleam California poppy), *Daucus carota* 'Dara' (Dara purple ammi), and *Euphorbia marginata* (snow-on-the-mountain).

**Selected images from Shrubs (2011-13)
Allison Cekala**

Fear of a Shrub Planet: Beyond the Bushes

Shrubs have become the definition of utility in a landscape, neutered into architectural figurines, stage props and dead zones. Formality has conscripted and coerced amenable species into precise hedgerows, geometrically wobbly tumors and goofy topiaries; a practice synonymous with extravagance and affluence. Unfortunately, the desire to inexpensively emulate success by imitating formal landscaping, particularly in suburban developments and commercial properties, only creates the feeling of depressing faux-decorum. The impenetrable, formidable shrubland is domesticated.

Generationally, shrubs have become the tedious things of constant maintenance. Trimming the hedges has become as obsessive a compulsion as cutting the lawn and while this is considered civilized and thoughtful,

Untitled, St. Johns, Portland, Oregon, USA
2012

Untitled, Northeast Portland, Oregon, USA
2012

Untitled, North Portland, Oregon, USA
2012

No camping on the poison oak (*Toxicodendron diversilobum*)

Atomic age junipers neglected and thriving outside an abandoned mid-century modern structure in Denver, Colorado. When forced into an architecturally specific movement, many shrubs become awkward relics of failed visions.

the unruly shrub can be a symbol of the progressive and counter-cultural. As new norms subsume the old, shrubs will continue to grow and thrive. As society advances into post-capitalism and our hastily produced infrastructure crumbles and is abandoned, the outlines of shrubs with which we have surrounded our homes will flourish and spread, creating shrubdivisions and shruburbs, the subdivision shaped shrublands of our own making. A skeletal version of an old civilization. A sympoietic suburban scrub. If the environments that we control, and the gardens as we create them, make up the matter of our reality, then shrubs are the anti-matter.

Palaiochora hillside on the island of Aegina, Greece; an ancient site of temples, houses and churches now being reclaimed by the holy phrygana.

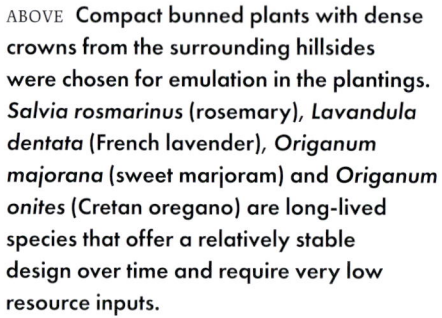

ABOVE **Compact bunned plants with dense crowns from the surrounding hillsides were chosen for emulation in the plantings.** *Salvia rosmarinus* (rosemary), *Lavandula dentata* (French lavender), *Origanum majorana* (sweet marjoram) and *Origanum onites* (Cretan oregano) **are long-lived species that offer a relatively stable design over time and require very low resource inputs.**

RIGHT, ABOVE **The land, sea, sky, plants and buildings each riff on the others' colors and textures. Dense shrubs of** *Salvia rosmarinus* (rosemary), *Sarcopoterium spinosum* (thorny burnet), *Pseudodictamnus acetabulosus* (Greek horehound), *Juniperus phoenicea* (Phoenician juniper), **and** *Centaurea spinosa* (spiny knapweed) **contain flares of** *Hyparhennia hirta* (thatching grass), **and** *Origanum onites* (Cretan oregano). **The harshness is an extension of function and compellingly beautiful.**

RIGHT, BELOW **The gardens were feathered into the soft-leaved maquis and surrounding garrigue shrublands to create a harmonious bonding of the intended and unintended.**

Landscapes of Cohabitation (Est 2000)
DESIGNERS: *Thomas Doxiadis, Terpsi Kremali, Aggeliki Mathioudaki, Ioanna Potiriadi, Chrisa Golemi, Eva Beristianou, Despoina Gkirti, and Aimilia Skoura.*
LOCATION: *Antiparos Island, Greece*

Landscapes of Cohabitation is an 80 hectare (197 acre) melding of designed shrubscapes with the surrounding maquis and garrigue shrublands. The doxiadis+ architecture and landscape team follows a philosophy of Forming Symbiosis which seeks inspiration in interdependency in order to transcend conflict in design. Landscapes of Cohabitation was built to synthesize the natural and cultural forms that were present in the landscape and find dynamic and supportive ways to bring new construction into an active and unique biome.

To emulate the wild systems of the site, the occurrence rates of the species surrounding the developments were identified, and those same ratios were followed in new plantings. The plants were then starburst out into the landscape, with the most densely planted sections located closest to houses, tapering out into the surrounding landscape, allowing the spaces to seamlessly weave together.

This is human wildness and plant wildness expressing something together. How can we start to create more of these spaces that show the diversity and value of humans and non-human Others?

The divine maquis: *Centaurea spinosa* (spiny knapweed), *Sarcopoterium spinosum* (thorny burnet), *Thymus capitatus* (conehead thyme), *Pistacia lentiscus* (mastic tree), *Cistus salvifolius* (sageleaf rock-rose), *Juniperus phoenicea* (Phoenician juniper), and *Helichrysum italicum* (curry plant) yield to a path that separates both the spined and scented, the irritating and irresistible.

Sky Scrub

Vegetated roofs offer polar and seemingly incongruous visions of our collective future: the post-apocalyptic ruins of modern capitalist society where our buildings serve as scaffolding for new life, or a utopian age where biophilic design is the norm. They force an unnatural and wild alliance between the human and plant domains, but we are just beginning to realize the possibilities inherent in this symbiosis.

Green roofs are tough environments for plants; high UV radiation, wild temperature fluctuations, and limited substrate moisture challenge traditional horticultural approaches. Succulents such as *Sedum* spp. (stonecrops) have been used extensively, often in monocultures, to vegetate roofs, and more recently, meadow-based systems inspired by the naturalistic design movement have proven to be adaptable and successful. Shrubland systems, much like green roofs, are often resource-scarce and represent an untapped reservoir of plant material fit for green-roof plantings. The possibility of leveraging shrubland ecologies such as nurse-plant phenomena is ripe for experimentation and may offer powerful design frameworks that result in resilient, self-sustaining rooftop vegetation.

Shrubs from semi-arid regions thrive on harsh rooftop conditions. *Artemisia tridentata* (big sagebrush), *Ericameria nauseosa* (rubber rabbitbrush) and *Holodiscus microphyllus* (cliff spiraea) are no strangers to heat, drought, and nutrient-poor, rocky soils. Moda Building, Bend, Oregon.

Moda Building (2007)

DESIGNERS: *Wintercreek Restoration & Nursery and We'H Pacific, Chelsea Schneider.*
LOCATION: *Bend, Oregon, USA.*

The Moda Building's plantings take direct inspiration from the shrub-steppe of central Oregon. The densely planted vegetation celebrates the tawny hues of spent inflorescences and silver sheen of tomentose foliage that typify shrubs in this semi-arid region. Designed as an accessible space for the building's occupants, this rooftop thicket provides refuge from the regimented spaces, both physical and virtual, that dominate our economy. The persistent structural forms of shrubs serve to make this green roof immersive and sheltered, despite its obvious exposure; they are like an impenetrable thicket turned inside out.

Thicket view office space. Dense and enveloping plantings make it feel as if the Moda building was dropped into the shrub-steppe of Central Oregon. *Sansevieria laurentii* (snakeplant) for corporate authenticity. Moda Building, Bend, Oregon.

Situated above the walking path in elevated beds, shrubs add dimension and a sense of immersion rarely felt on rooftop gardens. *Ericameria nauseosa* (rubber rabbitbrush) and *Artemisia tridentata* (big sagebrush) are emblematic of the shrub-steppe of central Oregon and become focal points of this rooftop garden. Moda Building, Bend, Oregon.

One South Van Ness Avenue (2010)

DESIGNERS: *Paul Kephart, Rana Creek, Douglas Ullman and Glenn Hunt, San Francisco Public Works.*
LOCATION: *San Francisco, California, USA.*

The first municipal green roof project in San Francisco, although carefully researched and planted, has the self-assured flair of spontaneous urban vegetation. The city of San Francisco uses the term living roof to describe green roofs, pointing to the intentional synergy and intimacy between architecture and biology. A sliver of substrate, just 15cm (6in) deep, supports low-growing shrubs including *Arctostaphylos edmundsii* (Little Sur manzanita) and *Eriogonum parvifolium* (seacliff buckwheat) among coastal forbs and grasses, reminiscent of nearby coastal scrub. The soft textures, flat grade, and dominance of grasses read visually like a meadow, but shrubs remain a crucial element, providing stable structure as perennial forbs ebb and flow.

Arctostaphylos edmundsii (Little Sur manzanita) and *Eriogonum parvifolium* (seacliff buckwheat) together with *Epilobium canum* (California fuchsia) form dense mats of vegetation with unexpected textural softness characteristic of coastal scrub plant communities. One South Van Ness Avenue, San Francisco, California.

MAKING SHRUBSCAPES

Interstitial forbs *Epilobium canum* (California fuchsia) and *Achillea millefolium* (yarrow) mix together, a combination reminiscent of coastal scrub.

Gardens of the Post-Anthropocene

Gardening towards the post-anthropocene happens when we garden with the intention of shifting the future stewardship of the earth away from human-dominated models and start a true collaboration with other creatures. To do this, we have to fight assumptions that horticulture has to be rooted in agriculture and that agriculture is the best way to ensure the future of humanity.

We don't have to turn the earth into something anthropocentrically functional in order to thrive. Humans and other animals have utilized shrublands since our emergence. Shrubscapes can remain wild and different and help to replace our global fingerprints. Accepting shrublands and making shrubscapes, creating beautiful, but possibly uncomfortable scenes, allowing gardens to take their own shapes, and inviting other creatures to push the uses of our gardens are ways to begin gardening for the post-anthropocene.

Redefining a foundation planting; *Dasiphora fruticosa* (shrubby cinquefoil) seeded into crumbling concrete on Windy Ridge above Alma, Colorado

LEFT Near the Spurwink River Fishing Wharf in Scarborough, Maine, the Rachel Carson National Wildlife Refuge is converting fallow fields into shrublands and woodlands. Early successional shrubland habitat in this region is critical for the survival of dozens of animal species including New England cottontail rabbits, American woodcock, ruffed grouse, eastern towhee and the brown thrasher [33]. Over 1100 shrubs were planted, including *Sambucus canadensis* (American black elderberry), *Rosa palustris* (swamp rose), *Rosa virginiana* (Virginia rose), *Aronia arbutifolia* (red chokeberry), *Aronia melanocarpa* (black chokeberry), *Cornus amomum* (silky dogwood) and *Cornus sericea* (red osier dogwood). The plantings in this photo are barely a month old.

BELOW An older, adjacent planting on the same site, with *Cornus amomum* (silky dogwood), *Salix discolor* (pussy willow), *Spiraea alba* (white meadowsweet), *Viburnum lentago* (nannyberry) and *Elaeagnus umbellata* (autumn olive). The sites were prepped with only an initial mowing, allowing the ground layer of grasses and forbs to regrow and hold the interstitial spaces while the shrubs matured.

Lands End Lookout (Est 2012)

DESIGNER: *Roderick Wyllie, Surfacedesign*
LOCATION: *San Francisco, California, USA*

The gardens of Lands End Lookout at Golden Gate National Recreation Area feel impressively not like a designed planting, but rather a remnant piece of coastal sage scrub that was protected during the development of the surrounding infrastructure. The result is a space that successfully reads like its wild counterparts, full of the contrast of intuitive rhythms and unbalanced forces, intention and neglect, permanence and disturbance. Like its surrounding planned and unplanned areas, it's a space that is alive and still finding its series of final forms to perch on.

The easy textural qualities of the dominant *Artemisia californica* (California sagebrush) bind together the design and contrast beautifully with interstitial subshrubs and forbs.

The slopes below the planted areas are full of adventive species like *Carpobrotus edulis* (sour fig) and *Paraserianthes lophantha* (Cape wattle), which serve the purpose of holding the cliff together. These same species have woven themselves through the gardens, further blurring the lines between horticulture and restoration, fantasy and reality. Like the Sutro Baths, which were placed upon the beach as ornament, but now crumble and feather into their surroundings, Lands End Lookout acts as an infusion and extension to influence, not dictate.

Gardens are not idealized versions of Nature, nor are they exact likenesses. It's worth remembering that they contain all of the flaws, traumas, intentions, biases, beauty and ambitions of their human and non-human creators.

Aptly named soft chaparral, this plant community is rife with gentle textures. Layers of *Artemisia pycnocephala* (coastal sagewort) and *Artemisia californica* (California sagebrush) move like the waves meeting the coastline below.

Piet's Bush. The northern end of the Flyover where a shrubscape takes the form of an expanded transitional edge bleeding into the Wildflower Field. The dusky autumn colors and diversity of leaf morphology is due to a dense mix of several shrubs and small, multi-stemmed trees including *Aesculus parviflora* (bottlebrush buckeye), *Sassafras albidum* (sassafras), *Viburnum prunifolium* (blackhaw), *Rhododendron viscosum* (swamp azalea), *Magnolia macrophylla* (bigleaf magnolia), *Magnolia tripetala* (umbrella magnolia), and *Rhus copallinum* (winged sumac).

The High Line (Est 2009)

DESIGNERS: *Piet Oudolf, James Corner Field Operations and Diller Scofidio + Renfro*
LOCATION: *New York City, New York, USA*

Stretching for almost 2.5km (1 ½ miles) through the west side of Manhattan, the High Line is possibly the most famous and important piece of naturalistic garden design in the world. Although it's known primarily as a grassland, inspired by a combination of the North American tallgrass prairie and the spontaneous vegetation that took hold in the railroad ballast and accumulated organic matter during its 30-year period of abandonment, the gardens of the High Line deftly transition through a series of successional plant communities including shrublands and woodlands.

The designers not only tapped into the emotional experience of being in a wild space, but successfully preserved the feelings evoked by exploring the High Line before it was developed into a park. That experience was one of surprise and excitement, privacy, discovery, illicitness and, in a controlled

Molten ejections of *Cotinus* 'Grace' smoketree through *Lespedeza thunbergii* 'Gibraltar' (Gibraltar bushclover)

The inclusion of shrubby elements in the herbaceous masses of the High Line invokes a shrub meadow. The herbaceous *Tricyrtis* 'Sinonome' (Sinonome toadlily) and seedheads of *Heuchera* (coralbell) glue together individuals of *Aronia melanocarpa* 'Viking' (Viking black chokeberry) and *Prunus virginiana* (chokecherry).

way, danger. In the planting schema, shrubs were invoked for this purpose. Beyond acting as visual breaks or as screening vignettes, the areas with the shrubbiest presence, namely the Washington Grasslands & Woodland Edge, Hudson River Overlook, Northern Spur Preserve, Chelsea Thicket and Flyover, are the most visually complicated and imposing. Although never emulating a full shrubland, these gardens echo the explosive shrub diversity of transitional edges, fully charged with the potential to invade and transform a field left fallow or a forest in the wake of disturbance. These areas are little gifts left for New York – promises that if the High Line is ever again abandoned, there is a plan in place. True wildness has been programmed into the flora, ready to turn grasslands into shrub meadows and swallow the toppled trees in urban thickets.

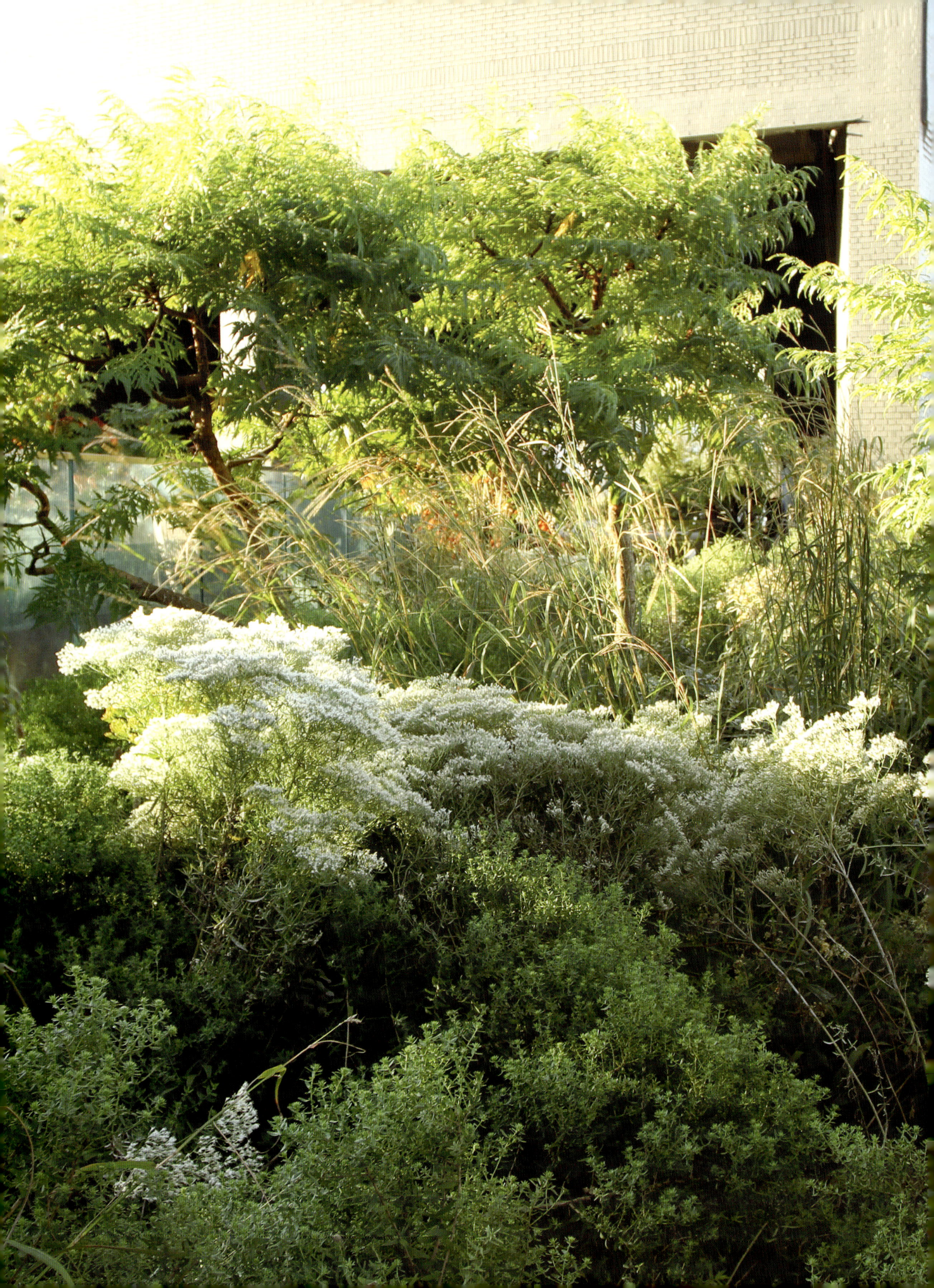

Rhus typhina 'Laciniata' (cutleaf staghorn sumac) with a foamy understory on the southern part of the High Line

RIGHT The Roads Water-Smart Garden at Denver Botanic Gardens, Colorado, is a stunning example of mature bioregional design achieved through the embodied values and experiences of its steward, Dan Johnson. Although the garden was installed in 1995 following a concept and design by Lauren Springer Ogden, Johnson has altered, advanced and harmonized the space daily for almost three decades. "The garden manifests the opportunities that come with subtle change and the nourishment I've found in exploration and experimentation," he says. Composed primarily of shrubs, subshrubs and succulent scrub, the garden mixes xeric plant material of desert, Mediterranean and steppe regions, creating a surprisingly stable oeuvre. The design prioritizes year-round color, texture and form, which pulsates and suffuses but never radically changes; instead, the seasonal highlights flow like rapids across the surface of boulders. "Every inch is, in a sense, contrived, but not artificial. This is about building a life in the arid world. It's a complex garden, filled with small moments, fleeting combinations and powerful vignettes. I wish I could take the time or make the space to expand those experiences."[34]

World Feels Weird (2017)
PENCIL AND WATERCOLOR ON PAPER
15.2 x 20.3cm
Kevin Philip Williams

Attunement in the space of dazzle camouflage where the organic and inorganic are merged together through intense patterning.

Tuning in

Gardening is a form of ritual embodiment, whether consciously or subconsciously. It's a process of partnering with plants to externalize our beliefs, emotions, visions and ideals into our physical world. Through this process we can begin to understand and more closely align ourselves with the plants that we work with. This phenomenon is described as attunement. Through attunement we adapt to the reality of other beings, often by incorporating or reflecting aspects of that being in ourselves. Through mimicry, futurecasting, and virtually all forms of expression and action, we are attuning ourselves to our environment and our environment is attuning to us.

Camouflage is one of the high temples of attunement. Wearing camouflage, or in the case of some organisms, actually being camouflaged, is an attempt to become the environment by mimicking its ambient noise. The point of camo is to become the Other, to lose or mask ourselves. The feeling can be intoxicating, empowering, and calming. By melding with the world we become omniscient, omnipresent observers. We are filled with the capacity of our environment to contain endless forms, expressions, evolutions and actions. Our space of nothing becomes a space of everything. Creating shrubscapes, and working with plants that shroud us, help to nestle us more deeply into our surroundings, separating us from other humans and human creations, priming us to attune more deeply with the Other.

This sentiment is echoed by Timothy Morton's inspection of the connection between withdrawal, appearance and being: "Things are exactly what they are, yet never how they appear, yet appearance is inseparable from being, so a thing is a twisted loop like a Möbius strip, in which the twist is everywhere, it has no starting or ending point. Appearance is the intrinsic twist in being."[35]

Shrubscapes offer us this type of understanding. Shrubs may make us more human by reflecting our varying capacities to hide and deceive, or provide and protect, and force us to confront those aspects of ourselves. Shrubs may make us less human by separating us from that which keeps us grounded in the human social world and rewilding our sensibilities towards the nonhuman. They can be a mask from which we observe the world, while being safely cloaked in thickets of obscurity.

BELOW An old hardened form of *Corokia cotoneaster* (korokio or wire-netting bush) on Mt Edward, New Zealand seemingly attuned in color and density with the neighboring lichen and the granite mountain itself.

Cyberpunk Shrubscapes (Est 2022)

DESIGNERS: *Stable Diffusion, Michael Guidi, Kevin Philip Williams*
LOCATION: *Cyberspace*

"Data travelers, electro wizards, techno anarchists . . ."[36]

Somewhere in the digital world, condensing in the cloud, or colonizing a server farm, a shrubscape exists, bound only by a memory of its earthly origins. Digital shrubscapes created by deep learning, text to image modeling software, or artificial intelligence, are evocative glimpses into our collective understanding of shrublands and gardens. By asking AI to create a shrubland-based garden, we are asking the program to learn what we would consider a shrubscape based on our own work in the physical realm. These images are composites, patterns, layouts, impressions, predictions, parodies and prophecies. Such shrubscapes have been willed into existence, and are snapshots of potential creations, conceptions and jumping-off points for wild systems.

BELOW AND OPPOSITE **Each image in this section is titled with the text prompt that was used to bring it into being.**

prompt://a dense and glowing and diverse wild scrubland garden in front of a suburban house.exe

prompt://a dense and glowing flowering garrigue wild scrubland garden in the backyard.exe

prompt://a dense and glowing garrigue wild shrubland designed dream backyard thicket garden.exe

prompt:// a dense and glowing thornscrub wild scrubland garden in front of a contemporary suburban house.exe

prompt://a dense and glowing thornscrub wild scrubland garden in the backyard full of shrubs.exe

prompt://a dense and glowing thornscrub wild scrubland garden in the backyard full of shrubs.exe

MAKING SHRUBSCAPES

prompt://a dense and glowing thornscrub wild scrubland garden in the backyard full of shrubs.exe

prompt://a dense and glowing wild scrubland garden in front of a contemporary suburban house.exe

prompt://wild shrubland garden backyard.exe

Artificial Intelligence is a tool. Like all tools, we can use it to further or alter our creations and investigations. Learning to partner with other intelligences to build worlds is at the heart of gardening, whether we work in digital or physical realms. Designing gardens with AI, a human-spawned intelligence, to achieve unpredictable, surprising results is a form of sympoietic wild systems emulation and whether or not they are translated into earthly gardens, they now exist in the realm of further representative modeling.

prompt://a hardcore punk shrubland garden.exe

prompt://a wild shrubland designed garden in the backyard.exe

Further Strategies for Naturalistic Design

Future naturalistic gardens will not be designed, but encouraged to become. Their starting points will not solely be human brains, but the intentions, wills and desires of many creatures. They will not be modeled after easy aesthetic rewards, but challenging, generative worlds.

Understanding how to meld the excitement and unpredictability of the natural world with the timelessness of gardens requires an expanded understanding of what it means to dissociate and deviate from the expected. We need a new definition of what it means to be wild.

Wildness and the Post-Humanities

The old definitions of wildness and wilderness have failed the Anthropocene. We do not live in the post-wild, we live as part of the new wild.

The standard definitions of wildness are both passionate and negative. They describe the character of being uncultivated, undomesticated, or inhospitable; having a lack of discipline, restraint and sound reasoning. Wildness is framed by either the prefix 'un', meaning contrary to, or it's framed as being a lack of something. This definition serves a society in which wildness is often not good. Our linguistics have evolved, or have been designed, to reinforce the idea that being apart from society in some way is bad. Much of the wildness in gardens (weeds, overgrowth, aggressive species, tangles, runners, suckers) is viewed negatively. Only aesthetically pleasing wildness is encouraged.

Positive treatments of wildness in the world of gardening are mostly concerned with ideas of autonomy[37], but self-governance and self-directed freedom, which is the definition of autonomy, is not the same as being wild. Making decisions for oneself is not wildness. Wildness is more concerned with the effects of those decisions.

We shall redefine wildness as "surprising thoughts or actions." When we refer to wildness, we mean the potential to be delighted and challenged by the surprising thoughts or actions of others or ourselves. Thus, the wild family becomes:

Wild – Something surprising
Wildness – Surprising thoughts or actions
Wilderness – Being subsumed by surprising thoughts or actions

MAKING SHRUBSCAPES 205

"That's how the light gets in." [39] Cushions of *Nardophyllum* (nardo) soften the razor-sharp volcanic substrate on the rolling hills and mesas of the Argentine Monte.

A riot of mesoflora in the dry, steppe foothills of the Kichi-Kemin Valley in eastern Kyrgyzstan, which support a huge diversity of shrubland communities. Here, *Clematis songarica* (Sungari leather flower) and *Clematis orientalis* (small-flowered virginsbower) spill over an unbelievable composition of *Ephedra equisetina* (bluestem jointfir), *Artemisia rutifolia* (afsanteen), *Salvia abrotanoides* (Russian sage) and *Atraphaxis virgata* (twiggy buckwheat).

If we can batch wild thoughts or actions into general categories or systems, we end up with three main groups: anthropogenic, non-anthropogenic and sympoietic wild systems.

Anthropogenic Wild Systems

These systems are created and enacted by humans, or surprising things that humans do. So, how can humans be wild?

The theory of agrilogistics, put forth by Timothy Morton as the Agrilogistic Viral Code or the Agrilogistic Sentence,[38] reveals that we live our lives following a program of self-preservation built upon the logic that the only way to protect ourselves in an unstable environment is to attempt to control it, which of course only destabilizes it further.

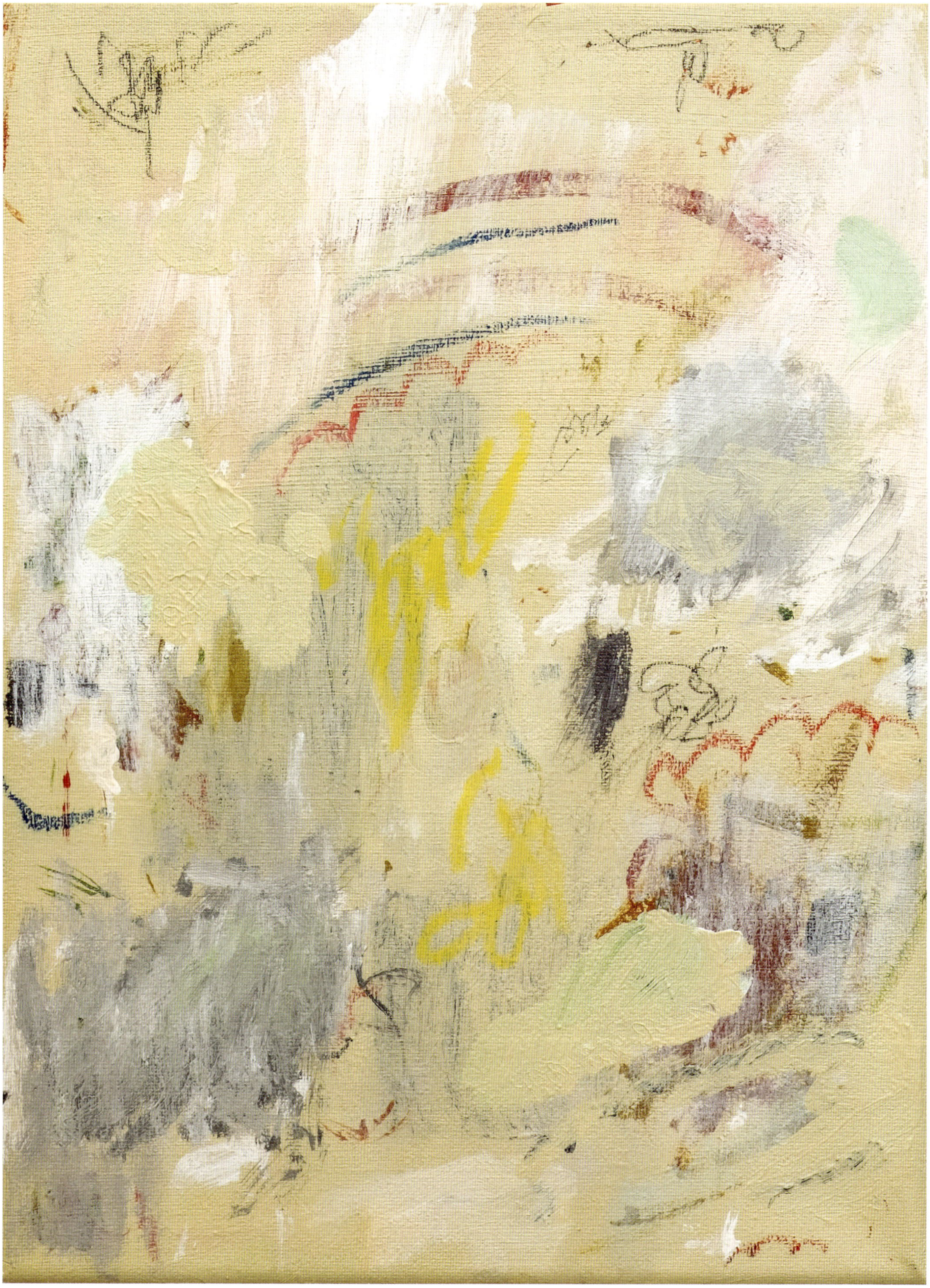

OPPOSITE *Christchurch Landscape No 1 (2018)*
ACRYLIC PAINT AND PENCIL ON STRETCHED CANVAS
21.6 x 27.9 cm.
Sean Robert McNamara
In abstract expressionism, artists do not discount the actions and effects of the materials and media with which they create. These partners in creation are given a sort of agency to affect the outcome, creating microcosms and universes within universes. We need to ask ourselves how many universes are in our gardens? And who is creating them?

ABOVE *Racomitrium lanuginosum* (woolly fringe-moss), *Veronica lycopodioides* (whipcord hebe), *Dracophyllum* (dragon-leaf), *Acrothamnus* sp. (beard-heath), and *Lycopodium fastigiatum* (mountain club moss) among others creating a fractured vegetative skin of shrubs, lichen, mosses and grasses coating the lower slopes of Mt Southey, New Zealand.

He argues that agrilogistics are the common thought process that we all share. It's the thought process that began with the first homebuilder, farmer or geoengineer; the idea that in order to ensure our survivability in an unstable environment, we began to alter the environment by changing it to fit our needs through clearing land, changing ambient temperatures, changing the course of rivers, and more, which all have the long-term effect of creating a truly unstable environment. It's what has been referred to as a progress trap. Agrilogistics is a cycle that we still cannot break and it has led to the Anthropocene, the age in which we now live, where humans have the greatest influence over Earth systems. Agrilogistics is for the most part unique to humanity and therefore, not surprising within the context of our society. This is at the heart of what it means to be a modern human.

BELOW, LEFT Detail of a metal security door in Barskoon, Kyrgyzstan. The effect of the elements and repeated attempts to change its color have resulted in an unpredictable and inspired patina. In this small section you can find pathways, plazas, plant masses, egresses and elevations all untethered by rote drafting tools.

MAKING SHRUBSCAPES

Wildness within human thought and action exists where we break with our own agrilogistics or we break societal norms. These are the places where we should look for influences to build our gardens, because they are where we are least like ourselves and therefore most likely to be able to successfully work with non-human Others.

Examples of Anthropogenic Wild Systems can be found in dissonant or self-generating music, feedback loops, algorithmic equations, graffiti, abstract expressionism, camouflage and the cross-temporal/multi-layered decay and regeneration of cities.

CENTRE, LEFT **TAZ 83, or Swiss alpenflage, was developed to blend soldiers into alpine plant communities. On the most superficial, albeit useful, level these camouflage patterns are garden designs. Their amorphous blobs, swaths, smudges, blotches, and spots reveal patterning, repetition and rhythm, and positive and negative space in a semi-randomized sense. This is a translation of naturalistic distribution patterns. The deeper implication in personal camouflage is that there are times when it's desirable to disappear into plants in their various stages and states of life. We are imbuing ourselves with the properties that we perceive in plants; innocuousness, peace and protection. Then we sometimes use this position to create danger, death and menace, which are usually unperceived but very real properties of plants.**

LEFT **In graffiti there is a new bloom and population every moment. Nothing is safe or permanent. We need this type of corrosion and regeneration in gardens.**

BELOW Computer glitches are surprising, unintentional breakdowns and expressions in systems that were created to function in predictable, reliable ways. Glitches can help us understand the potential for unintentional actions within an active and reactive space to create something beautiful. Could you imagine a garden set into motion using an algorithmic engine?

Non-Anthropogenic Wild Systems

Non-Anthropogenic wild systems are places where we are surprised by non-human Others. Sometimes this occurs in places that we might classically refer to as nature, natural areas, wilderness areas and parks. We see non-human Others acting wild all the time. Deer run into roadways, tree roots clog septic systems and uplift sidewalks, hurricanes destroy cities, butterflies migrate, forests exist, stalactites form.

RIGHT Can we find inspiration for soft, shifting and impermanent plantings in hard places? This stone face, with its various minerals and layers, contains several complex community schemes that are as beautiful as they are dizzying.

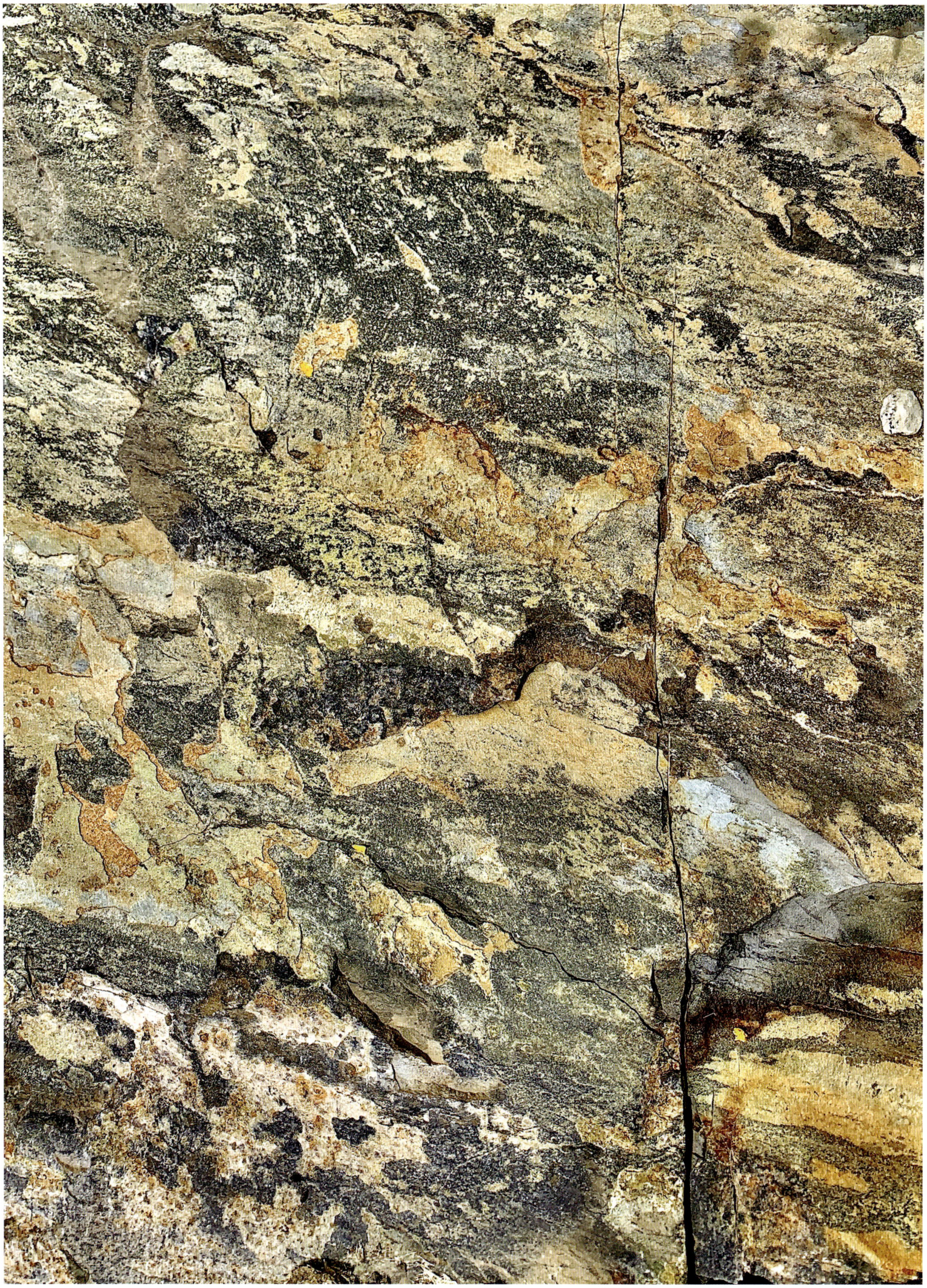

Duranta erecta 'Gold Edge' (Gold Edge golden dewdrop) reaches through a hedge of *Lavandula stoechas* (French lavender), offering an intensely gaudy contrast in Mexico City, Mexico.

Caesalpinia gilliesii (desert bird of paradise) occupies a dusty roadside median strip in a small town on the Argentine steppe. The feathery foliage of this xeric shrub evokes the tropics and it has become a popular ornamental in South America.

Sympoietic Systems

Sympoiesis is defined as "Collectively-producing systems that do not have self-defined spatial or temporal boundaries. Information and control are distributed among components. The systems are evolutionary and have the potential for surprising change."[40]

Sympoietic systems exist at the intersectionality of anthropogenic and non-anthropogenic wild systems. To work, live, laugh, play and create in sympoiesis requires sensitizing yourself to the needs and life processes of others as well as your own. Gardens and regenerated spaces, or what we often call ecologically restored spaces, have the potential to be sympoietic systems if stewarded correctly. These spaces can be acted upon by humans and non-humans to create something truly magnificent. Gardens are our crossroads, our shared common spaces and our meeting rooms with plants. The myriad techniques and styles referred to as naturalistic landscape design can be very useful in setting a sympoietic system in motion. However, certain styles of gardening are, quite frankly, not respectful to the potential of plants. High-touch, or ornamental gardens, can be beautiful in their own right, but they are echoes of humanity's most base definition of gardening: to constrain or control.

Embracing Wilderness

As the idea of the untouched, pristine, natural world, wilderness has been described as illogical and fantastical on a planet that is covered with our fingerprints [41]. However, within the context of these definitions, wilderness not only still exists, but can be created.

Wilderness exists in any moment when we feel fully absorbed in, or possibly overwhelmed by, a situation, creature, thought or moment that surprises us. It is a state of perception triggered by external or internal circumstances and leads to some of the most beautiful and ugly moments in our lives.

A shrubscape at The Huntington Library, Art Museum and Botanical Gardens in San Marino, California, merging succulent scrub and savannah by blending euphorbias and grasses – *Festuca mairei* (Atlas fescue), *Sporobolus airoides* (alkali sacaton) and *Muhlenbergia rigens* (deergrass) – with stately specimens of *Aloe ferox* (Cape aloe) and cycads.

Wilderness has always existed as the place where agrilogistic vectors are overwhelmed by non-agrilogistic vectors, or vice-versa. Wilderness for humans exists where we feel lost in what we perceive as non-human thought or action. For Others, it exists where they are overwhelmed by human thought or action. Wild systems are surprising systems, no matter who or what they surprise. Wilderness can happen on a mountain's sliding scree slope, in the eerie choral yips of coyotes echoing in a valley, on the crowded sidewalk of an unfamiliar city, in the jaws of a backhoe tearing through woodland undergrowth, in an oil slick on the ocean surface, in a cloud of pesticides being dropped over a jungle, in the gaze of a monster or in our own questioning minds. Humanity is as wild as any creature that has ever existed and we have created our own wilderness. Wilderness is a place or a state of being where we have lost control; where we are overwhelmed, all-encompassed or subsumed by the wildness of Others.

Wild Systems Emulation

Wild systems emulation seeks visual examples of surprising actions to inspire the arrangement of a design. These inspirations can be the result of intentional or unintentional forces from any source. Using constantly changing systems to guide the placement of plants, plant communities, architectural and hardscape elements has the short-term effect of creating a garden that feels as if it is already in motion and the long-term effect of encouraging a competitive, evolving space. This is garden-hacking. Using these wild, open-source examples of composition and expression as jumping-off points for planting helps to alleviate the heavy-handedness of the designer and encourages acceptance of wandering and competing plant communities.

Wild Systems Emulation challenges our first instincts and rejects our training and human impulses. Even when we try to make things seem as natural as possible, we can make them just seem like us. The sense of place is often not much more than a sense of someone. The curse of the design is the designer. As Spencer Moody yowls in the song 'Cruelty Abounds': "Does the singer wanna wreck the song? I do not know, but surely sometimes that's just how it sounds."[42] Wild Systems Emulation can help us create a sense of something else. The idea is to dissolve contrivances and, in a way, remove designers from the design.

MAKING SHRUBSCAPES

The unpredictable nature of mud splattered on to the side of a dumpster created emulatable drippy constellations.

Applying Wild Systems Emulation to the garden requires a resolve to trust and work with something more than human. Although simple in concept, this technique is not a reductive paint-by-numbers approach, but a complex starting place from which to weave together even more layers, concepts, species, phenologies, textures and reliefs. There is no magic bullet in garden design, no right or wrong answers, no gods and no masters. There are only compromises and revelations.

FOLLOWING SPREAD Using lichen, a symbiotic holobiont of algae, fungi and yeast, as a basis for naturalistic design filters the starting point for our work through a complex and collaborative decision-making process managed by multiple organisms.

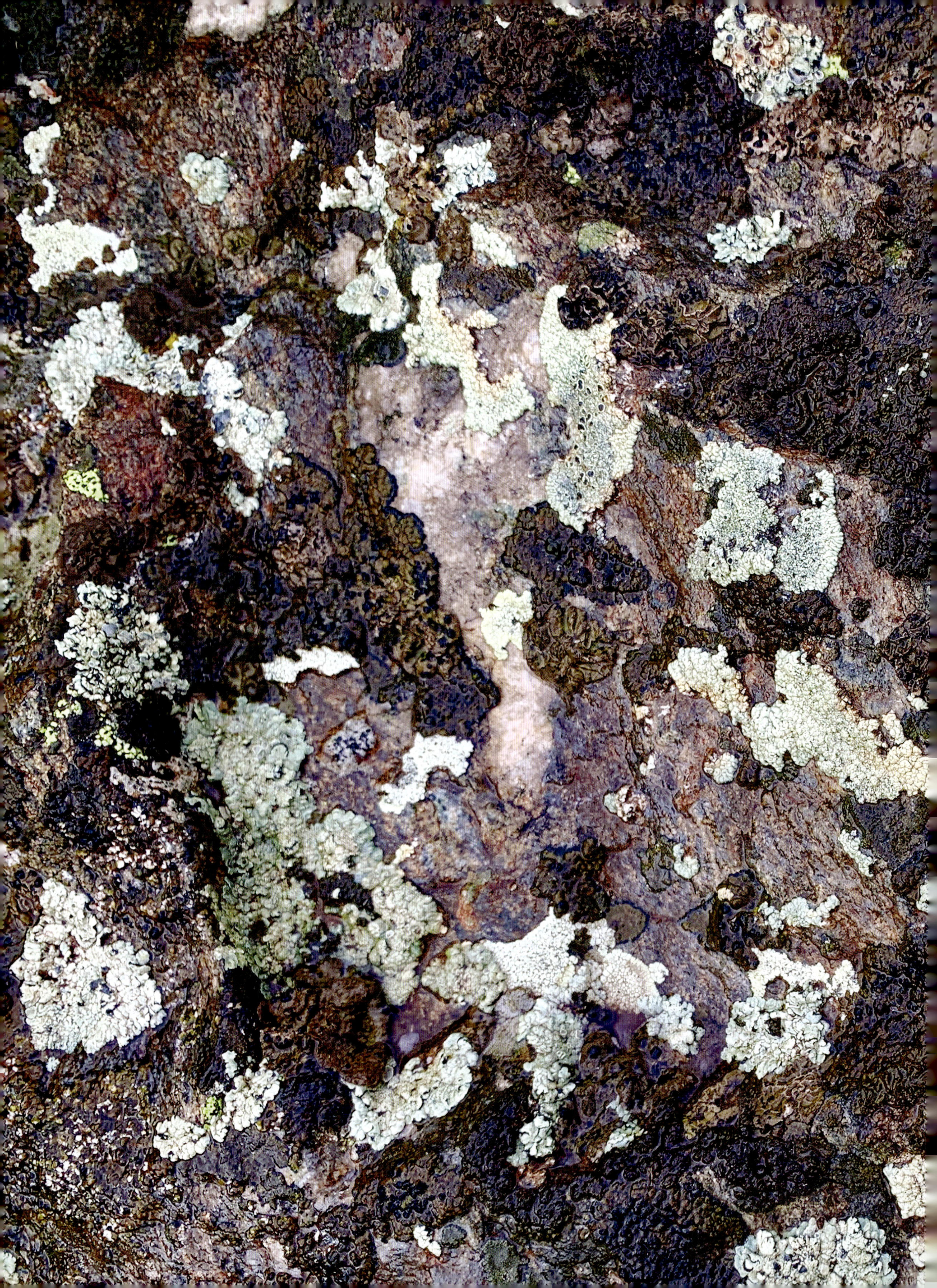

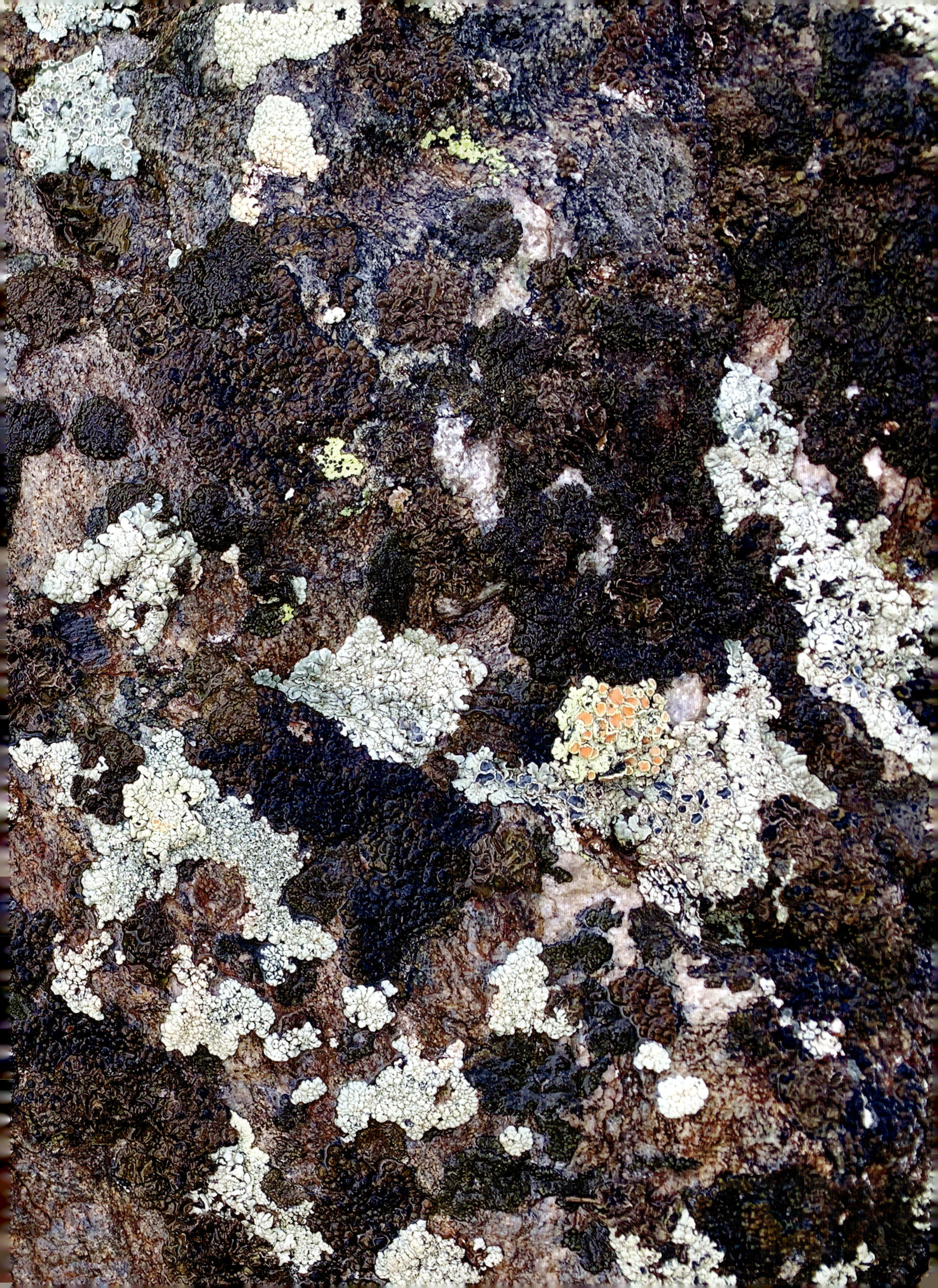

LEFT This wild system was found on a utility box in Ljubljana, Slovenia.

RIGHT SummerHome Garden. Denver, Colorado. The wild system fit to the site. Dominant and desired elements were identified including color-defined sections to use as spatial guides. Ten unique communities of about six species each were randomly planted within each section and seed mixtures were oversown with the intention of creating a thick, vibrant interstitial layer. Instead of assigning specific locations for each plant, approximate quantities were determined for the area of each space.

BELOW The result.

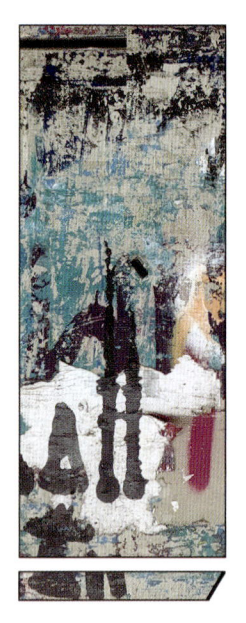

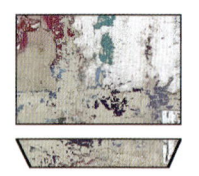

SummerHome Garden (Est 2020)

GARDEN DESIGNERS: *Kevin Philip Williams, Sonya Anderson and Lisa Negri*

The layout of the SummerHome Garden shrubscape was modeled on an instance of graffiti captured on a public utility box in Ljubljana, Slovenia. This radical object had been spray-painted, stickered, markered, wheat-pasted, sat upon, scraped, and battered by the elements for years. The result, much like the subsequent garden, was an urban collage that no singular being, person, or force could have planned.

MAKING SHRUBSCAPES 219

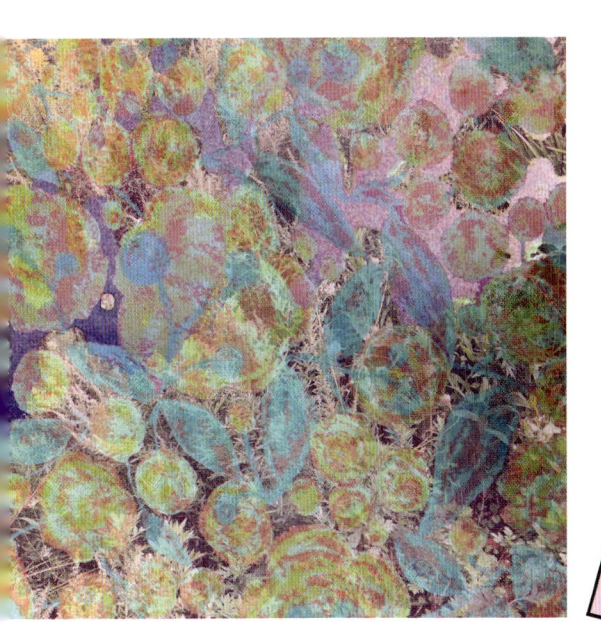

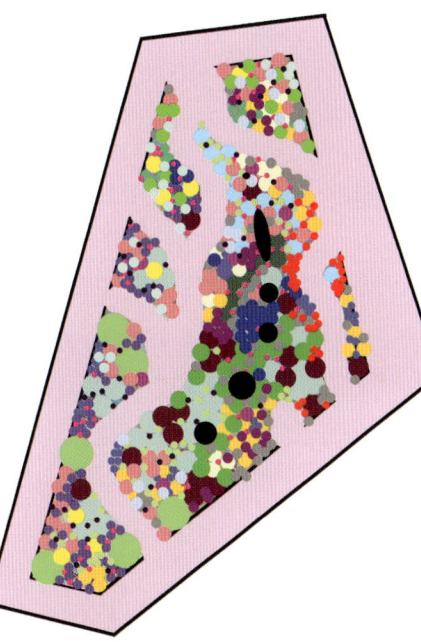

FAR LEFT The inspiration for this design was found in a collage of floral prints overlaid with a photograph of a wild weedscape found in a ditch.

LEFT After the wild system was fit to the polygonal site, pathways were carved out using an exhibit from the art space as inspiration. A complex planting and seeding arrangement was then designed, based on the superimposed interactions of the collage.

BELOW The result.

Alien Dream Worlds (Est 2022)
MEOW WOLF DENVER: *Convergence Station*
GARDEN DESIGNER: *Kevin Philip Williams*

Alien Dream Worlds, a habitat for the Plethodon, at Meow Wolf Denver: Convergence Station was modeled on a highly stylized digital collage emphasizing the themes of intersection, interaction and inclusion central to the art exhibit. Flora from the shrublands of the American southwest were combined with related species from analogous ecosystems around the world to create a unique ecosystem that challenges the viewer's sense of reality.

LEFT Salt, acid, oxidation, groundwater, weather, soil chemicals and microorganisms sketching a landscape design on a concrete foundation.

BELOW Although the three beds were assigned different planting themes using different species, they were also modeled on contiguous parts of the same wild system, resulting in dramatically different gardens with the same naturalistic effect.

OPPOSITE PAGE **The result.**

Denver Art Museum Sensory Garden (Est 2020)

GARDEN DESIGNERS: *Kevin Philip Williams, Angie Andrade and Didier Design Studio*

The Denver Art Museum Sensory Garden layout was patterned on a distressed and patinated section of concrete foundation, large and diverse enough to be interpreted over a series of planting beds. The plant list and visual aesthetics of the garden took inspiration from the garrigue and the steppe, combining soft-leaved shrubs, elegant grasses and fragrant perennials to create botanical touch tanks: gardens that encourage visitor interaction.

Mesh Not Matrix

The ideas of stitching and layering are central to shrublands and shrubscapes. Naturalistic landscapes, whether they are archetypally categorized as grassland, forest, shrubland or forbland, are always a mixture of heterogeneous elements. Even when the primary plant form is shrubby, interstitial non-shrubby species hold together the aesthetics and push the ecology.

Matrices have offered one of the most successful models for emulating wild archetypes in a naturalistic garden setting. In a matrix planting, an array of one or several species is set to provide rhythm and context while other species are interspersed, dotted, speckled, massed and spattered to enhance the base design. In short, a matrix is a grid, a binding structure, developed to help convey naturalistic gardening as an approachable concept. It simplifies complex arrangements, allowing anyone to access naturalistic aesthetics and, like the mass planting movement before it, can be universally applied across plant material, helping growers to sell large numbers of crops.

Unfortunately, most of our ideas related to gardening and horticulture are based on the desire to control, and the matrix is no different. While a matrix can be designed as an endlessly intricate dance, with multiple seasonal matrices and flowering themes, progressions of form and celebrations of liminality, it is often reduced to its ability to simplify, to make legible and save time. The application of a system is not the same as embracing a process. Gardening is a process; creation is a process; the world is a process.

The mesh offers a different starting place for a design. It is a true inter-lacing of parts and instead of presenting a style of gardening, it creates a complex starting point. Complexity in a garden imparts diversity, resilience and adaptive capacity, ensuring the long-term sustainability and survival of the design.

In its most basic form, a mesh can be implemented through a seed mix, either in a blank space or over an existing garden. Seed mixes, or seeded gardens like those championed by James Hitchmough in *Sowing Beauty*[43], do not offer an initial plant structure to bind everything together, but instead a loose agreement between the gardener and the seeds that they will work together to make something happen. At its most intricate, wild systems can be used to create overlays of complementary plant communities with combinations of intentional and undirected plant placements to create a complex system.

MAKING SHRUBSCAPES 223

One design informs the other in these two images. Both scenes swell and recede with a dance of seasonal color and impermanence.

LEFT The interstitial forbs of a montane sagebrush shrub-steppe featuring the brick-red stems of *Artemisia carruthii* (Carruth's sagewort), the green lightning of *Argemone hispida* (rough prickly poppy) and the yellow pop of a street sign in Salida, Colorado

BELOW The interstitial forbs of a designed shrubscape with *Artemisia ludoviciana* (white sagebrush), spreading like quicksilver through the speckled and august rusting of *Monarda punctata* (spotted beebalm), while *Solidago canadensis* (Canada goldenrod) signals in the background.

Do What You Want

Please use the methods, images and thoughts in this book as inspiration to create your own complex, emotionally arresting places. The forms, structures, colors, distribution patterns and the dynamics of these shrublands are energizing no matter where you live or what your shrub palette may be. Using regionally appropriate plant material, the compositional observations, design strategies, and encouragements are applicable anywhere.

Whatever type of shrubland you decide to set into motion, we encourage you to saturate the space with potential. Use a combination of seeding and planting to create a dense, vibrant garden. Allow plants to fill spaces, compete, wander and make their own decisions; the ecological archetypes used as the basis for most naturalistic designs fluctuate wildly from season to season, year to year, decade to decade.

It's important to think beyond a human timescale when implementing a neo-naturalistic garden. There are winners and losers in systems as conditions change in any plant community. Sometimes shrubs win and sometimes they lose. Successional states are real. Stable, or climax communities, are only temporary perceptions. In highly productive systems, grasslands tend to turn into shrublands, which tend to turn into forests. In high-stress systems, grasslands, shrublands or succulent scrub might be the stable form. In systems of high disturbance, the dynamics may flow in the opposite direction; a shrubland burns to the ground and annual grasses take over. The human element in these equations is also very real. In theory, there can exist, at all times, two parallel universes or realities of a garden: one in which humans directly and consistently act on a space and one in which they do not. These alternative stable states can exist along a spectrum of actions and intentions and should be embraced! This is our participation in nature, our communion with the non-human. Prepare for infinite change and celebrate the process.

Good Day Sunshine. Part 3.
Kelly Knaga

How do we make gardens? How do we add to, explore, edit, improve or disrupt spaces and what are the processes that we use? Can we begin by suggesting an alternate reality? Can we be invited? Can we respond and react to the change that is already in process?

MAKING SHRUBSCAPES

ENDNOTES

"Nothing is true. Everything is permitted."

Antoine Isaac Silvestre de Sacy (1838), Gustav Flügel (1864), Friedrich Nietzsche (1887)
Vladimir Bartol (1938), William S. Burroughs (1959)

Kevin Philip Williams

What will it take to reawaken our relationship with shrublands? To bring a habitat back into our lives? Will we (re)welcome shrublands into our landscapes if they feel unfamiliar? Will we respond to their beauty? Their ecological potential? Their psychological effects?

Like most biotemporal actions, the acceptance of a shrubby future may happen in the realm of creeping normality,[44] meaning that the change will be gradual, and if it happens, we may not notice that it's happening at all. That is, after all, how we lost touch with shrublands. The "cultural landscape amnesia" of the midwestern United States promotes images of endless grasslands rushing from the hardwood forests to the Rocky Mountains, when in reality extensive shrub corridors existed as cornerstone regional habitats.[45] The scattered remnant prairies that still exist are poor in such features, further promoting the incongruous feeling of shrubs in these landscapes. Elsewhere, shrubs grow where grasslands once flourished. Forests stand where farms once stood. Forbs flow over rubble.

The point is that things change. People change things. We adapt to the changes, normalize our new reality and forget. That's not necessarily a bad thing. We don't always need to restore the past or return to some previous reference state. Instead, we need to stay open, flexible and full of questions. It doesn't really matter what something was, as long as we can remain aware of what it could be. We need to remember that life is possible in all places, at all times, across an inconceivable spectrum. We need to embody an imperfect world, constantly in the process of becoming.

Michael Guidi

If you've finished this journey with more questions than answers, found more possibilities than prescriptions, and more uncertainties than guidelines, good. If our book is cast aside with nothing more than a reluctant veneration of the dusty, selenium-caked, windswept, aromatic, gritty, soft, thorny, arid, humid shrublands of the world, our goal has still been met. If, like us, you question what is or isn't a garden, refuse to define a shrub, or suddenly see shrubland garden designs in sidewalk oil slicks, know that this uncertainty is charged with more opportunities than limitations. After all, when we cease to understand the world[46] is when we can see the farthest; when what's expected, anticipated, or taken for granted no longer makes sense, there is a chance to build something new.

Shrublands don't just offer a fresh template for garden design, they provide a reconsideration of what gardens represent, who they are for, and what kind of experiences they can offer. Shrubs can be more than just the hedge around Eden. For certain, they are a refuge, but they are challenging, lonely, and vulnerable places too. And can't gardens express these things, just like the art, music, and poetry that are so central to lived experience?

When it comes to global vegetation, everything is different than it has ever been and therefore everything that comes after will be different than what's here now[47]. Our understanding of what's natural, what's best, or what's meant to be is just gained from snapshots in other people's lives, behind which there is a real, messy story. Our gardens should embody this opportunity for change inherent in all things, in their approach, styling, and evolution. Shrubscapes won't save the world. They won't save us. But intentional use of shrubland-styled garden design might help us build worlds that we don't quite recognize, that catch us off guard, and keep us open and flexible in an uncertain future.

GLOSSARY

Abiotic Non-living
Adaptive capacity The ability of a system to adjust to changing conditions.
Agrilogistics A self-preservation program in which humans actively try to change their environment in order to protect themselves from instability or uncertainty.
Alluvial fan A fan- or triangle-shaped outwash of sedimentary material often occurring at the mouths of restricted channels, such as canyons.
Anthocyanin Chemical compounds in plants that appear purple, red, black or blue.
Anthroflora Flora that are most related and relatable to the function of people.
Anthropocene The epoch in which humans have had a dominant influence over the Earth and its processes.
Anthropogenic wild systems Wild systems created and enacted by humans, or surprising things that humans do.
Anthropometric Relating to the size, shape and proportions of humans.
Arboreal Tree-like or relating to trees.
Attunement The process of harmonizing with, or taking on the characteristics of, another.
Backdune Sand dunes that are not directly adjacent to a coastline; a sand dune behind another.
Bajadas Several, coalesced alluvial fans.
Balds Hilltops and mountain summits that are not cold or tall enough to support alpine plant communities and, due to free-draining substrates and historical conditions, resist encroachment from forests.
Biome An extensive community of flora and fauna adapted to a specific environment.
Bioregion A large area distinguished by its climate and geology.
Biotemporal Time periods based on biological activities.
Biotic Living.
Black metal A genre of extreme music.
Box balls (see Green meatballs) A shrub sheared into a round ball.
Carotenoids Chemical compounds in plants that appear red, orange or yellow.
Caudex An enlarged stem used to store water and energy.
Chaparral A shrubland plant community occurring in a Mediterranean climate with cool, moist winters and hot, dry summers.
Chaparralscape A chaparral-based shrubscape.
Chasmophyte A plant growing in a crevice of a hard, inorganic material, such as stone or concrete.
Climax Community The notion of a point of relative ecological stability in a given climate.
Complex early seral forest Plant and animal communities that develop in and inhabit disturbed areas of a forest.
Convergent evolution When disparate species evolve similar adaptations and characteristics in response to comparable environmental conditions.
Coppice Pruning a shrub or tree to the ground; also, an area where shrubs or trees are pruned to the ground.
Creeping normality The phenomenon of accepting a major change as normal if it happens through slow, small, unnoticeable changes.
Crepuscular Relating to the activities or ambiance of dawn and dusk.
Cryptobiotic soil crust A hardened soil surface composed of living organisms and inorganic matter.
Desert An arid bioregion.
Disturbance An event that causes a change in the state, structure or species of an ecosystem. Many plant communities and species have evolved to depend on or tolerate disturbance events.
Divaricate A growth form where nodal growth happens at a wide angle from the previous growth, creating a tight mesh of branches.
Duff A layer of decaying organic matter, shed by plants, found beneath them.

Ecotone A sharp transition area between two ecosystems or biological communities.
Endemism When the natural distribution of a species is limited to a specific place or range.
Ensō A swiftly drawn or painted circle associated with Zen practice.
Epicuticular wax A waxy coating found on the surface of land plants with the primary function of reducing water loss.
Fertility islands The phenomenon of heightened soil productivity in a very localized area due to the accumulation of organic matter and nutrients beneath the canopies of shrubs and trees.
Forb An herbaceous, vascular, non-woody, flowering plant that is not a graminoid (grass or grass ally).
Forbland A landscape primarily composed of forbs.
Forest A landscape primarily composed of trees.
Fractals Recurring and repeating patterns at different scales.
Futurecasting Attempting to plan for the future by predicting upcoming needs, trends and opportunities.
Graft The practice of attaching two plants together so that they share a vascular system.
Graminoid A grass-like herbaceous plant. Most likely a grass (Poaceae), sedge (Cyperaceae) or rush (Juncaceae).
Grassland A landscape primarily composed of graminoids.
Green meatballs (see Box balls) A shrub sheared into a round ball.
Green Roof A roof that is covered in vegetation on top of a human-made structure.
Halophyte A salt-tolerant plant.
Herbaceous Any plant that does not produce woody stems.
Heterogeneous A state of diversity.
Homogeneous A state of uniformity.
Hostile horticulture A strategy that uses garden design or plants to guide or restrict behavior.
Icon A type of sign that has a physical resemblance to that which is being represented.
Index A type of sign that provides information about the thing being represented.
Interstitial The spaces between things.
Krummholz A term for a tree that has been stunted and deformed by the extreme conditions of high elevation.
Leeward The side of a mountain, structure or place that is sheltered from prevailing air currents or weather systems.
Lignified Becoming inflexible and woody.
Lovecraftian Related or referring to the work of novelist H.P. Lovecraft, who often wrote of the horror of the incomprehensible.
Mass path A pedestrian path etched into the ground by repeated use.
Matrix A binding structure, or a planting design strategy that utilizes several species as the basis for a naturalistic garden design.
Mediterranean A bioregion with cool, moist winters and hot, dry summers.
Mesa An isolated, flat-topped land mass bound by steep escarpments.
Mesh An interlacing of parts; a fully stitched-together community.
Morphology The study of forms and structures.
Natureculture A recognition of the inseparable relationship between the physical and social aspects of humans and non-humans.
Necroarchitecture The dead structures (stems, branches, trunks) that compose the interior of multi-stemmed plants.
NO CONTROL An ethos that embraces a limited ability to influence or direct an outcome.
Non-anthropogenic wild systems Wild systems created and enacted by non-humans, or surprising things that non-humans do.
Nurse plants Plants whose growth creates conditions that facilitate the growth of other plants.
Other (as in, *The Other* or *Non-human Other*) A distinct being. Also, the recognition of the existence and validity of the experiences of non-humans.
Phenology The study of the timing of cyclical biological events.
Pollard Pruning a shrub or tree to a defined point above ground in order to encourage young growth.
Post-Anthropocene The potential epoch in which humans no longer have the dominant influence over the Earth and its processes.

Posthumanism A philosophy that explores the decentralization of human thoughts and values and extends moral concern and agency to other beings.
Prairie A regional term for grasslands in the midwestern United States.
Pruning The act of cutting plants to control or direct growth.
Rain shadow A dry area caused by weather systems being blocked by mountains, buildings or significant vegetation.
Resilience The ability of a system to return to its previous state following a disruption or change.
Riparian Relating to wetlands, and lands surrounding and saturated by rivers and streams.
Sclerophyll A plant with hard, evergreen leaves adapted to extreme heat and drought.
Semiotics The study of language and signs and their meaning.
Shrubcore A type of shrubland that embraces the extreme elements and aesthetics of shrublands.
Shrubdivision A property or plot of land where shrubs occupy the spaces, or surround the negative spaces, formerly defined by human-built structures.
Shrubland A landscape primarily composed of shrubs.
Shruboid Something with a shrub-like shape or resemblance that is not consistently considered a shrub.
Shrubscape A designed landscape modeled after a shrubland.
Sigil A symbol imbued with power.
Signs Information directly related to the characteristics of something.
Sky Island Isolated ecosystems found on mountains and areas of high elevation surrounded by significantly different lowland conditions.
Steppe A semi-arid bioregion.
Stochastic A random or variable process.
Subshrub A shrub whose new growth is often herbaceous and dies back in periods of extreme cold or drought.
Sucker Growth shoots on a plant that arise from the roots.
Sweetwater Fresh water.
Symbiont A partner in a symbiotic relationship.

Symbiosis/Symbiotic A relationship between two or more organisms in close physical proximity.
Symbol A type of sign that bears no resemblance to the thing it is representing; its meaning needs to be learned through a cultural context.
Sympoiesis "Collectively-producing systems that do not have self-defined spatial or temporal boundaries. Information and control are distributed among components. The systems are evolutionary and have the potential for surprising change."[48]
Sympoietic wild systems Wild systems created and enacted by humans and non-humans, resulting in surprising, unpredictable outcomes.
Tomentose Covered with fine white hairs.
Topiary Plants that have been pruned or shaped into ornamental forms.
Transfunctional Having more than one purpose or state of being.
Tuckamore A regional term of eastern North America for a tree that has been stunted and deformed by coastal winds.
Uncanny valley A perceptual phenomenon which measures the emotional response felt in a human when viewing a humanoid Other.
Unproductive Referring to soils low in nutrients and organic matter.
Watersprout Growth shoots on a plant that arise from trunks or branches.
Wild Something surprising.
Wild systems emulation A design strategy that seeks visual examples of surprising actions to inspire the arrangement of a design.
Wilderness Being subsumed by surprising thoughts or actions.
Wildness Surprising thoughts or actions.
Windward The side of a mountain, structure, or area that is exposed to an air current or weather system.
Woodland A landscape primarily composed of tall shrubs and multi-stemmed trees. Also, a transitional landscape where shrublands and forests mix.

BIBLIOGRAPHIC REFERENCES

1 Stegner, Wallace. 'Thoughts in a dry land' *Where the Bluebird Sings to the Lemonade Springs: Living and Writing in the West.* Modern Library, 2002.

2 Le Guin, Ursula K. *Late in the Day: Poems, 2010–2014.* PM Press, 2016.

3 Gilbert, Scott F., et al. 'A Symbiotic View of Life: We Have Never Been Individuals.' *The Quarterly Review of Biology*, vol. 87, no. 4, 2012, pp. 325–341., https://doi.org/10.1086/668166.

4 Letter from Claude Monet to Alice Hoschedé, February 11, 1884, in Wildenstein 1979a, 237-38, here 238, Letter 415 in Philipp, Michael. *Claude Monet: The Truth of Nature.* Edited by Ortrud Westheider and Christoph Heinrich, Prestel, 2019.

5 Morton, Timothy. *Dark Ecology: For a Logic of Future Coexistence.* Columbia University Press, 2018.

6 https://www.greenfacts.org/en/biodiversity/figtableboxes/1012-richness.htm

7 The Cure. 'Just Like Heaven.' *Kiss Me, Kiss Me, Kiss Me.* Fiction Records, 1987.

8 Briggs, John M., et al. 'An Ecosystem in Transition: Causes and Consequences of the Conversion of Mesic Grassland to Shrubland.' BioScience, vol. 55, no. 3, 2005, p.243., https://doi.org/10.1641/0006-3568(2005)055[0243:aeitca]2.0.co;2

9 Dunnett, Nigel. *Naturalistic Planting Design: The Essential Guide.* Filbert Press, 2019.

10 Iggy and the Stooges. 'Gimme Danger.' *Raw Power.* Columbia, 1973.

11 Rainer, Thomas, and Claudia West. *Planting in a Post-Wild World: Designing Plant Communities That Evoke Nature.* Timber Press, 2015.

12 Mcandrew, Francis T., and Sara S. Koehnke. 'On the Nature of Creepiness.' *New Ideas in Psychology*, vol. 43, 2016, pp. 10–15., doi:10.1016/j.newideapsych.2016.03.003

13 Cohen, Jeffrey Jerome. *Monster Theory: Reading Culture.* University of Minnesota Press, 1997.

14 Buscher, Fred K., and Jot D. Carpenter. 'Outmoded Foundation Planting Haunts Landscape Design Progress.' Weeds, Trees & Turf, Mar. 1980, pp. 65–78., doi: http://archive.lib.msu.edu/tic/wetrt/article/1980mar65.pdf

15 Trap Them. 'Seizures in Barren Praise.' Deathwish, 2008.

16 Kohn, Eduardo. *How Forests Think: Toward an Anthropology beyond the Human.* University of California Press, 2013.

17 McCarthy, Cormac. 'The Kekulé Problem - Issue 47: Consciousness.' *Nautilus*, 17 Apr. 2017, https://nautil.us/the-kekul-problem-236574/

18 Cekala, Allison. 'American Pile.' https://www.allisoncekala.com/american-pile

19 Patti Smith Group. 'Pissing in a River.' *Radio Ethiopia.* Arista, 1976.

20 McArthur, E. Durant, and Stanley G. Kitchen. 'Shrubland ecosystems: importance, distinguishing characteristics, and dynamics.' In: Sosebee, Ronald E.; Wester, David B.; Britton, Carlton M.; McArthur, E. Durant; Kitchen, Stanley G., comps. Proceedings: Shrubland dynamics--fire and water; 2004 August 10-12; Lubbock, TX. Proceedings RMRS-P-47. Fort Collins, CO: US Department of Agriculture, Forest Service, Rocky Mountain Research Station. p. 3-10. 47 (2007).

21 Götmark, Frank, Elin Götmark, and Anna M. Jensen. 'Why be a shrub? A basic model and hypotheses for the adaptive values of a common growth form.' *Frontiers in Plant Science* 7 (2016): 1095. Buscher, Fred K., and Jot D. Carpenter. 'Outmoded Foundation Planting Haunts Landscape Design Progress.' Weeds, Trees & Turf, Mar. 1980, pp. 65–78., doi: http://archive.lib.msu.edu/tic/wetrt/article/1980mar65.pdf.

22 'Graveyard Fields' sign. United States Forest Service, Pisgah National Forest. Viewed 10 October 2022.

23 Sparklehorse, aka Mark Linkous (1962–2010), was an American recording artist who infused southern American gothic aesthetics into a lofi, indie rock sound.

24 Teenage Cool Kids. 'Landlocked State.' *Denton After Sunset.* Dull Tools, 2010.

25 Bad Religion. 'Los Angeles Is Burning.' *The Empire Strikes First.* Epitaph, 2004.

26 Tsing, Anna Lowenhaupt. *The Mushroom at the End of the World: On the Possibility of Life in Capitalist Ruins.* Princeton University Press, 2021.

27 Helzer, Chris. 'A Deep-Rooted Prairie Myth.' *The Prairie Ecologist,* 17 Sept. 2019, https://prairieecologist.com/2019/09/17/a-deep-rooted-prairie-myth/

28 Barker, Clive, and Christopher Figg. *Hellraiser.* Entertainment, 1987.

29 Agee, James. *The Night of the Hunter.* Paul Gregory Productions, 1955.

30 Hitchmough, James. *Sowing Beauty: Designing Flowering Meadows from Seed.* Timber Press, 2017.

31 Godshall, David. 'Horticultural Semiotics: Ugly Beautiful Los Angeles.' *Wonderground,* 23 Oct. 2018, https://wonderground.press/gardens/horticultural-semiotics-ugly-beautiful-los-angeles

32 Inside Out. 'No Spiritual Surrender.' *No Spiritual Surrender.* Revelation Records.

33 'Shrublands.' Extension, 23 Dec. 2021, https://extension.unh.edu/resource/shrublands

34 D. Johnson, personal communication, January 4, 2023.

35 Morton, Timothy. *Being Ecological.* MIT Press, 2019.

36 Carter, Chris, et al. *The X-Files*: 'Ghost in the Machine.' Season 1, episode 7, Fox, 29 Oct. 1993.

37 Robinson, W., and Rick Darke. *The Wild Garden.* Timber Press, 2009

38 Morton, Timothy. *Dark Ecology: For a Logic of Future Coexistence.* Columbia University Press, 2018.

39 Cohen, Leonard. 'Anthem.' The Future, Leonard Cohen, Columbia, 1992.

40 Haraway, Donna Jeanne. *Staying with the Trouble: Making Kin in the Chthulucene.* Duke University Press, 2016.

41 Cronon, William. 'The Trouble with Wilderness; or, Getting Back to the Wrong Nature.' https://www.williamcronon.net/writing/Trouble_with_Wilderness_Main.html.

42 The Murder City Devils. 'Cruelty Abounds.' *The White Ghost Has Blood on Its Hands Again.* Self-released, 2014.

43 Hitchmough, James. *Sowing Beauty: Designing Flowering Meadows from Seed.* Timber Press, 2017.

44 Diamond, Jared. Collapse: *How Societies Choose to Fail or Succeed.* Penguin Books Ltd., 2011.

45 Fisher, Adrian Ayres. 'Native Shrubs and Why They're Essential for Carbon Sequestration.' 28 Dec. 2018, www.ecologicalgardening.net/2018/12/native-shrubs-and-why-theyre-essential.html

46 Labatut Benjamín, and Adrian Nathan West. *When We Cease to Understand the World.* NYRB, New York Review Books, 2021.

47 Torres, Vladimir, et al. "Astronomical Tuning of Long Pollen Records Reveals the Dynamic History of Montane Biomes and Lake Levels in the Tropical High Andes during the Quaternary." *Quaternary Science Reviews*, vol. 63, 2013, pp. 59–72., https://doi.org/10.1016/j.quascirev.2012.11.004

48 Haraway, Donna Jeanne. *Staying with the Trouble: Making Kin in the Chthulucene.* Duke University Press, 2016.

ABOUT THE AUTHORS

TERPENE SNIFFIN / TRICHOME PETTIN / DRUPE KISSIN / PUBLIC GARDEN / HORTS

Kevin Philip Williams is a naturalistic gardener who collaborates with plants to create dynamic and challenging worlds. His unique style combines bioregional plant palettes, a hardcore punk ethos of NO CONTROL, and post-human aesthetics to craft wild and captivating spaces. Kevin's extensive work with Denver Botanic Gardens, as both a horticulturist and designer, has led to the creation of celebrated public gardens throughout the city.

Kevin was a Gardener on The High Line in Manhattan and studied as a Horticulture Intern at Brooklyn Botanic Garden. He holds a MS degree in Public Horticulture from the Longwood Graduate Program at the University of Delaware and a BA degree in The History and Philosophy of Science from Bard College.

Michael Guidi is an ecologist and horticulture researcher who is passionate about naturalistic plantings that embody the flexibility and resiliency of wild systems. His work draws inspiration from liminal urban spaces and wild areas alike to develop bioregional approaches to gardening. Preferring common and weedy plants to the rare and precious, Michael is a proponent of dynamic, self-sustaining gardens and green infrastructure as alternatives to static high-maintenance landscaping. His interdisciplinary research links ecological theory with horticultural techniques and designs to broaden the definition of gardens and gardening.

Michael took a circuitous path to horticulture, working as a field biologist before joining the Denver Botanic Gardens horticulture department. He holds a MS degree in Ecology from the Graduate Degree Program in Ecology at Colorado State University and a BS degree in Biology from Ithaca College.

INDEX

Page numbers in *italic* type refer to illustrations or their captions.

A
Abies fraseri 9
Acacia 22–3
acacia, bull horn *see Vachellia collinsii*
Acantholimon albertii 168
Acer
    A. circinatum 141, *154*
    A. rubrum 92–3
Achillea millefolium 149, *191*
Acrothamnus 207
Adenostoma fasciculatum 123, *123*, 126, 141
Aesculus parviflora 196
afsanteen *see Artemisia rutifolia*
Agastache
    A. rupestris 182
    A. urticifolia 110
Agave 138
    A. deserti 33
    A. lechuguilla 49
agrilogistics 205, 208, 214
Albany Pine Bush Preserve 84, *84*, 85, *86–7*, 89
alder
    green *see Alnus alnobetula*
    witch 138
algae 110
Alien Dream Worlds 219
alligator juniper *see Juniperus deppeana*
Alnus alnobetula 36
Aloe ferox 213
Aloidendron dichotomum *162–3*
Amelanchier
    A. alnifolia 65, 172, *173*
    A. lamarckii 11
ammi, Dara purple *see Daucus carota*
Amorpha canescens 54, 138, 144, 148, *149*
Amphicarpum amphicarpon 164
Anchorage, Alaska 49
Anderson, Sonya 182–3, 218
Andrade, Angie 221
Andromeda polifolia 166
Andropogon hallii 183
Angeles National Forest 123, *123*
anthroflora 42, 48
Anthropocene 18, 37, 192–3, 204–5, 209
Antonoff, Frank 180–2
Aralia racemosa 30
Arbutus xalapensis 35
Arctostaphylos *124–5*, 173
    A. canescens 140
    A. columbiana 45
    A. edmundsii 190, *190*
    A. glauca 29
    A. pajaroensis 176
    A. pumila 181
    A. pungens 71
    A. uva-ursi 141, *153*
    A. viscida 50, 57
Arethusa bulbosa 82
Argemone hispida 223
Argentina 27, 61, 72–3, 96, 164, 169, 205
aridity 70
Aristida
    A. purpurea 183
    A. tuberculosa 164
Arizona cypress *see Cupressus arizonica*
Arizona rosewood *see Vauquelinia californica*
Aronia
    A. arbutifolia 193
    A. melanocarpa 193, 197
Artemisia 16, 19, 141
    A. californica 131, *132–3*, 180, 194, *195*
    A. cana 68
    A. carruthii 223
    A. filifolia 182
    A. ludoviciana 223
    A. pycnocephala 130, *195*
    A. rutifolia 205
    A. tridentata 20, 71, 75, 77, 96, *97*, 97, 98–9, 102–3, 105, *105*, 138, 188, 189
    A. tridentata ssp. *vaseyana* *106–7*
ash, single-leaf *see Fraxinus anomala*
aspen, quaking *see Populus tremuloides*
Asplenium scolopendrium 11
aster
    California *see Corethrogyne filaginifolia*
    frost *see Symphyotrichum pilosum*
    Pacific *see Symphyotrichum chilense*
    parasol whitetop *see Doellingeria umbellata*
Astraeus hygrometricus 167
Astragalus angustifolius 171
Atlas fescue *see Festuca mairei*
Atraphaxis virgata 205
Atriplex 100
    A. canescens 138, 182, *183*
Australia 8, 22–3, 78, 134, *134*, 152, *174-5*
azalea
    alpine *see Kalmia procumbens*
    early *see Rhododendron prinophyllum*
    hybrid white spider 55
    swamp *see Rhododendron viscosum*
    western *see Rhododendron occidentale*
Azorella 72–3, 169
    A. prolifera 169

B
Baccharis 72–3, 100
    B. halimifolia 138, 156
    B. pilularis 128, *129*, 130, *130*, 132–3
Bahía Azul garden 10, *10*
Bald Head Island, North Carolina 63
balds 50, 90–5
banana yucca *see Yucca baccata*
barberry
    Fremont *see Berberis fremontii*
    Japanese *see Berberis thunbergii*
Barbican Beech Gardens 7, 9, 11
barometer earthstar fungus *see Astraeus hygrometricus*
Basilone, Nicole 76
bayberry, northern *see Myrica pensylvanica*
beard-heath *see Acrothamnus*
Beartooth Mountains, Wyoming 173
Beartooth Plateau, Wyoming 20
beautyberry, American *see Callicarpa americana*
beebalm, spotted *see Monarda punctata*
beloperone *see Justicia californica*
Berberis
    B. aquifolium 24
    B. fremontii 45
    B. repens 35, 67
    B. thunbergii 24
Beristianou, Eva 186–7
Big Bend National Park 49, *120–1*
bigpod ceanothus *see Ceanothus megacarpus*
Big Sur, California 61, 128, 131
bilberry 141
biodomes 168–71, 186
bitterbrush, antelope 138
bittersweet
    American *see Celastrus scandens*
    round-leaved *see Celastrus orbiculatus*
blackberry, smooth *see Rubus canadensis*
blackbrush *see Coleogyne ramosissima*
blackhaw *see Viburnum prunifolium*
blazing star *see Liatris*
blueberry 84
    Cascade *see Vaccinium deliciosum*
    highbush *see Vaccinium corymbosum*
    lowbush *see Vaccinium angustifolium*
blueblossom *see Ceanothus thyrsiflorus*
blue palo verde *see Parkinsonia florida*
bluestem
    little *see Schizachyrium scoparium*
    sand *see Andropogon hallii*
boardwalks 78
boglands 79, 89, 110, 157
Borrichia frutescens 159
bramble 141
Bridger Wilderness, Wyoming *102–3*
brittlebush *see Encelia farinosa*
Bromus inermis 68
broom, Scotch *see Cytisus scoparius*
broom snakeweed *see Gutierrezia sarothrae*
buckbrush *see Ceanothus cuneatus*
buckeye 138
    bottlebrush *see Aesculus parviflora*
buckwheat 141
    California *see Eriogonum fasciculatum*
    seacliff *see Eriogonum parvifolium*
    seaside *see Eriogonum latifolium*
    sulphurflower *see Eriogonum umbellatum*
    twiggy *see Atraphaxis virgata*
buffaloberry
    roundleaf *see Shepherdia rotundifolia*
    silver *see Shepherdia argentea*
bunneries 168, *170*, 186
burnet, thorny *see Sarcopoterium spinosum*
Burton Mesa Ecological Reserve 173
buttonbush, common *see Cephalanthus occidentalis*

C
cactus 101, 161
    Cereus 153
    fishhook *see Sclerocactus brevispinus*
    golden barrel *see Echinocactus grusonii*

organ pipe *see Stenocereus thurberi*
saguaro *see Carnegiea gigantea*
Caesalpinia gilliesii 212
California lilac *see Ceanothus*
Callicarpa americana 138, 158
Calluna 78
Calocedrus decurrens 155
Calochortus gunnisonii 109
Calochortus nuttallii 101
caman *see Ephedra ochreata*
Canyonlands National Park 98–9
Cape Cod National Seashore 153
carbon sequestration 38
Carex pensylvanica 164
caricature plant *see Graptophyllum pictum*
Carnegiea gigantea 30, 160–1
Carolina Sandhills National Wildlife Refuge 155, 157, 159
Carpobrotus edulis 131, 195
Cascabela thevetia 36
Cassiope 78
Castilleja
    C. miniata 114–15
    C. scabrida 101
Catananche caerulea 182
Ceanothus 29, 126, 141
    C. cuneatus 122, 126
    C. integerrimus var. *macrothyrsus* 180
    C. leucodermis 27, 126
    C. megacarpus 127
    C. thyrsiflorus 32, 128
cedar
    California incense *see Calocedrus decurrens*
    salt *see Tamarix ramosissima*
    southern red *see Juniperus virginiana*
Cekala, Allison 63, 184
Celastrus
    C. orbiculatus 84
    C. scandens 84
Centaurea spinosa 186, 187
Cephalanthus occidentalis 159
Cercocarpus
    C. intricatus 45
    C. ledifolius 182
    C. montanus 109, 138
Cereus 153
Chama, New Mexico 61
Chamaebatia foliolosa 155
Chamaedaphne calyculata 79, 79
chamise *see Adenostoma fasciculatum*
chaparral 8, 38, 70, 122–7
chastetree, simpleleaf *see Vitex trifolia*
chenopod shrubland 22–3
cherry
    fire *see Prunus pensylvanica*
    hollyleaf *see Prunus ilicifolia*
    sand *see Prunus pumila* 138
Chihuahuan Desert 49, 116–17, 117, 138
Chile 10, 10
chilicothe *see Marah macrocarpa*
Chilopsis linearis 53, 182
chinquapin, bush *see Chrysolepis sempervirens*
Chisos Mountains, Texas 116, 118–19
chokeberry 138
    black *see Aronia melanocarpa*

red *see Aronia arbutifolia*
Chrysolepis sempervirens 155
cinquefoil, shrubby *see Dasiphora fruticosa*
Cistus salvifolius 187
Clematis
    C. orientalis 205
    C. songarica 205
Clethra alnifolia 157, 158
clover, leafy prairie *see Dalea foliosa*
clubmoss, mountain *see Lycopodium fastigiatum*
coalesced dome bog 79
coastal bush lupine *see Lupinus arboreus*
coastal scrub 128–33
Coccoloba uvifera 150
Coconino National Forest 71
coffeeberry *see Frangula californica*
Coffin Bay National Park, South Australia 152
colapiche *see Nassauvia glomerulosa*
Coleogyne ramosissima 12–13, 141
Comptonia peregrina 84, 88
coneflower, pale purple *see Echinacea pallida*
coppicing 11, 148, 173
coralbell *see Heuchera*
coral bush *see Templetonia retusa*
Corethrogyne filaginifolia syn. *Lessingia filaginifolia* 130
Cornus
    C. amomum 193
    C. canadensis 166
    C. kousa var. *chinensis* 11
    C. racemosa 144
    C. sericea 193
Corokia cotoneaster 201
Corylus
    C. americana 144
    C. avellana 11, 138, 141
Cotinus 'Grace' 197
cottongrass, tawny *see Eriophorum virginicum*
cottonwood, eastern *see Populus deltoides*
coyote brush *see Baccharis pilularis*
crabapple, prairie 138
cranberry *see Vaccinium macrocarpon*
Creek, Rana 190–1
creosote bush *see Larrea tridentata*
Crested Butte, Colorado 110
Cretan hedge-hog heath *see Astragalus angustifolius*
Crisman, TS Mushin 67
Cupid's dart *see Catananche caerulea*
Cupressus arizonica 71
currant *see Ribes*
curry plant *see Helichrysum italicum*
cushion plants 168–71, 186
cycads 213
Cyrilla racemiflora 157, 159
Cytisus scoparius 126

D
Daboecia 78
daisy
    Hector's cushion *see Raoulia hectorii*
    seaside *see Erigeron glaucus*
Dalea foliosa 120–1
Dasiphora fruticosa 192
Dasylirion leiophyllum 116, 118–19

Daucus carota 183
deerbrush *see Ceanothus integerrimus* var. *macrothyrsus*
deergrass *see Muhlenbergia rigens*
deerweed 141
Delphinium barbeyi 114–15
Denali National Park and Preserve 165
Denver Art Museum Sensory Garden 220–1
desert bird of paradise *see Caesalpinia gilliesii*
desert scrub 27, 30, 33, 49, 70, 116–21
devil's club *see Oplopanax horridus*
Diplacus aurantiacus 55, 132–3
disturbance-based shrubland 70, 78, 84, 90, 90, 144–9
Doellingeria umbellata 91, 91
dogbane, bushy *see Cascabela thevetia*
dogfennel *see Eupatorium capillifolium*
dogwood 138
    creeping *see Cornus canadensis*
    gray *see Cornus racemosa*
    red osier *see Cornus sericea*
    silky *see Cornus amomum*
Dolly Sods Wilderness, West Virginia 31, 91, 91, 92–3
Dominguez-Escalante National Recreation Area 75
Doxiadis, Thomas 186–7
Dracophyllum 207
dragon-leaf *see Dracophyllum*
dragon's mouth orchid *see Arethusa bulbosa*
Drosera intermedia 89
dry montane shrublands 104–9
dune marsh-elder *see Iva imbricata*
dunes 84, 129, 130, 142–3, 148, 150–3, 164
Duranta erecta 212

E
Echinacea pallida 149
Echinocactus grusonii 160
ecotone 19, 84
Elaeagnus umbellata 193
elderberry 138
    American black *see Sambucus canadensis*
Encelia farinosa 160–1
Epacris 78
Ephedra 72–3, 141
    E. equisetina 205
Ephedra ochreata 36
Epilobium canum 190, 191
Eremurus 15
Erica 58–9, 78
Ericaceae 78
Ericameria 15, 16, 40–1, 138
    E. ericoides 32, 128, 130, 142–3
    E. nauseosa 24, 37, 53, 68, 77, 105, 105, 182, 182, 183, 188, 189
Erigeron
    E. elatior 110
    E. glaucus 130
Eriodictyon californicum 145
Eriogonum
    E. fasciculatum 27, 123, 123
    E. latifolium 142–3
    E. parvifolium 130, 190, 190
    E. umbellatum 37, 106–7

Eriophorum virginicum 136–7
Eriophyllum staechadifolium 32, 130
Eschscholzia californica 130
Eucalyptus 174–5
    E. coccifera 134
Euonymus europaeus 11
Eupatorium capillifolium 146
Euphorbia 161, 162–3
    E. acanthothamnos 171
    E. collina 46
    E. marginata 183
evening primrose, pale *see Oenothera pallida*
everlasting *see Helichrysum*

F
Fallugia paradoxa 53, 182
Feek, John 19
fern
    bracken 112, 155
    hart's tongue *see Asplenium scolopendrium*
    lip *see Myriopteris*
fernbush 141
fertility islands 30
Festuca mairei 213
Filippi, Olivier 10
fir 138
    Douglas *see Pseudotsuga menziesii*
    Fraser *see Abies fraseri*
Fitzgerald River National Park, Western Australia 152
flannelbush, California *see Fremontodendron californicum*
flax, blue *see Linum lewisii*
fleabane, tall *see Erigeron elatior*
flowers 52–5
forbs 110, 128, 130, 134, 148, 149, 179, 182, 190, 191, 193, 194, 223
forest understory 154–5
Fort Ord Dunes State Park 128, 129, 130
Fouquieria splendens 33, 117, 138, 160–1
Frangula californica 32, 124–5, 132–3
Frasera speciosa 109
Fraxinus anomala 97, 97
Fremontodendron californicum 126, 126
fruits 34–7
fuchsia, California *see Epilobium canum*
Fuchsia paniculata ssp. *paniculata* 35
fynbos 8

G
gallberry, big *see Ilex coriacea*
Gaultheria procumbens 167
Gaylussacia baccata 84, 155
Geranium viscosissimum 106–7
giant dagger *see Yucca faxoniana*
Gibraltar bushclover *see Lespedeza thunbergii*
Gkirti, Despoina 186–7
global warming 37, 38
golden dewdrop *see Duranta erecta*
goldenrod
    Canada *see Solidago canadensis*
    Roan Mountain *see Solidago roanesnsis*
    showy *see Solidago speciosa*
Golemi, Chrisa 186–7
graminoids 37, 148

grand repeater shrublands 74–5
grape, riverbank *see Vitis riparia*
Graptophyllum pictum 46
Graveyard Fields, North Carolina 90, 172
Grayia spinosa 71
greasewood 141
    black *see Sarcobatus vermiculatus*
Great Sagebrush Sea 102–3
Great Sand Dunes National Park 49, 77
Greece 171, 185, 186–7
Greek horehound *see Pseudodictamnus acetabulosus*
green roofs 188–91
Grimm, Juan 10, 10
Grob, Alpen 57
groundseltree *see Baccharis halimifolia*
growing season 70
Guidi, Michael 202
Gutierrezia sarothrae 116

H
Hadley, Massachusetts 63
halophytes 100, 159
Harrimanella hypnoides 166
hawthorn, black 141
hazel *see Corylus avellana*
hazelnut, American *see Corylus americana*
heath 58–9, 74, 78–85
heather 78
hebe, whipcord *see Veronica lycopodioides*
Hebe speciosa 179
Hedysarum boreale 96
Helichrysum 15
    H. italicum 187
    H. trilineatum 47
Helictotrichon sempervirens 183
Hennessy, Kevin 43
Hesperostipa comata 98–9
Hesperoyucca whipplei 126
Heteromeles arbutifolia 124–5, 126, 141
Heuchera 197
Hiawatha National Forest 112
High Line 196–9
Hitchmough, James 180, 222
Hogan, Sean 176
hokubetsi *see Helichrysum trilineatum*
holly 138
    grape 141
    mountain *see Ilex montana*
Holodiscus
    H. dumosus 37, 138
    H. microphyllus 188
honeycup 138
horsebrush 141
huckleberry, black *see Gaylussacia baccata*
Hudsonia 78
    H. ericoides 164
    H. tomentosa 153
Hunt, Glenn 190–1
Huntington Botanic Gardens, California 213
hydrangea, oakleaf 138
Hyparhennia hirta 186
Hypericum
    H. densiflorum 172
    H. × *hidcoteense* 11

I
ice plant 131
Ilex
    I. coriacea 157, 158
    I. glabra 157
    I. laevigata 83
    I. montana 91, 91
    I. verticillata 112
inkberry *see Ilex glabra*
inland barrens 84–9
Inulanthera thodei 14
Ipomopsis rubra 183
Iva imbricata 151

J
jarilla *see Larrea nitida*
Johnson, Dan 200
jointfir *see Ephedra*
    bluestem *see Ephedra equisetina*
jointweed, coast *see Polygonella articulata*
jojoba *see Simmondsia chinensis*
Juniperus 138, 185
    J. deppeana 49
    J. osteosperma 97, 97
    J. phoenicea 186, 187
    J. virginiana 156
    krummholz 138
Justicia californica 55

K
Kalmia
    K. angustifolia 79, 80–1, 82
    K. latifolia 53, 91, 91, 92–3, 138
    K. procumbens 165
Karner Barrens 84, 85
Kephart, Paul 190–1
kinnikinnick *see Arctostaphylos uva-ursi*
Knaga, Kelly 225
knapweed, spiny *see Centaurea spinosa*
Kniphofia caulescens 14
korokio *see Corokia cotoneaster*
Krascheninnikovia lanata 138, 182
Kremali, Terpsi 186–7
krummholz 138, 172, 173
kwongan 8
Kyrgyzstan 205, 208

L
labrador tea *see Rhododendron groenlandicum*
Landscapes of Cohabitation 186–7
Lands End Lookout 194–5
Larix laricina 78, 112
larkspur, subalpine *see Delphinium barbeyi*
Larrea
    L. nitida 36, 46
    L. tridentata 29, 30, 121, 138
laurel
    California bay *see Umbellularia californica*
    mountain *see Kalmia latifolia*
    sheep *see Kalmia angustifolia*
Lavandula 24
    L. dentata 186
    L. stoechas 176, 212
Laver, Mark 51
LA WAVE 180–1, 180–1

leadplant *see Amorpha canescens*
leatherleaf *see Chamaedaphne calyculata*
leaves 44–6
lebaila *see Pentzia cooperi*
lechuguilla *see Agave lechuguilla*
lelingoana *see Inulanthera thodei*
lemonade berry *see Rhus integrifolia*
Lesotho 47
Lespedeza thunbergii 197
Leucopogon 78
Liatris 15
lichen 18, 29, 50, 57, 110, 164, 201, 216–17
lily
    corn *see Veratrum californicum*
    foxtail *see Eremurus*
    Gunnison's Mariposa *see Calochortus gunnisonii*
    sego *see Calochortus nuttallii*
Linum lewisii 183
littleleaf pixiemoss *see Pyxidanthera barbulata*
Little Missouri National Grassland 65, 68
Lord's candle *see Hesperoyucca whipplei*
Los Padres National Forest 122, 124–5, 145
lungwort *see Pulmonaria*
Lupinus
    L. arboreus 54
    L. argenteus 102–3
Lycium pallidum 182
Lycopodaceae 82
Lycopodium fastigiatum 207
Lyonia mariana 157, 158

M
macchia 8, 70
McNamara, Sean Robert 17, 206
Magnolia
    M. macrophylla 196
    M. tripetala 196
    M. virginiana 157
mahogany, mountain *see Cercocarpus montanus*
    curl-leaf *see Cercocarpus ledifolius*
    little leaf *see Cercocarpus intricatus*
maidencane, blue *see Amphicarpum amphicarpon*
manzanita 141
    bigberry *see Arctostaphylos glauca*
    greenleaf 141
    hairy *see Arctostaphylos columbiana*
    hoary *see Arctostaphylos canescens*
    Little Sur *see Arctostaphylos edmundsii*
    Pajaro *see Arctostaphylos pajaroensis*
    pointleaf *see Arctostaphylos pungens*
    sandmat *see Arctostaphylos pumila*
    whiteleaf *see Arctostaphylos viscida*
maple 138
    red *see Acer rubrum*
maquis 8, 21, 70, 186, 187
Marah macrocarpa 126
marjoram, sweet *see Origanum majorana*
Maroon Bells-Snowmass Wilderness 114–15
mastic *see Pistacia lentiscus*
Mathioudaki, Aggeliki 186–7
matrix planting 222
mattoral 8
meadowsweet, white *see Spiraea alba*
Mediterranean climate 70
mesh planting 222

mesquite *see Prosopis glandulosa*
Mexico 179, 212
Mimosa borealis 54
mint
    horse *see Agastache urticifolia*
    licorice *see Agastache rupestris*
Moab, Utah 97, 97
mock heather *see Ericameria ericoides*
Moda Building 188–9
model shrublands 70, 77–133
Monarda punctata 89, 182, 183, 223
Monet, Claude 21
monkey-flower, sticky *see Diplacus aurantiacus*
Mono Lake, California 40–1
Monongahela National Forest 31, 90–1, 91, 92–3, 94, 136–7
Monte 72–3, 205
Monticello, Utah 96
monument plant *see Frasera speciosa*
Monument Valley, Utah 61
Morton, Timothy 26, 201, 205, 208
moss 110, 154, 164, 166
moss-plant *see Harrimanella hypnoides*
mountain andromeda *see Pieris floribunda*
mountain ash 138
    American *see Sorbus americana*
    western *see Sorbus scopulina*
mountain dryad 141
mountainlover *see Paxistima myrsinites*
mountain rosebay *see Rhododendron catawbiense*
mountain spray *see Holodiscus dumosus*
Mt. Field National Park, Tasmania 134, 134, 174–5
Mt. Sneffels Wilderness 173
Muhlenbergia
    M. dubia 181
    M. reverchonii 182, 183, 183
    M. rigens 213
muhly
    pine *see Muhlenbergia dubia*
    ruby *see Muhlenbergia reverchonii*
mule-ears *see Wyethia amplexicaulis*
mulinum *see Azorella*
Myrica
    M. cerifera 153
    M. pensylvanica 153
Myriopteris 121

N
Nags Head Woods Preserve 159
nannyberry *see Viburnum lentago*
nanoscrub 164–9
nardo *see Nardophyllum*
Nardophyllum 169, 205
Nassauvia glomerulosa 46
naturalism 6, 8, 204–5, 222
Navajo Nation 152
needle-and-thread grass *see Hesperostipa comata*
needle palm 138
Negri, Lisa 182–3, 218
neneo *see Azorella prolifera*
Neo-Expressionist remix 77
Newfoundland 83
New Jersey Pine Barrens 158, 164, 167
New Jersey tea 138

New Perennial movement 6
New Zealand 64, 135, 201, 207
nightshade, chaparral *see Solanum xanti*
non-Anthropogenic 210–11, 214
Notholithocarpus
    N. densiflorus 35
    N. densiflorus var. *echinoides* 140
nurse plants 30–3, 31, 33, 164

O
oak 141
    bear *see Quercus ilicifolia*
    black *see Quercus velutina*
    blackjack *see Quercus marilandica*
    dwarf chinquapin *see Quercus prinoides*
    Gambel *see Quercus gambelii*
    northern red *see Quercus rubra*
    poison *see Toxicodendron diversilobum*
    Rocky Mountain oak chaparral 104–5, 104, 105, 106–7
    scrub 126
    tanbark *see Notholithocarpus densiflorus*
    Tucker *see Quercus welshii*
    turkey *see Quercus laevis*
oat grass, blue *see Helictotrichon sempervirens*
ocotillo *see Fouquieria splendens*
Oenothera pallida 100–1
Ogden, Lauren Springer 200
olive, autumn *see Elaeagnus umbellata*
Olympic National Park 154
One South Van Ness Avenue 190–1
Oplopanax horridus 154
Opuntia 96, 138
    O. engelmannii 116, 117, 118–19, 120–1
Oregon grape *see Berberis*
Origanum
    O. majorana 186
    O. onites 186
Orthocarpus luteus 109
Oudolf, Piet 196–9
owl's-clover, yellow *see Orthocarpus luteus*
oxlip *see Primula elatior*
Oxydendrum arboreum 157

P
paintbrush
    giant red *see Castilleja miniata*
    rough *see Castilleja scabrida*
pandani *see Richea pandanifolia*
Panicum virgatum 164
Paraserianthes lophantha 195
Parkinsonia florida 160–1
parrot flower 161
paths 78
Pawnee National Grasslands 170
Paxistima myrsinites 155
Pea Island National Wildlife Refuge 159
peatland 78, 79
Pentzia cooperi 47
perennial plantings 6, 11
Persea palustris 157
petran 104–5, 104, 105, 106–7
Petrified Forest National Park 139
Pew, Preston 176
Philadelphus 'Belle Étoile' 11

philodendron, tree *see Thaumatophyllum bipinnatifidum*
Phlomis
    P. chrysophylla 176
    P. viscosa 176
Phyllodoce 78
Picea
    P. engelmannii 172
    P. mariana 78
    P. rubens 92–3, 95
Pichoga *see Euphorbia collina*
Pieris floribunda 29
Pike National Forest 172
pine
    eastern white *see Pinus strobus*
    longleaf *see Pinus palustris*
    pitch *see Pinus rigida*
    ponderosa *see Pinus ponderosa*
pine barren false heather *see Hudsonia ericoides*
pine barrens 84
Pinus
    P. palustris 146, 155
    P. ponderosa 155
    P. rigida 84
    P. strobus 80–1
Pisgah-Cherokee National Forest 141
Pisgah National Forest 172
Pistacia lentiscus 187
Pleurophora patagonica 27
plum 138
    American *see Prunus americana*
    beach *see Prunus maritima*
pocosin 157, 157
Polygonella articulata 164
Polytrichum 164
póñil *see Fallugia paradoxa*
poppy
    California *see Eschscholzia californica*
    rough prickly *see Argemone hispida*
Populus
    P. deltoides 97, 97
    P. tremuloides 111, 111, 173, 173
Potiriadi, Ioanna 186–7
prairie aesthetic 7
prickly pear *see Opuntia*
    desert *see Opuntia engelmannii*
Primula elatior 11
Prosopis glandulosa 30, 138
Prunus
    P. americana 35, 138
    P. ilicifolia 126
    P. maritima 35, 138, 153
    P. pensylvanica 30, 86–7, 138, 172
    P. pumila 88, 182
Pseudodictamnus acetabulosus 186
Pseudotsuga menziesii 155
Psittacanthus calyculatus 161
Pulmonaria 'Blue Ensign' 11
Purshia stansburiana 53
Pyxidanthera barbulata 167

Q

Quercus 172
    Q. gambelii 104, 172, 173
    Q. ilicifolia 84, 153
    Q. laevis 146, 155
    Q. marilandica 46, 55
    Q. prinoides 84, 86–7
    Q. rubra 155
    Q. velutina 155
    Q. welshii 152
quiver tree *see Aloidendron dichotomum*

R

rabbitbrush, rubber *see Ericameria nauseosa*
Rachel Carson National Wildlife Refuge 193
Racomitrium lanuginosum 207
Rancho Cistus Med Bed 176
range grasses 68
Raoulia hectorii 135
raspberry *see Rubus*
red-hot poker *see Kniphofia caulescens*
Rhododendron 31, 138
    R. canadense 36, 79, 80–1, 82, 83
    R. catawbiense 29, 95
    R. groenlandicum 79
    R. x (hybrid white spider azalea) 55
    R. occidentale 140
    R. prinophyllum 55
    R. viscosum 92–3, 157, 196
rhodora *see Rhododendron canadense*
Rhus
    R. aromatica 65, 155
    R. copallinum 153, 157, 196
    R. glabra 88, 148
    R. integrifolia 180
    R. typhina 86–7, 198–9
    R. virens 118–19
Ribes 141
    R. aureum 20
    R. cereum 37
    R. roezlii 36
Richea pandanifolia 174–5
Roads Water-Smart Garden, Denver 200
Roan Mountain Rhododendron Gardens, North Carolina 95
Rock Creek State Park 144
rock-rose, sageleaf *see Cistus salvifolius*
Rocky Mountain oak chaparral 104–5, 104, 105, 106–7
Rocky Mountains 39
Rosa
    Northern Accents 'Sven' 53
    R. acicularis 54
    R. palustris 193
    R. virginiana 193
Rosaceae 8
rose
    swamp *see Rosa palustris*
    Virginia *see Rosa virginiana*
rosemary *see Salvia rosmarinus*
    bog *see Andromeda polifolia*
Routt National Forest 110
Rubus 138, 153
    R. canadensis 141
    R. hispidus 136–7, 166
Ruth Bancroft Garden & Nursery 179

S

sacaton, alkali *see Sporobolus airoides*
Saco Heath Preserve 78, 79, 79, 155
sage
    black *see Salvia mellifera*
    golden-leaved Jerusalem *see Phlomis chrysophylla*
    Mojave *see Salvia pachyphylla*
    Russian *see Salvia yangii*
    viscid Jerusalem *see Phlomis viscosa*
    West Texas grass *see Salvia reptans*
    white *see Salvia apiana*
sagebrush
    big *see Artemisia tridentata*
    California *see Artemisia californica*
    coastal *see Artemisia pycnocephala*
    sand *see Artemisia filifolia*
    silver *see Artemisia cana*
    white *see Artemisia ludoviciana*
sagewort
    Carruth's *see Artemisia carruthii*
    coastal *see Artemisia pycnocephala*
Saguaro National Park 31
St. John's wort, bushy *see Hypericum densiflorum*
salal 141
Salix 113
    S. arctica 54
    S. brachycarpa 114–15
    S. discolor 193
    S. geyeriana 111, 111
    S. humilis 88, 138, 144
    S. monticola 111, 111
    S. petrophila 166
    S. wolfii 111, 111
saltbush *see Atriplex*
    fourwing *see Atriplex canescens*
salt crystal formations 57
Salvia
    S. apiana 180
    S. mellifera 123, 123, 141
    S. pachyphylla 182
    S. reptans 182
    S. rosmarinus 186
    S. yangii 182
Sambucus
    S. canadensis 193
    S. nigra f. *porphyrophylla* 11
San Bruno Mountain State & County Park 132–3
Sanseviera laurentii 189
San Simeon, California 61
Sarcobatus 100
    S. vermiculatus 75, 97, 97
Sarcopoterium spinosum 186, 187
Sassafras albidum 84, 86–7, 196
saw palmetto 138
Schizachyrium scoparium 146, 148, 164
Schneider, Chelsea 188–9
Sclerocactus brevispinus 101
scrub 8
seagrape *see Coccoloba uvifera*
sedge, Pennsylvania *see Carex pensylvanica*
Sedum 188
serviceberry 138
    western *see Amelanchier alnifolia*
shadscale 141

Shepherdia
   S. argentea 65, 138
   S. rotundifolia 45
Sheyenne National Grassland 148
shrubby cinquefoil 138
shrub growth strategy 26
shrub-meadow 148–9, 148, 149
shrub-steppe 8, 11, 19, 26, 27, 65, 70, 96–103
Sibbaldia procumbens 166
Sierra gooseberry *see Ribes roezlii*
silver seaside wooly sunflower *see Eriophyllum staechadifolium*
silvery lupine *see Lupinus argenteus*
Simmondsia chinensis 160–1
Sinonome toadlily *see Tricyrtis* 'Sinonome'
Siskiyou Mountains, Oregon 140
Skoura, Aimilia 186–7
skunkbush 138
Smith Rock State Park 71
smoketree *see Cotinus*
snakeplant *see Sansevieria laurentii*
snowberry 141
snow-on-the-mountain *see Euphorbia marginata*
soft chaparral 195
soil 70
Solanum xanti 126
Solidago
   S. canadensis 223
   S. roanensis 141
   S. speciosa 182
Sorbus
   S. americana 92–3
   S. scopulina 54, 112
Sorghastrum nutans 149
sotol, smooth-leaf *see Dasylirion leiophyllum*
sour fig *see Carpobrotus edulis*
sourwood *see Oxydendrum arboreum*
South Africa 162–3
spicebush, northern 138
spikenard, American *see Aralia racemosa*
spiny hopsage *see Grayia spinosa*
spiraea, cliff *see Holodiscus microphyllus*
Spiraea alba 193
Sporobolus airoides 213
spruce 138
   black *see Picea mariana*
   Engelmann *see Picea engelmannii*
   red *see Picea rubens*
spurge *see Euphorbia*
   Greek spiny *see Euphorbia acanthothamnos*
staggerbush *see Lyonia mariana*
Stansbury's cliffrose *see Purshia stansburiana*
Steamboat Springs, Colorado 111, 111
Stenocereus thurberi 160–1
steppe *see* shrub-steppe
stonecrop *see Sedum*
succulent scrub 160–3
suckering 8, 90, 154, 173
sumac 138
   cutleaf staghorn *see Rhus typhina*
   evergreen *see Rhus virens*
   fragrant *see Rhus aromatica*
   poison *see Toxicodendron vernix*
   smooth *see Rhus glabra*
   staghorn *see Rhus typhina*
   winged *see Rhus copallinum*
SummerHome Garden 182–3, 218
sundew, spoonleaf *see Drosera intermedia*
Sungari leather flower *see Clematis songarica*
swamp 156–9
swamp bay *see Persea palustris*
swamp dewberry *see Rubus hispidus*
swamp titi *see Cyrilla racemiflora*
Sweden 58–9
sweetbay magnolia *see Magnolia virginiana*
sweetfern *see Comptonia peregrina*
sweet pepperbush *see Clethra alnifolia*
sweetspire, Virginia 138
sweetvetch, northern *see Hedysarum boreale*
Swiss alpenflage 208
switchgrass *see Panicum virgatum*
Symphyotrichum
   S. chilense 181
   S. pilosum 84
sympoietic systems 212

T
tamarack *see Larix laricina*
Tamarix ramosissima 40–1, 97, 97
tanoak, bush *see Notholithocarpus densiflorus var. echinoides*
tansy, bushy seaside *see Borrichia frutescens*
Taos, New Mexico 63
Tasmanian snow gum *see Eucalyptus coccifera*
teaberry, eastern *see Gaultheria procumbens*
temperature 70
Templetonia retusa 152
Texas madrone *see Arbutus xalapensis*
Texas plume *see Ipomopsis rubra*
thatching grass *see Hyparrhenia hirta*
Thaumatophyllum bipinnatifidum 179
thornscrub 160–3
three-awn
   purple *see Aristida purpurea*
   seaside *see Aristida tuberculosa*
thrift, prickly *see Acantholimon albertii*
Thymus capitatus 187
Tibet, China 61
Tien Shan Mountains 168
Tiger Mountain State Forest 147
titirangi *see Hebe speciosa*
tomillo rosa *see Pleurophora patagonica*
topiary 74
Toxicodendron
   T. diversilobum 141, 184
   T. vernix 157
toyon *see Heteromeles arbutifolia*
Trans-Pecos Desert 138
Trentham Gardens, Staffordshire 11
Tricyrtis 'Sinonome' 197
Tsing, Anna Lowenhaupt 144
tundra 37
twinberry 138

U
Ullman, Douglas 190–1
Umbellularia californica 140, 146
uncanny valley 48
United Kingdom 7, 8, 9, 11, 75, 78

V
Vaccinium 58–9, 138, 155
   V. angustifolium 55, 92–3, 141
   V. corymbosum 79, 80–1, 91, 92–3, 172
   V. deliciosum 140
   V. macrocarpon 136–7, 138, 166
Vachellia collinsii 161
Vauquelinia californica 45
Veratrum californicum 110
Veronica lycopodioides 207
Viburnum 138
   V. × *bodnantense* 11
   V. lentago 193
   V. 'Pragense' 45
   V. prunifolium 196
Viola odorata 11
virginsbower, small-flowered *see Clematis orientalis*
Vitex trifolia 179
Vitis riparia 88

W
wattle *see Acacia*
   Cape *see Paraserianthes lophantha*
waxmyrtle, southern *see Myrica cerifera*
wet montane shrublands 110–15
whitethorn, chaparral *see Ceanothus leucodermis*
wildfires 37, 38, 123, 126, 146, 148
wild systems emulation 214–15
Williams, Kevin Philip 62, 66, 180–2, 200, 202, 218, 219, 221
willow 37, 138, 141
   Arctic *see Salix arctica*
   barren-ground *see Salix brachycarpa*
   desert *see Chilopsis linearis*
   Geyer's *see Salix geyeriana*
   mountain *see Salix monticola*
   prairie *see Salix humilis*
   pussy *see Salix discolor*
   rock *see Salix petrophila*
   Wolf's *see Salix wolfii*
wind 70
winterberry *see Ilex*
   smooth *see Ilex laevigata*
Wintercreek Restoration & Nursery 188–9
winterfat *see Krascheninnikovia lanata*
wire-netting bush *see Corokia cotoneaster*
wolfberry, pale *see Lycium pallidum*
Woodman Hollow State Preserve 155
woolly beach-heather *see Hudsonia tomentosa*
woolly fringe-moss *see Racomitrium lanuginosum*
Wyethia amplexicaulis 108
Wyllie, Roderick 194–5

Y
yarrow *see Achillea millefolium*
yellow prairie grass *see Sorghastrum nutans*
yerba santa, California *see Eriodictyon californicum*
Yosemite National Park 50, 57
Yucca 138
   Y. baccata 71
   Y. faxoniana 121
   Y. rostrata 182

ACKNOWLEDGMENTS

For sheltering and feeding two road-ravaged scrubs
Frank Antonoff and Stephanie Philson Antonoff
Lenora McNamara and Sean McNamara
George Urquiola and Monica Urquiola
Stephanie Aldrich and Todd Aldrich
Bryan Thompsonowak and Sharon Thompsonowak
Arlene Williams and Phil Williams

For generously sharing photographs, knowledge, perspectives and time
Frank Antonoff
Maria Aschenbrener, Danielle Schulz, and Emily Willkom of the Denver Art Museum
Bryant Baker
Janet E. Bare
Timothy A. Block
Mike Bone
Owen Conlow
Cathy Cunliffe
Denver Botanic Gardens
Thomas Doxiadis, Alexia Karakassis, Maria Paneta and the doxiadis+ team.
Ryan Drake
Bruce Dvorak
Murray Fagg and the Centre for Australian National Biodiversity Research and the Australian National Botanic Gardens
Alyssa Farrier
Olivier Filippi
David Godshall and the Terremoto team
Holly Gayle Haynes
Dale Hills
Sean Hogan
Dan Johnson
Russell Juelg
Martha Keen
Panayoti Kelaidis
Mike Kintgen
Wesley Knapp
Cindy Newlander
Clive Nichols
Kelly D. Norris
Jill Ratzenberger
Karl Stromayer, Kate O'Brien, Sarah Dudek, Colin McKevitt and the team at the Rachel Carson National Wildlife Refuge
Graham W. Taylor
Tim Thibault
Rafael Tiffany
Jen Toews
Maeve Turner

For your partnership and artwork
Nicole Basilone
Volodea Biri
Stephen Booth
Seán Boylan
Allison Cekala
TS Mushin Crisman
John Feek
Alpen Grob
Kevin Hennessy
Kelly Knaga
Mark Laver, Alejandra Russi and the Ricco/Maresca Gallery
Sean Robert McNamara
Stability AI

For supporting our vision (quest)
The Denver Botanic Gardens Employee Engagement & Wellness Committee
Sonya Anderson
Carina Bañuelos-Harrison
Georgie Brooks-Myrtle and Dan Parker of Saint John's Cathedral and Dominick Park
Diana Bush
Phil Douglas
Nigel Dunnett
Kati Fay
Tom Fischer
Nicholas Giaquinto
Jessica Hannah Jones
The Hooples of Camp Four
Sarada Krishnan
Anna Mumford and Filbert Press
Lisa Negri
Pat Roth
Brian Vogt

Photo credits
Frank Antonoff 180 btm, **Bryant Baker** cover, 27 btm, 29 top left, 29 btm left, 38, 56, 122, 124-5, 126 top right, 126 btm centre, 127, 142-3, 145, 146 btm, 173 top left; **Janet E. Bare/Denver Botanic Gardens** 53 btm middle; **Mike Bone** 14, 40-1, 46 top right, 46 bottom left, 47, 72-3, 121 middle, 153 top left, 200 top, 212 btm; **Cathy Cunliffe/doxiadis+** 186 top left; **Nigel Dunnett** 7, 9, 10; **Bruce Dvorak** 188, 189, 190, 191; **M. Fagg** 22-3, 134, 152 top and centre, 174-5; **Holly Gayle Haynes/Denver Botanic Gardens** 53 top middle; **Sean Hogan** 140, 176; **Dan Johnson** 27 top, 36 top middle, 36 top right, 46 top middle, 164 top, 169, 205 top; **Martha Keen** 35 top middle; **Panayoti Kelaidis** 64, 135, 162-3, 171, 185 btm, 201, 207; **Mike Kintgen** 33, 111, 112, 172 top right, 173 btm; **Cindy Newlander** 45 top left, 152 btm; **Clive Nichols/doxiadis+** 186 left and btm, 187; **Kelly Norris** 144, 149, 155 top left; **Rafael Tiffany** 179, 196, 197, 198-9, 213; **Jen Toews** 109 top right, 170, 233